Spring 5.0 By Example

Grasp the fundamentals of Spring 5.0 to build modern, robust, and scalable Java applications

Claudio Eduardo de Oliveira

BIRMINGHAM - MUMBAI

Spring 5.0 By Example

Copyright © 2018 Packt Publishing

Commissioning Editor: Aaron Lazar
Acquisition Editor: Chaitanya Nair
Content Development Editor: Lawrence Veigas
Technical Editor: Adhithya Haridas
Copy Editor: Safis Editing
Project Coordinator: Prajakta Naik
Proofreader: Safis Editing
Indexer: Tejal Daruwale Soni
Graphics: Jisha Chirayil
Production Coordinator: Aparna Bhagat

First published: February 2018

Production reference: 1230218

Published by Packt Publishing Ltd.
Livery Place
35 Livery Street
Birmingham
B3 2PB, UK.

ISBN 978-1-78862-439-8

www.packtpub.com

I dedicate this book to my loving wife for her continued support, patience, and encouragement throughout the long process of writing this book.

`mapt.io`

Mapt is an online digital library that gives you full access to over 5,000 books and videos, as well as industry leading tools to help you plan your personal development and advance your career. For more information, please visit our website.

Why subscribe?

- Spend less time learning and more time coding with practical eBooks and Videos from over 4,000 industry professionals

- Improve your learning with Skill Plans built especially for you

- Get a free eBook or video every month

- Mapt is fully searchable

- Copy and paste, print, and bookmark content

PacktPub.com

Did you know that Packt offers eBook versions of every book published, with PDF and ePub files available? You can upgrade to the eBook version at `www.PacktPub.com` and as a print book customer, you are entitled to a discount on the eBook copy. Get in touch with us at `service@packtpub.com` for more details.

At `www.PacktPub.com`, you can also read a collection of free technical articles, sign up for a range of free newsletters, and receive exclusive discounts and offers on Packt books and eBooks.

Contributors

About the author

Claudio Eduardo de Oliveira is a software architect and software developer working for Sensedia. He works with APIs, microservices, and cloud-centric applications. He has more than ten years of experience in software development with Java and JVM languages. He is a speaker at some important events in Brazil about Spring and other Java Frameworks.

> *I want to thank the people who have worked with me during my career; people who have taught me during my journey, who have helped me acquire knowledge.*
>
> *Also, I would like to thank my parents, who educated and supported me during my studies. I will always be grateful for that.*

About the reviewer

Paulo Zanco is a solution architect working for Daitan Labs. He is also a system architect with over 25 years of experience at national and international large/middle-sized companies. He has led many complex projects consisting of medium and large teams. He has extensive experience of designing and developing object-oriented and services systems. He is also certified by Sun and Oracle, in J2EE and SOA technologies. He holds a Master's degree in Management Information Systems from Pontifícia Universidade Católica de Campinas.

Packt is searching for authors like you

If you're interested in becoming an author for Packt, please visit authors.packtpub.com and apply today. We have worked with thousands of developers and tech professionals, just like you, to help them share their insight with the global tech community. You can make a general application, apply for a specific hot topic that we are recruiting an author for, or submit your own idea.

Table of Contents

Preface

With growing demands, organizations are looking for systems that are robust and scalable. Hence the Spring Framework has become the most popular framework for Java development. It not only simplifies software development but also improves developer productivity. This book covers effective ways to develop robust applications in Java using Spring.

Who this book is for

Developers who are starting out with Spring will learn about the new Spring 5.0 framework concepts followed by their implementation in Java and Kotlin. The book will also help experienced Spring developers gain insights into the new features added in Spring 5.0.

What this book covers

Chapter 1, *Journey to the Spring World*, will guide you through the main concepts of Spring Framework. Here we learn to setup the environment by installing OpenJDK, Maven, IntelliJ IDEA, and Docker. By the end, we will create our first Spring application.

Chapter 2, *Starting in the Spring World – the CMS Application*, will begin by getting our hands dirty with Spring Initializr to create configurations for our CMS application. We will then learn how to create REST resources, add the service layer and finally integrate with AngularJS.

Chapter 3, *Persistence with Spring Data and Reactive Fashion*, will build upon our CMS application created in the previous chapter. Here we will learn how to persist data on a real database by learning about Spring Data Reactive MongoDB and PostgresSQL. We will finally learn about Project Reactor which will help you to create a non-blocking application in the JVM ecosystem.

Chapter 4, *Kotlin Basics and Spring Data Redis*, will give you a basic introduction to Kotlin while presenting the benefits of the language. We will then learn how to use Redis which will be used as a message broker using the publish-subscribe feature.

Chapter 5, *Reactive Web Clients*, will teach you how to use the Spring Reactive Web Client and make HTTP calls in a reactive fashion. We will also be introduced to RabbitMQ and Spring Actuator.

Chapter 6, *Playing with Server-Sent Events*, will help you develop an application which will filter tweets by text content. We will accomplish this by consuming the tweeter steam using Server-Sent Events which is a standard way to send data streams from a server to clients

Chapter 7, *Airline Ticket System*, will teach you to use Spring Messaging, WebFlux, and Spring Data components to build a airline ticket system. You will also learn about circuit breakers and OAuth in this chapter. By the end, we will create a system with many microservices to ensure scalability.

Chapter 8, *Circuit Breakers and Security*, will help you discover how to apply service discovery features for our business microservices while also understanding how the Circuit Breaker pattern can help us to bring resilience to our applications.

Chapter 9, *Putting It All Together*, will bring the entire book into perspective while also teaching you about the Turbine server. We will also look into the Hystrix Dashboard to monitor our different microservices to ensure maintainability and optimum performance of our applications.

To get the most out of this book

The readers are expected to have a basic knowledge of Java. Notion about Distributed Systems is an added advantage.

To execute code files in this book, you would need to have the following software/dependencies:

- IntelliJ IDEA Community Edition
- Docker CE
- pgAdmin
- Docker Compose

You will be assisted with installation processes,etc through this book.

Download the example code files

You can download the example code files for this book from your account at `www.packtpub.com`. If you purchased this book elsewhere, you can visit `www.packtpub.com/support` and register to have the files emailed directly to you.

You can download the code files by following these steps:

1. Log in or register at `www.packtpub.com`.
2. Select the **SUPPORT** tab.
3. Click on **Code Downloads & Errata**.
4. Enter the name of the book in the **Search** box and follow the onscreen instructions.

Once the file is downloaded, please make sure that you unzip or extract the folder using the latest version of:

- WinRAR/7-Zip for Windows
- Zipeg/iZip/UnRarX for Mac
- 7-Zip/PeaZip for Linux

The code bundle for the book is also hosted on GitHub at `https://github.com/PacktPublishing/Spring-5.0-By-Example`. We also have other code bundles from our rich catalog of books and videos available at `https://github.com/PacktPublishing/`. Check them out!

Download the color images

We also provide a PDF file that has color images of the screenshots/diagrams used in this book. You can download it here: `https://www.packtpub.com/sites/default/files/downloads/Spring50ByExample_ColorImages.pdf`.

Conventions used

There are a number of text conventions used throughout this book.

`CodeInText`: Indicates code words in text, database table names, folder names, filenames, file extensions, pathnames, dummy URLs, user input, and Twitter handles. Here is an example: "It includes the infrastructure connections which are configured in the default profile in `application.yaml`."

A block of code is set as follows:

```
<dependency>
  <groupId>org.springframework.boot</groupId>
  <artifactId>spring-boot-starter-amqp</artifactId>
</dependency>
```

When we wish to draw your attention to a particular part of a code block, the relevant lines or items are set in bold:

```
management:
  endpoints:
    web:
      expose: "*"
```

Any command-line input or output is written as follows:

```
docker-compose up -d
```

Bold: Indicates a new term, an important word, or words that you see onscreen. For example, words in menus or dialog boxes appear in the text like this. Here is an example: "The next screen will be shown and we can configure the **Environment Variable**:"

Warnings or important notes appear like this.

Tips and tricks appear like this.

Get in touch

Feedback from our readers is always welcome.

General feedback: Email feedback@packtpub.com and mention the book title in the subject of your message. If you have questions about any aspect of this book, please email us at questions@packtpub.com.

Errata: Although we have taken every care to ensure the accuracy of our content, mistakes do happen. If you have found a mistake in this book, we would be grateful if you would report this to us. Please visit www.packtpub.com/submit-errata, selecting your book, clicking on the Errata Submission Form link, and entering the details.

Piracy: If you come across any illegal copies of our works in any form on the Internet, we would be grateful if you would provide us with the location address or website name. Please contact us at copyright@packtpub.com with a link to the material.

If you are interested in becoming an author: If there is a topic that you have expertise in and you are interested in either writing or contributing to a book, please visit authors.packtpub.com.

Reviews

Please leave a review. Once you have read and used this book, why not leave a review on the site that you purchased it from? Potential readers can then see and use your unbiased opinion to make purchase decisions, we at Packt can understand what you think about our products, and our authors can see your feedback on their book. Thank you!

For more information about Packt, please visit packtpub.com.

1
Journey to the Spring World

Spring is an open source modular framework for the JVM platform. A framework is a collection of libraries whose primary goal is to address common software development problems. The framework should solve these problems in a generic form.

Rod Johnson created the Spring Framework in 2002 together with his book publication, which was called *Expert One-on-One J2EE Design and Development*. The idea behind the creation of the framework was to tackle the complexities of Java Enterprise Edition.

At that time, this kind of solution-focused a lot on the details of the infrastructure, and a developer using the solution would spend a lot of time writing code to solve infrastructural problems. Since its creation, one of Rod Johnson's primary concerns has been to increase developer productivity.

The framework was first seen as a lightweight container for Java Runtime Environment, and it became popular in the community, especially because of the dependency injection feature. The framework made dependency injection incredibly easy. Developers hadn't seen such a feature before, and as a consequence, people the world over adopted the project. Year by year, its popularity within the software development world has been increasing.

In the earliest versions, the framework had to work with the XML file to configure the container. At the time, this was so much better than J2EE applications, where it was necessary to create many `Ant` files to create the boilerplate classes and interfaces.

The framework was always seen as an advanced technology for the Java platform, but in 2014, the Spring team launched the Spring Boot platform. This platform was incredibly successful in the Java Enterprise ecosystem, and it changed the way in which developers built Java Enterprise applications.

Today, Spring is the *de facto* framework for Java development, and companies around the world use it in their systems. The community is vibrant and contributes to development in different ways, such as opening issues, adding the code, and discussing the framework in the most important Java conferences around the world. Let's look at and play with the famous framework for Java developers.

We will cover the following topics in this chapter:

- Main modules of the Spring Framework
- Spring annotations for each module
- Setting up the development environment
- Docker and Docker commands

Spring modularity

Since its foundation, the framework has had a particular focus on modularity. It is an important framework characteristic because it makes the framework an excellent option for different architectural styles and different parts of applications.

It means the framework is not an opinionated, full-stack framework that dictates the rules to make everything work. We can use the framework as we need and integrate it with a wide range of specification and third-party libraries.

For example, for portal web applications, the Spring MVC supports features such as template engines and REST endpoints and integrates them with the popular JavaScript framework, AngularJS.

Also, if the application needs support for a distributed system, the framework can supply an amazing module called Spring Cloud, which has some essential features for distributed environments, such as service registration and discovery, a circuit breaker, intelligent routing, and client-side load balancing.

Spring makes the development applications for Java Runtime easy with different languages, such as Java, Kotlin, and Groovy (with which you can choose the flavor and make the development task fun).

It is divided into various modules. The main modules are as follows:

- Spring Core
- Spring Data

- Spring Security
- Spring Cloud
- Spring Web-MVC

In this book, we will cover the most common solutions involved in Java Enterprise applications, including the awesome Spring Cloud project. Also, we can find some interesting projects such as Spring Batch and Spring Integration, but these projects are for specific needs.

Spring Core Framework

This module is the base of the framework and contains the essential support for dependency injection, web features supported by Spring **MVC (model-view-controller)** and the pretty new WebFlux frameworks, and aspect-oriented programming. Also, this module supports the foundation for JDBC, JMS, JPA and a declarative way to manage transactions. We will explore it and understand the main projects of this module. So let's do it!

Core container

The core container is the basis of the whole Spring ecosystem and comprehends four components—core, beans, context, and expression language.

Core and beans are responsible for providing the fundamentals of the framework and dependency injection. These modules are responsible for managing the IoC container, and the principal functions are the instantiation, configuration, and destruction of the object residents in the Spring container.

Spring contexts are also called Spring IoC containers, which are responsible for instantiating, configuring, and assembling beans by reading configuration metadata from XML, Java annotations, and/or Java code in the configuration files.

There are two critical interfaces inside these modules—BeanFactory and ApplicationContext. The BeanFactory takes care of the bean lifecycle, instantiating, configuring, managing, and destroying, and the ApplicationContext helps developers to work with files resources in a generic way, enable to publish events to registered listeners. Also, the ApplicationContext supports internationalization and has the ability to work with messages in different Locales.

These modules help the context component to provide a way to access the objects inside the container. The context component has the `ApplicationContext` interface with the essential class for the container.

 Some common annotations are `@Service`, `@Component`, `@Bean`, and `@Configuration`.

Spring Messaging

Spring Framework supports a wide range of messaging systems. The Java platform is recognized as providing excellent support for messaging applications, and Spring Framework follows this approach and offers a variety of projects to help developers to write powerful applications with more productivity and fewer lines of infrastructure code. The basic idea of these projects is to provide some template classes that have the convenience methods to interact with the messaging systems.

Also, the project supplies some listener annotations to provide support for listening to messages from the brokers. The framework maintains the standard for different projects. In general, the prefix of the annotations is the name of the messaging system, for example, `@KafkaListener`.

The framework supplies many abstractions to create messaging applications in a generic way. This is interesting stuff because the application requirements change during the application lifecycle and the message broker solution may change as well. Then, with small changes, the application built with the Spring message module can work in different brokers. This is the goal.

Spring AMQP

This subproject supports the AMQP protocol in Spring Framework. It provides a template to interact with the message broker. A template is like a super high-level API that supports the `send` and `receive` operations.

There are two projects in this set: `spring-amqp`, which can be used for ActiveMQ for instance, and `spring-rabbit`, which adds support for the RabbitMQ broker. This project enables broker administration through the APIs to declare queues, bindings, and exchanges.

These projects encourage the extensive use of dependency injection provided by the core container, because they make the configuration more declarative and easy to understand.

Nowadays, the RabbitMQ broker is the popular choice for the messaging applications, and Spring provides full support for client interactions up to the level of administration tasks.

Some common annotations are `@Exchange` and `@QeueueBinding`.

Spring for Apache Kafka

Spring for Apache Kafka supports the broker-based Apache Kafka applications. It provides a high-level API to interact with Apache Kafka. Internally, the projects use the Kafka Java APIs.

This module supports the annotation programming model. The basic idea is that with a couple of annotations and some POJO models, we can bootstrap the application and start listening to and producing messages.

`KafkaTemplate` is a central class of this project. It enables us to send messages to Apache Kafka with a high-level API. Asynchronous programming is supported as well.

This module offers support for transactions via annotations. This feature is enabled via standard transactional annotations used in Spring-based applications, such as `@Transactional`.

We also learned about Spring AMQP. This project adds the Spring concept of creating applications based on this broker. The dependency injection features are supported as well.

Some common annotations are `@EnableKafka` and `@KafkaListener`.

Spring JMS

The idea of this project provides a JMS integration with ideas of Spring Framework projects and supplies a high-level API to interact with brokers. The worst part of a JMS specification is that it has a lot of boilerplate code to manage and close connections.

The `JmsTemplate` is a central class for this module, and it enables us to send messages to the broker. The JMS specification has a lot of intrinsic behaviors to handle the creation and releases resources, for instance, the `JmsTemplate` class do this tasks automatically for developers.

The module also supports transactional requirements. The `JmsTransactionManager` is the class that handles the transactional behavior of the Spring JMS module.

Spring removes the boilerplate code with a couple of annotations. The framework increases the readability of the code and makes the code more intuitive as well.

Some common annotations are `@JmsListener` and `@EnableJms`.

Spring Web MVC

This module is the first one built by the Spring Team to support the web applications in Spring Framework. This module uses the Servlet API as its foundation, and then these web applications must follow the Servlet Specification and be deployed into servlet containers. In version 5.0, the Spring Team created a Reactive web framework, which will be covered later in this book.

The Spring Web MVC module was developed using the front controller pattern. When the framework was created, this pattern was a common choice for many frameworks, such as Struts and JSF, among others. Under the hood, there is the main servlet in Spring called `DispatcherServlet`. This servlet will redirect through an algorithm to do the desired work.

It enables developers to create amazing web applications on the Java platform. This portion of the framework provides full support to develop this kind of application. There are some interesting features for this purpose, such as support for internationalization and support for handling cookies. Also, multipart requests are an exciting feature for when the application needs to handle upload files and support routing requests.

These characteristics are common for most web applications, and the framework has excellent support for these features. This support makes the framework a good choice for this kind of application. In Chapter 2, *Starting in the Spring World - The CMS Application*, we will create an application using this module and the main features will be explored in depth.

The module has full support for annotation programming since to declare HTTP endpoints until to wrap the request attribute in an HTTP request. It makes the application extremely readable without the boilerplate code to get the request parameter, for example.

Web application-wise, it enables developers to work with robust template engines such as Thymeleaf and Freemarker. It is entirely integrated with routing features and bean validation.

Also, the framework allows developers to build REST APIs with this module. Given all of this support, the module has become a favorite in the Spring ecosystem. Developers have started to create APIs with this stack, and some important companies have started to use it, especially given that the framework provides an easy way to navigate through the annotations. Because of this, the Spring Team added the new annotation `@RestController` in version 4.0.

We will work a lot with this module. Chapter by chapter, we will learn interesting things about this part of the framework.

 Some common annotations are `@RequestMapping`, `@Controller`, `@Model`, `@RestController`, and `@RequestBody`.

Spring WebFlux

A new module introduced in Spring 5.0, Spring WebFlux, can be used to implement web applications built with Reactive Streams. These systems have nonblocking characteristics and are deployed in servers built on top of Netty, such as Undertown and servlet containers that support + 3.1.

 Netty is an open source framework that helps developers to create network applications—that is, servers and clients using the asynchronous, event-driven pattern. Netty provides some interesting advantages, such as lower latency, high throughput, and less resource consumption. You can find more information at `https://netty.io`.

This module supports annotations based on Spring MVC modules, such as `@GetMapping`, `@PostMapping`, and others. This is an important feature that enables us to migrate to this new version. Of course, some adjustments are necessary, such as adding Reactor classes (Mono or Flux).

This module meets the modern web requirements to handle a lot of concurrent channels where the thread-per-request model is not an option.

We will learn about this module in Chapter 3, *Adding Persistence with Spring Data and Putting it into Reactive Fashion* and implement a fully Reactive application based on Reactive Streams.

 Some common annotations are @RequestMapping, @RestController, and @RequestBody.

Spring Data

Spring Data is an interesting module that provides the easiest way to manage application data with Spring-based programming. The project is an umbrella project, with subprojects to support different databases technologies, even relational and nonrelational databases. The Spring Team supports some databases technologies, such as Apache Cassandra, Apache Solr, Redis, and JPA Specification, and the community maintains the other exciting projects, such as ElasticSearch, Aerospike, DynamoDb, and Couchbase. The full list of projects can be found at http://projects.spring.io/spring-data.

The goal is to remove the boilerplate code from the persistence code. In general, the data access layer is quite similar, even in different projects, differing only in the project model, and Spring Data provides a powerful way to map the domain model and repository abstraction.

There are some central interfaces; they're a kind of marker to instruct the framework to choose the correct implementation. Under the hood, Spring will create a proxy and delegate the correct implementation. The amazing thing here is that developers don't have to write any persistence code and then take care of this code; they simply choose the required technology and Spring takes care of the rest.

The central interfaces are CrudRepository and PagingAndSortingRepository, and their names are self-explanatory. CrudRepository implements the CRUD behaviors, such as create, retrieval, update, and delete. PagingAndSortingRepository is an extension of CrudRepository and adds some features such as paging and sorting. Usually, we will find derivations of these interfaces such as MongoRepository, which interacts with MongoDB database technology.

Some common annotations are @Query, @Id, and @EnableJpaRepositories.

Spring Security

Security for Java applications was always a pain for developers, especially in Java Enterprise Edition. There was a lot of boilerplate code to look up objects in the application servers, and the security layer was often heavily customized for the application.

In that chaotic scenario, the Spring Team decided to create a Spring Security project to help developers handle the security layer on the Java application.

In the beginning, the project had extensive support for Java Enterprise Edition and integration with EJB 3 security annotations. Nowadays, the project supports many different ways to handle authorization and authentication for Java applications.

Spring Security provides a comprehensive model to add authorization and authentication for Java applications. The framework can be configured with a couple of annotations, which makes the task of adding a security layer extremely easy. The other important characteristics concern how the framework can be extended. There are some interfaces that enable developers to customize the default framework behaviors, and it makes the framework customized for different application requirements.

It is an umbrella project, and it is subdivided into these modules:

- spring-security-core
- spring-security-remoting
- spring-security-web
- spring-security-config
- spring-security-ldap
- spring-security-acl
- spring-security-cas
- spring-security-openid
- spring-security-test

These are the main modules, and there are many other projects to support a wide range of types of authentication. The module covers the following authentication and authorization types:

- LDAP
- HTTP Basic
- OAuth
- OAuth2
- OpenID
- CAAS
- JAAS

The module also offers a **domain-specific language (DSL)** to provide an easy configuration. Let's see a simple example:

```
http
  .formLogin()
    .loginPage("/login")
     .failureUrl("/login?error")
      .and()
    .authorizeRequests()
      .antMatchers("/signup","/about").permitAll()
      .antMatchers("/admin/**").hasRole("ADMIN")
      .anyRequest().authenticated();
```

 The example was extracted from the spring.io blog. For more details, go to https://spring.io/blog/2013/07/11/spring-security-java-config-preview-readability/.

As we can see, the DSL makes the configuration task extremely easy and very understandable.

Spring Security's main features are as follows:

- Session management
- Protection against attacks (CSRF, session fixation, and others)
- Servlet API integration
- Authentication and authorization

We will learn more about Spring Security in `Chapter 8`, *Circuit Breakers and Security*. We will also put it into practice.

 `@EnableWebSecurity` is a common annotation.

Spring Cloud

Spring Cloud is another umbrella project. The primary goal of this project is to help developers create distributed systems. Distributed systems have some common problems to solve and, of course, a set of patterns to help us, such as service discovery, circuit breakers, configuration management, intelligent route systems, and distributed sessions. Spring Cloud tools have all these implementations and well-documented projects.

The main projects are as follows:

- Spring Cloud Netflix
- Spring Cloud Config
- Spring Cloud Consul
- Spring Cloud Security
- Spring Cloud Bus
- Spring Cloud Stream

Spring Cloud Netflix

Spring Cloud Netflix is perhaps the most popular Spring module nowadays. This fantastic project allows us to integrate the Spring ecosystem with the Netflix OSS via Spring Boot AutoConfiguration features. The supported Netflix OSS libraries are Eureka for service discovery, Ribbon to enable client-side load balancing, circuit breaker via Hystrix to protect our application from external outages and make the system resilient, the Zuul component provides an intelligent routing and can act as an edge service. Finally, the Feign component can help developers to create HTTP clients for REST APIs with a couple of annotations.

Let's look at each of these:

- **Spring Cloud Netflix Eureka**: The focus of this project is to provide service discovery for applications while conforming to Netflix standards. Service discovery is an important feature and enables us to remove hardcoded configurations to supply a hostname and ports; it is more important in cloud environments because the machine is ephemeral, and thus it is hard to maintain names and IPs. The functionality is quite simple, the Eureka server provides a service registry, and Eureka clients will contact its registers themselves.

    Some common annotations are @EnableEurekaServer and @EnableEurekaClient.

- **Spring Cloud Feign**: The Netflix team created the Feign project. It's a great project that makes the configuration of HTTP clients for REST applications significantly easier than before. These implementations are based on annotations. The project supplies a couple of annotations for HTTP paths, HTTP headers, and much more, and of course, Spring Cloud Feign integrates it with the Spring Cloud ecosystem through the annotations and autoconfiguration. Also, Spring Cloud Feign can be combined with the Eureka server.

    Some common annotations are @EnableFeignClients and @FeignClient.

- **Spring Cloud Ribbon**: Ribbon is a client-side load balancer. The configuration should mainly provide a list of servers for the specific client. It must be named. In Ribbon terms, it is called the **named client**. The project also provides a range of load-balancing rules, such as Round Robin and Availability Filtering, among others. Of course, the framework allows developers to create custom rules. Ribbon has an API that works, integrated with the Eureka server, to enable service discovery, which is included in the framework. Also, essential features such as fault tolerance are supported because the API can recognize the running servers at runtime.

Some common annotations are @RibbonClient and @LoadBalanced.

- **Spring Cloud Hystrix**: An acclaimed Netflix project, this project provides a circuit breaker pattern implementation. The concept is similar to an electrical circuit breaker. The framework will watch the method marked with @HystrixCommand and watch for failing calls. If the failed calls number more than a figure permitted in configuration, the circuit breaker will open. While the circuit is open, the fallback method will be called until the circuit is closed and operates normally. It will provide resilience and fault-tolerant characteristics for our systems. The Spring ecosystem is fully integrated with Hystrix, but it works only on the @Component and @Service beans.

Some common annotations are @EnableCircuitBreaker and @HystrixCommand.

Spring Cloud Config

This exciting project provides an easy way to manage system configurations for distributed systems, and this is a critical issue in cloud environments because the file system is ephemeral. It also helps us to maintain different stages of the deployment pipeline. Spring profiles are fully integrated with this module.

We will need an application that will provide the configuration for other applications. We can understand its workings by thinking of the concepts of the **server** and the **client**, the server will provide some configurations through HTTP and the client will look up the configuration on the server. Also, it is possible to encrypt and decrypt property values.

There are some storage implementations to provide these property files, and the default implementation is Git. It enables us to store our property files in Git, or we can use the file system as well. The important thing here is that the source does not matter.

Git is a distributed version control. The tool is commonly used for development purposes, especially in the open-source community. The main advantage, when you compare it to some market players, such as SVN, is the *distributed architecture*.

There is an interesting integration between **Spring Cloud Bus** and this module. If they are integrated, it is possible to broadcast the configuration changes on the cluster. This is an important feature if the application configuration changes with frequency. There are two annotations that tell Spring to apply changes at runtime: @RefreshScope and @ConfigurationProperties.

In Chapter 7, *Airline Ticket System*, we will implement an exciting service to provide external configurations for our microservices using this module. Server concepts will be explained in more detail. The client details will be presented as well.

 @EnableConfigServer is a common annotation.

Spring Cloud Consul

Spring Cloud Consul provides integrations with Hashicorp's Consul. This tool addresses problems in the same way as service discovery, a distributed configuration, and control bus. This module allows us to configure Spring applications and Consul with a few annotations in a Spring-based programming model. Autoconfiguration is supported as well. The amazing thing here is that this module can be integrated with some Netflix OSS libraries, such as Zuul and Ribbon, via Spring Cloud Zuul and Spring Cloud Ribbon respectively (for example).

 @EnableDiscoveryClient is a common annotation.

Spring Cloud Security

This module is like an extension from Spring Security. However, distributed systems have different requirements for security. Normally, they have central identity management, or the authentication lies with the clients in the case of REST APIs. Normally, in distributed systems, we have microservices, and these services might have more than one instance in the runtime environment whose characteristics make the authentication module slightly different from monolithic applications. The module can be used together with Spring Boot applications and makes the OAuth2 implementation very easy with a couple of annotations and a few configurations. Also, some common patterns are supported, such as single sign-on, token relay, and token exchange.

For the microservice applications based on the Spring Cloud Netflix, it is particularly interesting because it enables downstream authentication to work with a Zuul proxy and offers support from Feign clients. An interceptor is used to fetch tokens.

 Some commons annotations are `@EnableOAuth2Sso` and `@EnableResourceServer`.

Spring Cloud Bus

The main goal of this project is to provide an easy way to broadcast changes spread throughout the cluster. The applications can connect the distributed system nodes through the message broker.

It provides an easy way for developers to create a publish and subscribe mechanism using the `ApplicationContext` provided by Spring Container. It enables the possibility to create applications using the event-driven architecture style with the Spring Ecosystem.

To create custom events, we need to create a child class from `RemoteApplicationEvent` and mark the class to be scanned via `@RemoteApplicationEventScan`.

The projects support three message brokers as the transport layer:

- AMQP
- Apache Kafka
- Redis

> `@RemoteApplicationEventScan` is a common annotation.

Spring Cloud Stream

The idea behind this module is to provide an easy way to build message-driven microservices. The module has an opinionated way of configuration. It means we need to follow some rules to create these configurations. In general, the application is configured by the `yaml|properties` file.

The module supports annotations as well. This means that a couple of annotations are enough to create consumers, producers, and bindings; it decouples the application and makes it easy to understand. It supplies some abstractions around the message brokers and channels, and it makes the developer's life more comfortable and productive as well.

Spring Cloud Stream has Binder implementations for RabbitMQ and Kafka.

> Some common annotations are `@EnableBinding`, `@Input`, and `@Output`.

Spring Integration

This module supports a lot of Enterprise Application patterns and brings the Spring programming model to this topic. The Spring programming model enables extensive dependence injection support and is annotations programming-centric. The annotations instruct us as to how the framework needs to be configured and defines framework behaviors.

The POJO model is suggested because it is simple and widely known in the Java development world.

This project has some intersections with the other modules. Some other projects use these module concepts to do their work. There is a project called Spring Cloud Stream, for instance.

The Enterprise Integration patterns are based on a wide range of communication channels, protocols, and patterns. This project supports some of these.

The modules support a variety of features and channels, such as the following:

- Aggregators
- Filters
- Transformers
- JMS
- RabbitMQ
- TCP/UDP
- Web services
- Twitter
- Email
- And much more

There are three main concepts of Enterprise application integration:

- Messages
- Message channel
- Message endpoint

Finally, the Spring Integration module offers a comprehensive way to create application integration and enables developers to do it using amazing support.

 Some common annotations are `@EnableIntegration`, `@IntegrationComponentScan`, and `@EnablePublisher`.

Spring Boot

Spring Boot was released in 2014. The idea behind this project was to present a way to deploy the web application outside of any container, such as Apache Tomcat, Jetty, and so on. The benefit of this kind of deployment is the independence from any external service. It allows us to run the web applications with one JAR file. Nowadays, this is an excellent approach because this forms the most natural way to adopt DevOps culture.

Spring Boot provides embedded servlet containers, such as Apache Tomcat, Jetty, and Undertow. It makes the development process more productive and comfortable when testing our web applications. Also, customizations during configuration are allowed via a configuration file, or by providing some beans.

There are some advantages when adopting the Spring Boot framework. The framework does not require any XML for configuration. This is a fantastic thing because we will find all the dependencies in the Java files. This helps the IDEs to assist developers, and it improves the traceability of the code. Another important advantage is that the project tries to keep the configuration as automatic as possible. Some annotations make the magic happen. The interesting thing here is that Spring will inject the implementation of any code that is generated at runtime.

The Spring Boot framework also provides interesting features to help developers and operations, such as health checks, metrics, security, and configuration. This is indispensable for modern applications where the modules are decomposed in a microservices architecture.

There are some other interesting features that can help the developers DevOps-wise. We can use the `application-{profile}.properties` or `application.yaml` files to configure different runtime profiles, such as development, testing, and production. It is a really useful Spring Boot feature.

Also, the project has full support for the tests, since the web layer up to the repository layer.

The framework provides a high-level API to work with unit and integration tests. Also, the framework supplies many annotations and helpers classes for developers.

The Spring Boot project is a production-ready framework with default optimized configurations for the web servers, metrics, and monitoring features to help the development team deliver high-quality software.

We can develop applications by coding in the Groovy and Java languages. Both are JVM languages. In version 5.0, the Spring Team announced the full support for Kotlin, the new language for JVM. It enables us to develop consistent and readable codes. We will look at this feature in depth in `Chapter 7`, *Airline Ticket System*.

Microservices and Spring Boot

The microservices architectural style, in general, is distributed, must be loosely coupled, and be well-defined. These characteristics must be followed when you want a microservices architecture.

Much of Spring Boot is aimed at developer productivity by making common concepts, such as RESTful HTTP and embedded web application runtimes, easy to wire up and use. In many respects, it also aims to serve as a *micro-framework*, by enabling developers to pick and choose the parts of the framework they need, without being overwhelmed by bulky or otherwise unnecessary runtime dependencies. This also enables Boot applications to be packaged into small units of deployment, and the framework is able to use build systems to generate those deployables as runnable Java archives.

The main characteristics of microservices are:

- Small-grained components
- Domain responsibility (orders, shopping carts)
- Programming-language agnostic
- Database agnostic

Spring Boot enables us to run an application on embedded web servers such as Tomcat, Jetty, and Undertow. This makes it extremely easy to deploy our components because it is possible to expose our HTTP APIs in one JAR.

The Spring Team even thinks in terms of developer productivity, and they offer a couple of projects called **starters.** These projects are groups of dependencies with some compatibilities. These awesome projects additionally work with the convention over configuration. Basically, they are common configurations that developers need to make on every single project. We can change these settings in our `application.properties` or `application.yaml` files.

Another critical point for microservices architecture is monitoring. Let's say that we're working on an e-commerce solution. We have two components, shopping cart and payments. The shopping cart probably needs to have several instances and payments need to have fewer instances. How can we check these several instances? How can we check the health of these services? We need to fire an alarm when these instances go down. This is a common implementation for all services. The Spring Framework supplies a module called Spring Boot Actuator that provides some built-in health checks for our application, databases, and much more.

Setting up our development environment

Before we start, we need to set up our development environment. Our development environment consists of the following four tools:

- JDK
- Build tool
- IDE
- Docker

We will install JDK version 8.0. This version is fully supported in Spring Framework 5. We will present the steps to install Maven 3.3.9, the most famous build tool for Java development, and in the last part, we will show you some detailed instructions on how to install IntelliJ IDEA Community Edition. We will use Ubuntu 16.04, but you can use your favorite OS. The installation steps are easy.

Installing OpenJDK

OpenJDK is a stable, free, and open source Java development kit. This package will be required for everything related to code compilation and runtime environments.

Also, it is possible to use an Oracle JDK, but you should pay attention to the **License and Agreements**.

To install OpenJDK, we will open a terminal and run the following command:

```
sudo apt-get install openjdk-8-jdk -y
```

We can find more information on how to install Java 8 JDK in the installation section (`http://openjdk.java.net/install/`) of the OpenJDK page.

Check the installation using the following command:

```
java -version
```

You should see the OpenJDK version and its relevant details displayed as follows:

```
ubuntu@ubuntu-xenial:~$ java -version
openjdk version "1.8.0_131"
OpenJDK Runtime Environment (build 1.8.0_131-8u131-b11-2ubuntu1.16.04.3-b11)
OpenJDK 64-Bit Server VM (build 25.131-b11, mixed mode)
ubuntu@ubuntu-xenial:~$ 
```

Now that we have installed the Java development kit, we are ready for the next step. In the real world, we must have a build tool to help developers to compile, package, and test the Java applications.

Let's install Maven in the next section.

Installing Maven

Maven is a popular build tool for Java development. Some important open source projects were built using this tool. There are features that facilitate the build process, standardize the project structure, and provide some guidelines for best practices development.

We will install Maven, but the installation step should be executed after the OpenJDK installation.

Open a terminal and execute the following:

```
sudo apt-get install maven -y
```

Check the installation using this command:

```
mvn -version
```

You should see the following output, although the version may be different for you:

```
ubuntu@ubuntu-xenial:~$ mvn -version
Apache Maven 3.3.9
Maven home: /usr/share/maven
Java version: 1.8.0_131, vendor: Oracle Corporation
Java home: /usr/lib/jvm/java-8-openjdk-amd64/jre
Default locale: en_US, platform encoding: ANSI_X3.4-1968
OS name: "linux", version: "4.4.0-97-generic", arch: "amd64", family: "unix"
ubuntu@ubuntu-xenial:~$
```

Well done. Now we have Maven installed. Maven has a vibrant community that produces many plugins to help developers with important tasks. There are plugins to execute a unit test and plugins to prepare the project for the release event that can be integrated with SCM software.

We will use the `spring boot maven` plugin and `docker maven` plugin. The first converts our application to a JAR file and the second enables us to integrate with Docker Engine to create images, run containers, and much more. In the next few chapters, we will learn how to configure and interact with these plugins.

Installing IDE

The IDE is an important tool to help developers. In this book, we will use the IntelliJ IDEA as an *official* tool for developing our projects. There are no restrictions for other IDEs because the project will be developed using Maven as a build tool.

The IDE is a personal choice for developers, and in general, it involves passion; what some people love, other developers hate. Please feel free to use your favorite.

IntelliJ IDEA

IntelliJ IDEA is a JetBrains product. We will use the Community Edition, which is open source and a fantastic tool with which to code Java and Kotlin. The tool offers a fantastic autocomplete feature, and also fully supports Java 8 features.

Go to `https://www.jetbrains.com/idea/download/#section=linux` and download the Community Edition. We can extract the `tar.gz` and execute it.

Spring Tools Suite

The Spring Tools Suite is based on Eclipse IDE, provided by the Eclipse Foundation, of course. The goal is to provide support for the Spring ecosystem and make the developer's life easier. Interesting features such as Beans Explorer are supported in this tool.

Download the tool at the following link:
`http://download.springsource.com/release/STS/3.6.4.RELEASE/dist/e4.4/groovy-grails-tool-suite-3.6.4.RELEASE-e4.4.2-linux-gtk-x86_64.tar.gz`

Installing Docker

Docker is an open source project that helps people to run and manage containers. For developers, Docker helps in different stages of the development lifecycle.

During the development phase, Docker enables developers to spin up different infrastructure services such as databases and service discoveries like Consul without installation in the current system operational. It helps the developers because developers do not need to install these kinds of systems in the operating system layer. Usually, this task can cause conflicts with the libraries during the installation process and consumes a lot of time.

Sometimes, developers need to install the exact version. In this case, it is necessary to reinstall the whole application on the expected version. It is not a good thing because the developer machine during this time becomes slow. The reason is quite simple, there are many applications that are used during software development.

Docker helps developers at this stage. It is quite simple to run a container with MongoDB. There is no installation and it enables developers to start the database with one line. Docker supports the image tag. This feature helps to work with different versions of the software; this is awesome for developers who need to change the software version every time.

Another advantage is that when the developers need to deliver the artifacts for test or production purposes, Docker enables these tasks via Docker images.

Docker helps people to adopt the DevOps culture and delivers amazing features to improve the performance of the whole process.

Let's install Docker.

The easiest way to install Docker is to download the script found at `https://get.docker.com`:

```
curl -fsSL get.docker.com -o get-docker.sh
```

After the download is completed, we will execute the script as follows:

```
sh get-docker.sh
```

Wait for the script execution and then check the Docker installation using the following command:

```
docker -v
```

The output needs to look like the following:

```
ubuntu@ubuntu-xenial:~$ docker -v
Docker version 17.10.0-ce, build f4ffd25
ubuntu@ubuntu-xenial:~$
```

Sometimes, the version of Docker can be increased, and the version should be at least **17.10.0-ce**.

Finally, we will add the current user to the Docker group, and this enables us to use the Docker command line without the `sudo` keyword. Type the following command:

```
sudo usermod -aG docker $USER
```

We need to log out to effect these changes. Confirm whether the command works as expected by typing the following. Make sure that the `sudo` keyword is not present:

```
docker ps
```

The output should be as follows:

```
ubuntu@ubuntu-xenial:~$ docker ps
CONTAINER ID      IMAGE        COMMAND      CREATED      STATUS      PORTS      NAMES
ubuntu@ubuntu-xenial:~$
```

Introducing Docker concepts

Now, we will introduce some Docker concepts. This book is not about Docker, but some basic instructions on how to use Docker are necessary to interact with our containers during the next few chapters. Docker is a de facto tool that is used to manage containers.

Docker images

The Docker image is like a template for a Docker container. It contains a set of folders and files that are necessary to start the Docker container. We will never have an image in execution mode. The image provides a template for Docker Engine to start up the container. We can create an analogy with object orientation to understand the process better. The image is like a class that provides an *infrastructure* to instantiate some objects, and instances are like a container.

Also, we have a Docker registry to store our images. These registries can be public or private. Some cloud vendors provide these private registries. The most famous is Docker Hub. It can be free, but if you choose this option, the image should be public. Of course, Docker Hub supports private images, but in this case, you have to pay for the service.

Containers

Docker containers are a *lightweight* virtualization. The term lightweight means that Docker uses the SO functionalities to cage the system process and manager memory, processors, and folders. This is different from virtualization with VMs because, in this mode, the technology needs to simulate the whole SO, drivers, and storage. This task consumes a lot of computational power and can sometimes be inefficient.

Docker networks

A Docker network is a layer that provides runtime isolation for containers. It is a kind of sandbox in which to run containers that are isolated from other containers. When the Docker is installed, by default it creates three networks that should not be removed. These three networks are as follows:

- `bridge`
- `none`
- `host`

Also, Docker provides the user with an easy way to create your network. For this purpose, Docker offers two drivers—**bridge** and **overlay**.

Bridge can be used for the local environment, and it means this kind of network is allowed on a single host. It will be useful for our applications because it promotes isolation between containers regarding security. This is a good practice. The name of the container attached to this kind of network can be used as a **DNS** for the container. Internally, Docker will associate the container name with the container IP.

The overlay network provides the ability to connect containers to different machines. This kind of network is used by Docker Swarm to manage the container in a clustered environment. In the newest version, the Docker Compose tool natively supports Docker Swarm.

Docker volumes

Docker volumes are the suggested way to persist data outside of a container. These volumes are fully managed by Docker Engine, and these volumes can be writable and readable depending on the configuration when they are used with a Docker command line. The data of these volumes is persisted on a directory path on a host machine.

There is a command-line tool to interact with volumes. The base of this tool is the `docker volume` command; the `--help` argument on the end shows the help instructions.

Docker commands

Now we will take a look at Docker commands. These commands are used mainly in the development life cycle, commands such as `spin up container`, `stop containers`, `remove`, and `inspect`.

Docker run

`docker run` is the most common Docker command. This command should be used to start the containers. The basic structure of a command is as follows:

```
docker run [OPTIONS] IMAGE[:TAG|@DIGEST] [COMMAND] [ARG...]
```

The options arguments enable some configurations for the container, for instance, the `--name` argument permits you to configure a name for a container. It is important for DNS when the container is running in a bridge network.

The network settings can be configured on the `run` command as well, and the parameter is `-- net`. This enables us to configure the network to which the container will be attached.

Another important option is `detached`. It indicates whether the container will run in the background. The `-d` parameter instructs Docker to run a container in the background.

Docker container

The `docker container` command permits you to manage the containers. There are many commands, as shown in the following list:

- docker container attach
- docker container commit
- docker container cp
- docker container create
- docker container diff
- docker container exec
- docker container export
- docker container inspect
- docker container kill
- docker container logs
- docker container ls
- docker container pause
- docker container port
- docker container prune
- docker container rename

- docker container restart
- docker container rm
- docker container run
- docker container start
- docker container stats
- docker container stop
- docker container top
- docker container unpause
- docker container update
- docker container wait

There are some important commands here. The docker container exec permits you to run commands on a running container. This is an important task to debug or look inside the container files. The docker container prune removes the stopped containers. It is helpful in the development cycle. There are some known commands, such as docker container rm, docker container start, docker container stop, and docker container restart. These commands are self-explanatory and have similar behaviors.

Docker network

The docker network commands enable you to manage the Docker network stuff via the command line. There are six basic commands, and the commands are self-explanatory:

- docker network create
- docker network connect
- docker network ls
- docker network rm
- docker network disconnect
- docker network inspect

docker network create, docker network ls, and docker network rm are the main commands. It is possible to compare them with the Linux commands, where the rm command is used to remove things and the ls command is usually used to list things such as folders. The create command should be used to create networks.

The docker network connect and docker network disconnect commands allow you to connect the running container to the desired network. They may be useful in some scenarios.

Finally, the `docker network inspect` command provides detailed information on the requested network.

Docker volume

The `docker volume` command permits you to manage the Docker volumes via the command-line interface. There are five commands:

- `docker volume create`
- `docker volume inspect`
- `docker volume ls`
- `docker volume prune`
- `docker volume rm`

The `docker volume create`, `docker volume rm` and `docker volume ls` commands are effectively used to manage the `docker volume` by Docker Engine. The behaviors are quite similar to those of the networks, but for volumes. The `create` command will create a new volume with some options allowed. The `ls` command lists all volumes and the `rm` command will remove the requested volume.

Summary

In this chapter, we looked at the main concepts of Spring Framework. We understood the main modules of the framework and how these modules can help developers to build applications in different kinds of architecture, such as messaging applications, REST APIs, and web portals.

We also spent some time preparing our development environment by installing essential tools, such as Java JDK, Maven, and IDE. This was a critical step to take before we continue to the next chapters.

We used Docker to help us to set up a development environment, such as containers for databases and delivery for our application in Docker images. We installed Docker and looked at the main commands for managing containers, networks, and volumes.

In the next chapter, we will create our first Spring application and put it into practice!

2
Starting in the Spring World – the CMS Application

Now, we'll create our first application; at this point, we have learned the Spring concepts, and we are ready to put them into practice. At the beginning of this chapter, we'll introduce the Spring dependencies to create a web application, also we know that Spring Initializr is a fantastic project that enables developers to create Spring skeleton projects, with as many dependencies as they want. In this chapter, we will learn how to put up our first Spring application on IDE and command line, expose our first endpoint, understand how this works under the hood, and get to know the main annotations of Spring REST support. We will figure out how to create a service layer for the **CMS (Content Management System)** application and understand how Dependency Injection works in a Spring container. We will meet the Spring stereotypes and implement our first Spring bean. At the end of this chapter, we will explain how to create a view layer and integrate that with AngularJS.

In this chapter, the following topics will be covered:

- Creating the project structure
- Running the first Spring application
- Introducing the REST support
- Understanding the Dependency Injection in Spring

Creating the CMS application structure

Now we will create our first application with the Spring Framework; we will create a basic structure for the CMS application with Spring Initializr. This page helps to bootstrap our application, it's a kind of guide which allows us to configure the dependencies on Maven or Gradle. We can also choose the language and version of Spring Boot.

The page looks like this:

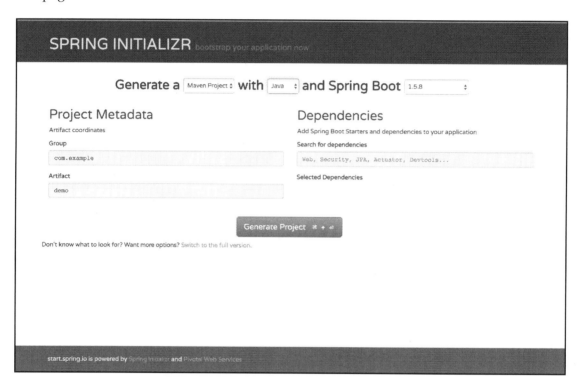

In the **Project Metadata** section, we can put the coordinates for Maven projects; there is a group field which refers to the `groupId` tag, and we have artifacts which refer to the `artifactId`. This is all for the Maven coordinates.

The dependencies section enables the configuration of the Spring dependencies, the field has the autocomplete feature and helps developers to put in the correct dependency.

The CMS project

Before we start to code and learn amazing things, let's understand a little bit about the CMS project, the main purpose of this project is to help companies manage the CMS content for different topics. There are three main entities in this project:

- The News class is the most important, it will store the content of the news.
- It has a *category* which makes the search easier, and we can also group news by category, and of course, we can group by the user who has created the news. The news should be approved by other users to make sure it follows the company rules.
- The news has some *tags* as well, as we can see the application is pretty standard, the business rules are easy as well; this is intentional because we keep the focus on the new things we will learn.

Now we know how Spring Initializr (https://start.spring.io) works and the business rules we need to follow, we are ready to create the project. Let's do it right now.

Project metadata section

Insert spring-five in the **Group** field and cms in the **Artifact** field. If you want to customize it, no problem, this is a kind of informative project configuration:

```
Project Metadata

Artifact coordinates

Group

  spring-five


Artifact

  cms
```

The dependencies section

Type the MVC word in the **Search for Dependencies** field. The Web module will appear as an option, the Web module contains the full-stack web development with Embedded Tomcat and Spring MVC, select it. Also, we need to put Thymeleaf dependencies in this module. It is a template engine and will be useful for the view features at the end of this chapter. Type Thymeleaf, it includes the Thymeleaf templating engine, and includes integration with Spring. The module will appear, and then select it as well. Now we can see **Web** and **Thymeleaf** in the **Selected Dependencies** pane:

Generating the project

After we have finished the project definition and chosen the project dependencies, we are ready to download the project. It can be done using the **Generate Project** button, click on it. The project will be downloaded. At this stage, the project is ready to start our work:

The zip file will be generated with the name cms.zip (the **Artifact** field input information) and the location of the downloaded file depends on the browser configuration.

>Before opening the project, we must uncompress the artifact generated by **Spring Initializr** to the desired location. The command should be: `unzip -d <target_destination> /<path_to_file>/cms.zip`. Follow the example: `unzip -d /home/john /home/john/Downloads/cms.zip`.

Now, we can open the project in our IDE. Let's open it and take a look at the basic structure of the project.

Running the application

Before we run the application, let's have a walk through our project structure.

Open the project on IntelliJ IDEA using the **Import Project** or **Open** options (both are similar), the following page will be displayed:

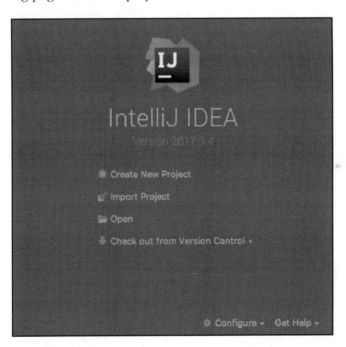

Then we can open or import the `pom.xml` file.

The following project structure should be displayed:

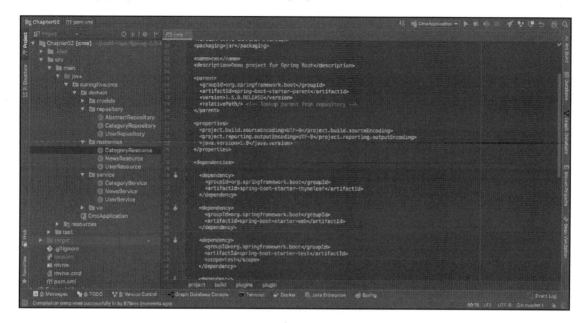

Open the `pom.xml`, we have three dependencies, `spring-boot-starter-thymeleaf`, `spring-boot-starter-web`, `spring-boot-starter-test`, and an interesting plugin, `spring-boot-maven-plugin`.

These `starter` dependencies are a shortcut for developers because they provide full dependencies for the module. For instance, on the `spring-boot-starter-web`, there is `web-mvc`, `jackson-databind`, `hibernate-validator-web`, and some others; these dependencies must be on the classpath to run the web applications, and starters make this task considerably easier.

Let's analyze our `pom.xml`, the file should look like this:

```
<?xml version="1.0" encoding="UTF-8"?>
<project xmlns="http://maven.apache.org/POM/4.0.0"
  xmlns:xsi="http://www.w3.org/2001/XMLSchema-instance"
  xsi:schemaLocation="http://maven.apache.org/POM/4.0.0
http://maven.apache.org/xsd/maven-4.0.0.xsd">
  <modelVersion>4.0.0</modelVersion>

  <groupId>spring-five</groupId>
  <artifactId>cms</artifactId>
  <version>0.0.1-SNAPSHOT</version>
```

```xml
<packaging>jar</packaging>

<name>cms</name>
<description>Demo project for Spring Boot</description>

<parent>
  <groupId>org.springframework.boot</groupId>
  <artifactId>spring-boot-starter-parent</artifactId>
  <version>1.5.8.RELEASE</version>
  <relativePath/> <!-- lookup parent from repository -->
</parent>

<properties>
  <project.build.sourceEncoding>UTF-8</project.build.sourceEncoding>
<project.reporting.outputEncoding>UTF-8</project.reporting.outputEncoding>
  <java.version>1.8</java.version>
</properties>

<dependencies>

  <dependency>
    <groupId>org.springframework.boot</groupId>
    <artifactId>spring-boot-starter-thymeleaf</artifactId>
  </dependency>

  <dependency>
    <groupId>org.springframework.boot</groupId>
    <artifactId>spring-boot-starter-web</artifactId>
  </dependency>

  <dependency>
    <groupId>org.springframework.boot</groupId>
    <artifactId>spring-boot-starter-test</artifactId>
    <scope>test</scope>
  </dependency>

  <dependency>
    <groupId>org.projectlombok</groupId>
    <artifactId>lombok</artifactId>
    <version>1.16.16</version>
    <scope>provided</scope>
  </dependency>

  <dependency>
    <groupId>io.springfox</groupId>
    <artifactId>springfox-swagger2</artifactId>
    <version>2.7.0</version>
  </dependency>
```

```
        <dependency>
          <groupId>io.springfox</groupId>
          <artifactId>springfox-swagger-ui</artifactId>
          <version>2.7.0</version>
        </dependency>

    </dependencies>

    <build>
      <plugins>
        <plugin>
          <groupId>org.springframework.boot</groupId>
          <artifactId>spring-boot-maven-plugin</artifactId>
        </plugin>
      </plugins>
    </build>

</project>
```

Also, we have a `spring-boot-maven-plugin`, this awesome plugin provides Spring Boot support for Maven. It enables you to package the application in a Fat-JAR, and the plugin supports the run, start, and stop goals, as well interacting with our applications.

 Fat-JAR: a JAR which contains all project class files and resources packed together with all its dependencies.

For now, that is enough on Maven configurations; let's take a look at the Java files.

The Spring Initializr created one class for us, in general, the name of this class is artifact name plus `Application`, in our case `CmsApplication`, this class should look like this:

```java
package springfive.cms;

import org.springframework.boot.SpringApplication;
import org.springframework.boot.autoconfigure.SpringBootApplication;

@SpringBootApplication
public class CmsApplication {

  public static void main(String[] args) {
    SpringApplication.run(CmsApplication.class, args);
  }
}
```

Looking under the hood

We have some interesting things here, let's understand them. The
`@SpringBootApplication` is the essential annotation for the Spring Boot application; it's a
kind of alias for `@Configuration`, `@EnableAutoConfiguration`, and
`@Component` annotations. Let's dig in:

- The first annotation, `@Configuration` indicates that the class can produce a
  beans definitions for the Spring container. This is an interesting annotation to
  work with external dependencies such as `DataSources`; this is the most common
  use case for this annotation.
- The second annotation, `@EnableAutoConfiguration` means that with the
  Spring `ApplicationContext` container, it will try to help us configure the
  default beans for the specific context. For instance, when we create the web MVC
  application with Spring Boot, we will probably need a web server container to
  run it. In a default configuration, the Spring container, together with
  `@EnableAutoConfiguration`, will configure a bean Tomcat-embedded
  container for us. This annotation is very helpful for developers.
- The `@Component` is a stereotype, the container understands which class is
  considered for auto-detection and needs to instantiate it.

The `SpringApplication` class is responsible for bootstrapping the Spring application from
the main method, it will create an `ApplicationContext` instance, take care of
configurations provided by the configuration files, and finally, it will load the singleton
beans that are defined by annotations.

> **Stereotype Annotations** denote a conceptual division in an architecture
> layer. They help the developers understand the purpose of the class and
> the layer which the beans represent, for example, `@Repository` means the
> data access layer.

Running the application

We will run the application in IntelliJ IDEA and command line. It is an important task to
learn because we are working in different development environments; sometimes the
configurations of the application are a little bit complicated, and we are not able to run it
with IDEs, or sometimes the companies have different IDEs as standard, so we will learn
about two different ways.

IntelliJ IDEA

In general, the IntelliJ IDEA recognizes the main class annotated with `@SpringBootApplication` and creates a run configuration for us, but it depends on the version of the tool, let's do it.

Command line

The command line is a more generic tool to run the project. Also, this task is easy, thanks to the Spring Boot Maven plugin. There are two ways to run, and we will cover both.

Command line via the Maven goal

The first one is a goal of the Spring Boot Maven plugin, and it is straightforward; open the terminal then go to the root project folder, pay attention as this is the same folder where we have the `pom.xml,` and execute the following command:

```
mvn clean install spring-boot:run
```

The Maven will now compile the project and run the main class, the class `CmsApplication,` and we should see this output:

Command line via the JAR file

To run it through the Java file, we need to compile and package it, and then we can run the project with the Java command line. To compile and package it, we can use the pretty standard Maven command like this:

```
mvn clean install
```

After the project is compiled and packaged as a Fat-JAR, we can execute the JAR file, go to the target folder and check the files from this folder, probably the result will look like this:

```
classes/              generated-sources/    generated-test-sources/ maven-archiver/    maven-status/       surefire-reports/    test-classes/
ubuntu@ubuntu-xenial:/vagrant/cms$ cd target/
ubuntu@ubuntu-xenial:/vagrant/cms/target$ ls -l
total 20808
drwxr-xr-x 1 ubuntu ubuntu      128 Oct 28 16:44 classes
-rw-r--r-- 1 ubuntu ubuntu 21301788 Oct 28 16:44 cms-0.0.1-SNAPSHOT.jar
-rw-r--r-- 1 ubuntu ubuntu     2745 Oct 28 16:44 cms-0.0.1-SNAPSHOT.jar.original
drwxr-xr-x 1 ubuntu ubuntu       96 Oct 28 16:44 generated-sources
drwxr-xr-x 1 ubuntu ubuntu       96 Oct 28 16:44 generated-test-sources
drwxr-xr-x 1 ubuntu ubuntu       96 Oct 28 16:44 maven-archiver
drwxr-xr-x 1 ubuntu ubuntu       96 Oct 28 16:44 maven-status
drwxr-xr-x 1 ubuntu ubuntu      128 Oct 28 16:44 surefire-reports
drwxr-xr-x 1 ubuntu ubuntu       96 Oct 28 16:44 test-classes
ubuntu@ubuntu-xenial:/vagrant/cms/target$
```

We have two main files in our target folder, the cms-0.0.1-SNAPSHOT.jar and the cms-0.0.1-SNAPSHOT.jar.original, the file with the .original extension is not executable. It is the original artifact resulting from the compilation, and the other is our executable file. It is what we are looking for, let's execute it, type the following command:

```
java -jar cms-0.0.1-SNAPSHOT.jar
```

The result should be as displayed. The application is up and running:

That is it for this part, in the next section, we will create the first **REST** (**Representational State Transfer**) resources and understand how the REST endpoints work.

Creating the REST resources

Now, we have an application up and running in this section, and we will add some REST endpoints and model some initial classes for the CMS application, the REST endpoints will be useful for the AngularJS integration.

One of the required characteristics for the APIs is the documentation, and a popular tool to help us with these tasks is Swagger. The Spring Framework supports Swagger, and we can do it with a couple of annotations. The project's Spring Fox is the correct tool to do this, and we will take a look at the tool in this chapter.

Let's do this.

Models

Before we start to create our class, we will add the `Lombok` dependency in our project. It is a fantastic library which provides some interesting things such as `GET/SET` at compilation time, the `Val` keyword to make variables final, `@Data` to make a class with some default methods like getters/setters, `equals`, and `hashCode`.

Adding Lombok dependency

Put the following dependency in a `pom.xml` file:

```
<dependency>
  <groupId>org.projectlombok</groupId>
  <artifactId>lombok</artifactId>
  <version>1.16.16</version>
  <scope>provided</scope>
</dependency>
```

The `provided` scope instructs Maven not to include this dependency in the JAR file because we need it at compile time. We do not need it at runtime. Wait for Maven to download the dependency, that is all for now.

Also, we can use the **Reimport All Maven Projects** provided by IntelliJ IDEA, located in the Maven Projects tab, as shown here:

Creating the models

Now, we will create our models, which are Java classes annotated with `@Data`.

Tag

This class represents a tag in our system. There isn't necessarily any repository for it because it will be persisted together with our `News` entity:

```
package springfive.cms.domain.models;

import lombok.Data;

@Data
public class Tag {

  String value;

}
```

Category

A category model for our CMS application can be used to group the news. Also, the other important thing is that this makes our news categorized to make the search task easy. Take a look at the following code:

```
package springfive.cms.domain.models;

import lombok.Data;

@Data
public class Category {

  String id;

  String name;

}
```

User

It represents a user in our domain model. We have two different profiles, the author who acts as a news writer, and another one is a reviewer who must review the news registered at the portal. Take a look at the following example:

```
package springfive.cms.domain.models;

import lombok.Data;

@Data
public class User {

    String id;

    String identity;

    String name;

    Role role;

}
```

News

This class represents news in our domain, for now, it does not have any behaviors. Only properties and getters/setters are exposed; in the future, we will add some behaviors:

```
package springfive.cms.domain.models;

import java.util.Set;
import lombok.Data;

@Data
public class News {

    String id;

    String title;

    String content;

    User author;

    Set<User> mandatoryReviewers;
    Set<Review> reviewers;
```

```
    Set<Category> categories;

    Set<Tag> tags;

}
```

The `Review` class can be found at GitHub: (`https://github.com/PacktPublishing/Spring-5.0-By-Example/tree/master/Chapter02/src/main/java/springfive/cms/domain/models`).

As we can see, they are simple Java classes which represent our CMS application domain. It is the heart of our application, and all the domain logic will reside in these classes. It is an important characteristic.

Hello REST resources

We have created the models, and we can start to think about our REST resources. We will create three main resources:

- `CategoryResource` which will be responsible for the `Category` class.
- The second one is `UserResource`. It will manage the interactions between the `User` class and the REST APIs.
- The last one, and more important as well, will be the `NewsResource` which will be responsible for managing news entities, such as reviews.

Creating the CategoryResource class

We will create our first REST resource, let's get started with the `CategoryResource` class which is responsible for managing our `Category` class. The implementation of this entity will be simple, and we will create CRUD endpoints such as create, retrieve, update, and delete. We have two important things we must keep in mind when we create the APIs. The first one is the correct HTTP verb such as `POST`, `GET`, `PUT` and `DELETE`. It is essential for the REST APIs to have the correct HTTP verb as it provides us with intrinsic knowledge about the API. It is a pattern for anything that interacts with our APIs. Another thing is the status codes, and it is the same as the first one we must follow, this is the pattern the developers will easily recognize. The *Richardson Maturity Model* can help us create amazing REST APIs, and this model introduces some levels to measure the REST APIs, it's a kind of thermometer.

Firstly, we will create the skeleton for our APIs. Think about what features you need in your application. In the next section, we will explain how to add a service layer in our REST APIs. For now, let's build a `CategoryResource` class, our implementation could look like this:

```java
package springfive.cms.domain.resources;

import java.util.Arrays;
import java.util.List;
import org.springframework.http.HttpStatus;
import org.springframework.http.ResponseEntity;
import org.springframework.web.bind.annotation.DeleteMapping;
import org.springframework.web.bind.annotation.GetMapping;
import org.springframework.web.bind.annotation.PathVariable;
import org.springframework.web.bind.annotation.PostMapping;
import org.springframework.web.bind.annotation.PutMapping;
import org.springframework.web.bind.annotation.RequestMapping;
import org.springframework.web.bind.annotation.ResponseStatus;
import org.springframework.web.bind.annotation.RestController;
import springfive.cms.domain.models.Category;
import springfive.cms.domain.vo.CategoryRequest;

@RestController
@RequestMapping("/api/category")
public class CategoryResource {

  @GetMapping(value = "/{id}")
  public ResponseEntity<Category> findOne(@PathVariable("id") String id){
    return ResponseEntity.ok(new Category());
  }

  @GetMapping
  public ResponseEntity<List<Category>> findAll(){
    return ResponseEntity.ok(Arrays.asList(new Category(),new Category()));
  }

  @PostMapping
  public ResponseEntity<Category> newCategory(CategoryRequest category){
    return new ResponseEntity<>(new Category(), HttpStatus.CREATED);
  }

  @DeleteMapping("/{id}")
  @ResponseStatus(HttpStatus.NO_CONTENT)
  public void removeCategory(@PathVariable("id") String id){
  }

  @PutMapping("/{id}")
```

```
    public ResponseEntity<Category> updateCategory(@PathVariable("id") String
id,CategoryRequest category){
      return new ResponseEntity<>(new Category(), HttpStatus.OK);
    }


  }
```

The `CategoryRequest` can be found at GitHub (`https://github.com/PacktPublishing/ Spring-5.0-By-Example/tree/master/Chapter02/src/main/java/springfive/cms/ domain/vo`).

We have some important concepts here. The first one is `@RestController`. It instructs the Spring Framework that the `CategoryResource` class will expose REST endpoints over the Web-MVC module. This annotation will configure some things in a framework, such as `HttpMessageConverters` to handle HTTP requests and responses such as XML or JSON. Of course, we need the correct libraries on the classpath, to handle JSON and XML. Also, add some headers to the request such as `Accept` and `Content-Type`. This annotation was introduced in version 4.0. It is a kind of syntactic sugar annotation because it's annotated with `@Controller` and `@ResponseBody`.

The second is the `@RequestMapping` annotation, and this important annotation is responsible for the HTTP request and response in our class. The usage is quite simple in this code when we use it on the class level, it will propagate for all methods, and the methods use it as a relative. The `@RequestMapping` annotation has different use cases. It allows us to configure the HTTP verb, params, and headers.

Finally, we have `@GetMapping`, `@PostMapping`, `@DeleteMapping`, and `@PutMapping`, these annotations are a kind of shortcut to configure the `@RequestMapping` with the correct HTTP verbs; an advantage is that these annotations make the code more readable.

Except for the `removeCategory`, all the methods return the `ResponseEntity` class which enables us to handle the correct HTTP status codes in the next section.

UserResource

The `UserResource` class is the same as `CategoryResource`, except that it uses the `User` class. We can find the whole code on the GitHub (`https://github.com/PacktPublishing/ Spring-5.0-By-Example/tree/master/Chapter02`).

NewsResource

The `NewsResource` class is essential, this endpoint enables users to review news previously registered, and it also provides an endpoint to return the updated news. This is an important feature because we are interested only in the relevant news. Irrelevant news cannot be shown on the portal. The resource class should look like this:

```
package springfive.cms.domain.resources;

import java.util.Arrays;
import java.util.List;
import org.springframework.http.HttpStatus;
import org.springframework.http.ResponseEntity;
import org.springframework.web.bind.annotation.DeleteMapping;
import org.springframework.web.bind.annotation.GetMapping;
import org.springframework.web.bind.annotation.PathVariable;
import org.springframework.web.bind.annotation.PostMapping;
import org.springframework.web.bind.annotation.PutMapping;
import org.springframework.web.bind.annotation.RequestMapping;
import org.springframework.web.bind.annotation.ResponseStatus;
import org.springframework.web.bind.annotation.RestController;
import springfive.cms.domain.models.News;
import springfive.cms.domain.models.Review;
import springfive.cms.domain.vo.NewsRequest;

@RestController
@RequestMapping("/api/news")
public class NewsResource {

  @GetMapping(value = "/{id}")
  public ResponseEntity<News> findOne(@PathVariable("id") String id){
    return ResponseEntity.ok(new News());
  }

  @GetMapping
  public ResponseEntity<List<News>> findAll(){
    return ResponseEntity.ok(Arrays.asList(new News(),new News()));
  }

  @PostMapping
  public ResponseEntity<News> newNews(NewsRequest news){
    return new ResponseEntity<>(new News(), HttpStatus.CREATED);
  }

  @DeleteMapping("/{id}")
  @ResponseStatus(HttpStatus.NO_CONTENT)
  public void removeNews(@PathVariable("id") String id){
```

```
    }

    @PutMapping("/{id}")
    public ResponseEntity<News> updateNews(@PathVariable("id") String
id,NewsRequest news){
        return new ResponseEntity<>(new News(), HttpStatus.OK);
    }

    @GetMapping(value = "/{id}/review/{userId}")
    public ResponseEntity<Review> review(@PathVariable("id") String
id,@PathVariable("userId") String userId){
        return ResponseEntity.ok(new Review());
    }

    @GetMapping(value = "/revised")
    public ResponseEntity<List<News>> revisedNews(){
        return ResponseEntity.ok(Arrays.asList(new News(),new News()));
    }

}
```

The `NewsRequest` class can be found at `GitHub`.

Pay attention to the HTTP verbs and the HTTP status code, as we need to follow the correct semantics.

Adding service layer

Now, we have the skeleton for the REST layer ready, and in this section, we will start to create a service layer for our application. We will show how the Dependency Injection works under the hood, learn the stereotype annotations on Spring Framework and also start to think about our persistence storage, which will be presented in the next section.

Changes in the model

We need to make some changes to our model, specifically in the News class. In our business rules, we need to keep our information safe, then we need to review all the news. We will add some methods to add a new review done by a user, and also we will add a method to check if the news was reviewed by all mandatory reviewers.

Adding a new review

For this feature, we need to create a method in our `News` class, the method will return a `Review` and should look like this:

```
public Review review(String userId,String status){
    final Review review = new Review(userId, status);
    this.reviewers.add(review);
    return review;
}
```

We do not need to check if the user, who performs the review action, is a mandatory reviewer at all.

Keeping the news safely

Also, we need to check if the news is fully revised by all mandatory reviewers. It is quite simple, we are using Java 8, and it provides the amazing `Stream` interface, which makes the collections interactions easier than before. Let's do this:

```
public Boolean revised() {
    return this.mandatoryReviewers.stream().allMatch(reviewer ->
this.reviewers.stream()
        .anyMatch(review -> reviewer.id.equals(review.userId) &&
"approved".equals(review.status)));
}
```

Thanks, Java 8, we appreciate it.

Before starting the service layer

Our application needs to have a persistence storage where our records can be loaded, even if the application goes down. We will create the fake implementation for our repositories. In chapter 3, *Persistence with Spring Data and Reactive Fashion*, we will introduce the Spring Data projects which help developers create amazing repositories with a fantastic DSL. For now, we will create some Spring beans to store our elements in memory, let's do that.

CategoryService

Let's start with our simplest service, the `CategoryService` class, the behaviors expected of this class are CRUD operations. Then, we need a representation of our persistence storage or repository implementation, for now, we are using the ephemeral storage and `ArrayList` with our categories. In the next chapter, we will add the real persistence for our CMS application.

Let's create our first Spring service. The implementation is in the following snippet:

```
package springfive.cms.domain.service;

import java.util.List;
import org.springframework.stereotype.Service;
import springfive.cms.domain.models.Category;
import springfive.cms.domain.repository.CategoryRepository;

@Service
public class CategoryService {

  private final CategoryRepository categoryRepository;

  public CategoryService(CategoryRepository categoryRepository) {
    this.categoryRepository = categoryRepository;
  }

  public Category update(Category category){
    return this.categoryRepository.save(category);
  }

  public Category create(Category category){
    return this.categoryRepository.save(category);
  }

  public void delete(String id){
    final Category category = this.categoryRepository.findOne(id);
    this.categoryRepository.delete(category);
  }

  public List<Category> findAll(){
    return this.categoryRepository.findAll();
  }

  public Category findOne(String id){
    return this.categoryRepository.findOne(id);
  }
```

```
}
```

There is some new stuff here. This class will be detected and instantiated by the Spring container because it has a @Service annotation. As we can see, there is nothing special in that class. It does not necessarily extend any class or implement an interface. We received the CategoryRepository on a constructor, this class will be provided by the Spring container because we instruct the container to produce this, but in Spring 5 it is not necessary to use @Autowired anymore in the constructor. It works because we had the only one constructor in that class and Spring will detect it. Also, we have a couple of methods which represent the CRUD behaviors, and it is simple to understand.

UserService

The UserService class is quite similar to the CategoryService, but the rules are about the User entity, for this entity we do not have anything special. We have the @Service annotation, and we received the UserRepository constructor as well. It is quite simple and easy to understand. We will show the UserService implementation, and it must be like this:

```
package springfive.cms.domain.service;

import java.util.List;
import java.util.UUID;
import org.springframework.stereotype.Service;
import springfive.cms.domain.models.User;
import springfive.cms.domain.repository.UserRepository;
import springfive.cms.domain.vo.UserRequest;

@Service
public class UserService {

  private final UserRepository userRepository;

  public UserService(UserRepository userRepository) {
    this.userRepository = userRepository;
  }

  public User update(String id,UserRequest userRequest){
    final User user = this.userRepository.findOne(id);
    user.setIdentity(userRequest.getIdentity());
    user.setName(userRequest.getName());
    user.setRole(userRequest.getRole());
    return this.userRepository.save(user);
  }
```

```
public User create(UserRequest userRequest){
  User user = new User();
  user.setId(UUID.randomUUID().toString());
  user.setIdentity(userRequest.getIdentity());
  user.setName(userRequest.getName());
  user.setRole(userRequest.getRole());
  return this.userRepository.save(user);
}

public void delete(String id){
  final User user = this.userRepository.findOne(id);
  this.userRepository.delete(user);
}

public List<User> findAll(){
  return this.userRepository.findAll();
}

public User findOne(String id){
  return this.userRepository.findOne(id);
}

}
```

Pay attention to the class declaration with `@Service` annotation. This is a very common implementation in the Spring ecosystem. Also, we can find `@Component`, `@Repository` annotations. `@Service` and `@Component` are common for the service layer, and there is no difference in behaviors. The `@Repository` changes the behaviors a little bit because the frameworks will translate some exceptions on the data access layer.

NewsService

This is an interesting service which will be responsible for managing the state of our news. It will interact like a *glue* to call the domain models, in this case, the `News` entity. The service is pretty similar to the others. We received the `NewsRepository` class, a dependency and kept the repository to maintain the states, let's do that.

The `@Service` annotation is present again. This is pretty much standard for Spring applications. Also, we can change to the `@Component` annotation, but it does not make any difference to our application.

Configuring Swagger for our APIs

Swagger is the de facto tool for document web APIs, and the tool allows developers to model APIs, create an interactive way to play with the APIs, and also provides an easy way to generate the client implementation in a wide range of languages.

The API documentation is an excellent way to engage developers to use our APIs.

Adding dependencies to pom.xml

Before we start the configuration, we need to add the required dependencies. These dependencies included Spring Fox in our project and offered many annotations to configure Swagger properly. Let's add these dependencies.

The new dependencies are in the pom.xml file:

```
<dependency>
  <groupId>io.springfox</groupId>
  <artifactId>springfox-swagger2</artifactId>
  <version>2.7.0</version>
</dependency>

<dependency>
  <groupId>io.springfox</groupId>
  <artifactId>springfox-swagger-ui</artifactId>
  <version>2.7.0</version>
</dependency>
```

The first dependency is the core of Swagger with annotations and related kinds of stuff. Spring Fox Swagger UI dependency provides a rich interface in HTML which permits developers to interact with the APIs.

Configuring Swagger

The dependencies are added, now we can configure the infrastructure for Swagger. The configuration is pretty simple. We will create a class with @Configuration to produce the Swagger configuration for the Spring container. Let's do it.

Take a look at the following Swagger configuration:

```
package springfive.cms.infra.swagger;

import org.springframework.context.annotation.Bean;
import org.springframework.context.annotation.Configuration;
import org.springframework.web.bind.annotation.RestController;
import springfox.documentation.builders.ParameterBuilder;
import springfox.documentation.builders.PathSelectors;
import springfox.documentation.builders.RequestHandlerSelectors;
import springfox.documentation.spi.DocumentationType;
import springfox.documentation.spring.web.plugins.Docket;
import springfox.documentation.swagger2.annotations.EnableSwagger2;

@Configuration
@EnableSwagger2
public class SwaggerConfiguration {

  @Bean
  public Docket documentation() {
    return new Docket(DocumentationType.SWAGGER_2)
        .select()
.apis(RequestHandlerSelectors.withClassAnnotation(RestController.class))
        .paths(PathSelectors.any())
        .build();
  }

}
```

The @Configuration instructs the Spring to generate a bean definition for Swagger. The annotation, @EnableSwagger2 adds support for Swagger. @EnableSwagger2 should be accompanied by @Configuration, it is mandatory.

The Docket class is a builder to create an API definition, and it provides sensible defaults and convenience methods for configuration of the Spring Swagger MVC Framework.

The invocation of method .apis(RequestHandlerSelectors.withClassAnnotation(RestController.class)) instructs the framework to handle classes annotated with @RestController.

There are many methods to customize the API documentation, for example, there is a method to add authentication headers.

That is the Swagger configuration, in the next section, we will create a first documented API.

First documented API

We will start with the `CategoryResource` class, because it is simple to understand, and we need to keep the focus on the technology stuff. We will add a couple of annotations, and the magic will happen, let's do magic.

The `CategoryResource` class should look like this:

```
package springfive.cms.domain.resources;

import io.swagger.annotations.Api;
import io.swagger.annotations.ApiOperation;
import io.swagger.annotations.ApiResponse;
import io.swagger.annotations.ApiResponses;
import java.util.List;
import org.springframework.http.HttpStatus;
import org.springframework.http.ResponseEntity;
import org.springframework.web.bind.annotation.DeleteMapping;
import org.springframework.web.bind.annotation.GetMapping;
import org.springframework.web.bind.annotation.PathVariable;
import org.springframework.web.bind.annotation.PostMapping;
import org.springframework.web.bind.annotation.PutMapping;
import org.springframework.web.bind.annotation.RequestBody;
import org.springframework.web.bind.annotation.RequestMapping;
import org.springframework.web.bind.annotation.ResponseStatus;
import org.springframework.web.bind.annotation.RestController;
import springfive.cms.domain.models.Category;
import springfive.cms.domain.service.CategoryService;
import springfive.cms.domain.vo.CategoryRequest;

@RestController
@RequestMapping("/api/category")
@Api(tags = "category", description = "Category API")
public class CategoryResource {

  private final CategoryService categoryService;

  public CategoryResource(CategoryService categoryService) {
    this.categoryService = categoryService;
  }

  @GetMapping(value = "/{id}")
  @ApiOperation(value = "Find category",notes = "Find the Category by ID")
  @ApiResponses(value = {
      @ApiResponse(code = 200,message = "Category found"),
      @ApiResponse(code = 404,message = "Category not found"),
  })
```

```java
    public ResponseEntity<Category> findOne(@PathVariable("id") String id){
        return ResponseEntity.ok(new Category());
    }

    @GetMapping
    @ApiOperation(value = "List categories",notes = "List all categories")
    @ApiResponses(value = {
        @ApiResponse(code = 200,message = "Categories found"),
        @ApiResponse(code = 404,message = "Category not found")
    })
    public ResponseEntity<List<Category>> findAll(){
        return ResponseEntity.ok(this.categoryService.findAll());
    }

    @PostMapping
    @ApiOperation(value = "Create category",notes = "It permits to create a
new category")
    @ApiResponses(value = {
        @ApiResponse(code = 201,message = "Category created successfully"),
        @ApiResponse(code = 400,message = "Invalid request")
    })
    public ResponseEntity<Category> newCategory(@RequestBody CategoryRequest
category){
        return new ResponseEntity<>(this.categoryService.create(category),
HttpStatus.CREATED);
    }

    @DeleteMapping("/{id}")
    @ResponseStatus(HttpStatus.NO_CONTENT)
    @ApiOperation(value = "Remove category",notes = "It permits to remove a
category")
    @ApiResponses(value = {
        @ApiResponse(code = 200,message = "Category removed successfully"),
        @ApiResponse(code = 404,message = "Category not found")
    })
    public void removeCategory(@PathVariable("id") String id){
    }

    @PutMapping("/{id}")
    @ResponseStatus(HttpStatus.NO_CONTENT)
    @ApiOperation(value = "Update category",notes = "It permits to update a
category")
    @ApiResponses(value = {
        @ApiResponse(code = 200,message = "Category update successfully"),
        @ApiResponse(code = 404,message = "Category not found"),
        @ApiResponse(code = 400,message = "Invalid request")
    })
    public ResponseEntity<Category> updateCategory(@PathVariable("id") String
```

```
   id,CategoryRequest category){
       return new ResponseEntity<>(new Category(), HttpStatus.OK);
   }


}
```

There are a lot of new annotations to understand. The `@Api` is the root annotation which configures this class as a Swagger resource. There are many configurations, but we will use the tags and description, as they are enough.

The `@ApiOperation` describes an operation in our API, in general against the requested path. The `value` attribute is regarding as the summary field on Swagger, it is a brief of the operation, and `notes` is a description of an operation (more detailed content).

The last one is the `@ApiResponse` which enables developers to describe the responses of an operation. Usually, they want to configure the status codes and message to describe the result of an operation.

Before you run the application, we should compile the source code. It can be done using the Maven command line using the `mvn clean install`, or via IDE using the **Run Application**.

Now, we have configured the Swagger integration, we can check the API documentation on the web browser. To do it, we need to navigate to `http://localhost:8080/swagger-ui.html` and this page should be displayed:

We can see APIs endpoints configured in our CMS application. Now, we will take a look at **category** which we have configured previously, click on the **Show/Hide** link. The output should be:

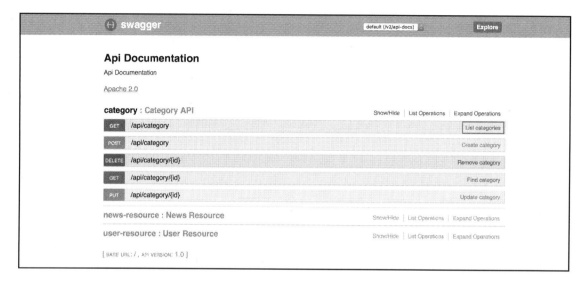

As we can see, there are five operations in our **Category API**, the operation has a path and a summary to help understand the purpose. We can click on the requested operation and see detailed information about the operation. Let's do it, click on **List categories** to see detailed documentation. The page looks like this:

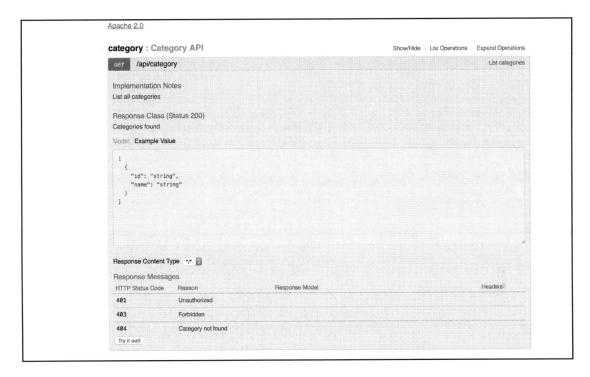

Outstanding job. Now we have an amazing API with excellent documentation. Well done.

Let's continue creating our CMS application.

Integrate with AngularJS

The AngularJS Framework has been becoming a trend for a few years, the community is super active, the project was created by Google.

The main idea of the framework is to help developers handle the complexities of the frontend layer, especially in the HTML part. The HTML markup language is static. It is a great tool to create static documents, but today it is not a requirement for modern web applications. These applications need to be dynamic. The UX teams around the world, work hard to create amazing applications, with different effects, these guys try to keep the applications more comfortable for the users.

AngularJS adds the possibility of extending the HTML with some additional attributes and tags. In this section, we will add some interesting behaviors on the frontend application. Let's do it.

AngularJS concepts

In our CMS application, we will work with some Angular components. We will use `Controllers` which will interact with our HTML and handle the behavior of some pages, such as those that show error messages. The `Services` is responsible for handling the infrastructure code such as interacting with our CMS API. This book is not intended to be an AngularJS guide. However, we will take a look at some interesting concepts to develop our application.

The AngularJS common tags are:

- `ng-app`
- `ng-controller`
- `ng-click`
- `ng-hide`
- `ng-show`

These tags are included in the AngularJS Framework. There are many more tags created and maintained by the community. There is, for example, a library to work with HTML forms, we will use it to add dynamic behaviors in our CMS Portal.

Controllers

Controllers are part of the framework to handle the business logic of the application. They should be used to control the flow of data in an application. The controller is attached to the DOM via the `ng-controller` directive.

To add some actions to our view, we need to create functions on controllers, the way to do this is by creating functions and adding them to the `$scope` object.

The controllers cannot be used to carry out DOM manipulations, format data and filter data, it is considered best practice in the AngularJS world.

Usually, the controllers inject the service objects to delegate handling the business logic. We will understand services in the next section.

Services

Services are the objects to handle business logic in our application. In some cases, they can be used to handle state. The services objects are a singleton which means we have only one instance in our entire application.

In our application, the services are responsible for interacting with our CMS APIs built on Spring Boot. Let's do that.

Creating the application entry point

The Spring Boot Framework allows us to serve static files. These files should be in the classpath in one of these folders, `/static`, `/public`, `/resources`, or `/META-INF/resources`.

We will use the `/static` folder, in this folder, we will put our AngularJS application. There are some standards to modularize the AngularJS application folder structure which depends on the application size and requirements. We will use the most simple style to keep the attention on Spring integration. Look at the project structure:

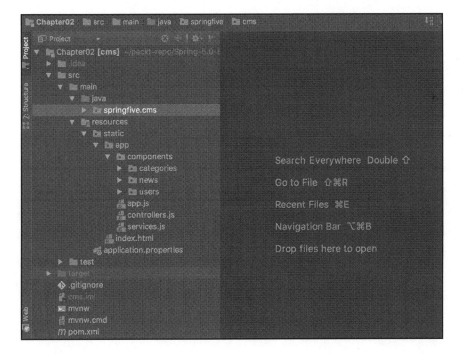

There are some assets to start and run an AngularJS application. We will use the Content Delivery Network (CDN) to load the AngularJS Framework, the Angular UI-Router which helps to handle routing on our web application, and the Bootstrap Framework which helps to develop our pages.

 Content Delivery Network is distributed proxy servers around the world. It makes the content more high availability and improves performance because it will be hosted nearer the end user. The detailed explanation can be found at CloudFare Page (https://www.cloudflare.com/learning/cdn/what-is-a-cdn/).

Then we can start to configure our AngularJS application. Let's start with our entry point, index.html:

```
<!DOCTYPE html>
<html lang="en">
<head>
  <meta charset="utf-8">
  <meta http-equiv="X-UA-Compatible" content="IE=edge">
  <meta name="viewport" content="width=device-width, initial-scale=1">
  <title>Spring Boot Security</title>
  <link rel="stylesheet"
href="https://maxcdn.bootstrapcdn.com/bootstrap/3.3.7/css/bootstrap.min.css
">
</head>
<body ng-app="cms">

<!-- Header -->
<nav class="navbar navbar-default navbar-fixed-top">
  <div class="container">
    <div class="navbar-header">
      <button type="button" class="navbar-toggle collapsed" data-
toggle="collapse" data-target="#navbar"
              aria-expanded="false" aria-controls="navbar">
        <span class="sr-only">Toggle navigation</span>
        <span class="icon-bar"></span>
        <span class="icon-bar"></span>
        <span class="icon-bar"></span>
      </button>
      <a class="navbar-brand" href="#">CMS</a>
    </div>
    <div id="navbar" class="collapse navbar-collapse">
      <ul class="nav navbar-nav">
        <li class="active"><a href="#">Home</a></li>
        <li><a href="#users">Users</a></li>
        <li><a href="#categories">Categories</a></li>
```

```
        <li><a href="#news">News</a></li>
      </ul>
    </div>
  </div>
</nav>

<!-- Body -->
<div class="container">
  <div ui-view></div>
</div>

<script
src="https://ajax.googleapis.com/ajax/libs/angularjs/1.4.8/angular.min.js">
</script>
<script
src="https://cdnjs.cloudflare.com/ajax/libs/angular-ui-router/1.0.3/angular
-ui-router.js"></script>

<script type="text/javascript" src="app/app.js"></script>

<script type="text/javascript" src="app/controllers.js"></script>
<script type="text/javascript" src="app/services.js"></script>

<script type="text/javascript" src="app/components/categories/category-
controller.js"></script>
<script type="text/javascript" src="app/components/categories/category-
service.js"></script>

<script type="text/javascript" src="app/components/news/news-
controller.js"></script>
<script type="text/javascript" src="app/components/news/news-
service.js"></script>

<script type="text/javascript" src="app/components/users/user-
controller.js"></script>
<script type="text/javascript" src="app/components/users/user-
service.js"></script>

</body>
</html>
```

There are some important things here. Let's understand them.

The ng-app tag is a directive which is used to bootstrap the AngularJS application. This tag is the root element of the application and is usually placed on the <body> or <html> tags.

The `ui-view` tag instructs the Angular UI-Router about which portion of the HTML document will be handled by the application states, in other words, the designated part has the dynamic behaviors and change depends on the routing system. Look at the following code snippet:

```
<!-- Body -->
<div class="container">
  <div ui-view></div>
</div>
```

This part of the code can be found at `index.hml` file.

Following the `ui-view`, we have our JavaScript files, the first one is the AngularJS Framework, in this version the file is minified. Look at our JavaScript files, the files were created in the `/static/app/components` folder. Take a look at the image here:

The second one is the UI-Router which helps us to manage our routes. Finally, we have our JavaScript files which configure the AngularJS application, our controllers, and the services to interact with our CMS APIs.

Also, we have some Bootstrap classes to align fields and make design easier.

Creating the Category Controller

Now, we need to create our controllers. We will start with the simplest to make the example more easy to understand. The CategoryController has the responsibility of controlling the data of the Category entity. There are two controllers, one enables us to create a category, and another lists all categories stored in the database.

The category-controller.js should be like this:

```
(function (angular) {
  'use strict';

  // Controllers
  angular.module('cms.modules.category.controllers', []).

  controller('CategoryCreateController',
      ['$scope', 'CategoryService','$state',
        function ($scope, CategoryService,$state) {

          $scope.resetForm = function () {
            $scope.category = null;
          };

          $scope.create = function (category) {
            CategoryService.create(category).then(
                function (data) {
                  console.log("Success on create Category!!!")
                  $state.go('categories')
                }, function (err) {
                  console.log("Error on create Category!!!")
                });
          };
      }]).

  controller('CategoryListController',
      ['$scope', 'CategoryService',
        function ($scope, CategoryService) {
          CategoryService.find().then(function (data) {
            $scope.categories = data.data;
          }, function (err) {
            console.log(err);
          });
      }]);
})(angular);
```

We have created an AngularJS module. It helps us to keep the functions organized. It acts as a kind of namespace for us. The `.controller` function is a constructor to create our controller's instances. We received some parameters, the AngularJS framework will inject these objects for us.

Creating the Category Service

The `CategoryService` objects is a singleton object because it is an AngularJS service. The service will interact with our CMS APIs powered by the Spring Boot application.

We will use the `$http` service. It makes the HTTP communications easier.

Let's write the `CategoryService`:

```
(function (angular) {
  'use strict';

  /* Services */
</span>  angular.module('cms.modules.category.services', []).
  service('CategoryService', ['$http',
    function ($http) {

      var serviceAddress = 'http://localhost:8080';
      var urlCollections = serviceAddress + '/api/category';
      var urlBase = serviceAddress + '/api/category/';

      this.find = function () {
        return $http.get(urlCollections);
      };

      this.findOne = function (id) {
        return $http.get(urlBase + id);
      };

      this.create = function (data) {
        return $http.post(urlBase, data);
      };

      this.update = function (data) {
        return $http.put(urlBase + '/id/' + data._id, data);
      };

      this.remove = function (data) {
        return $http.delete(urlBase + '/id/' + data._id, data);
      };
```

```
      }
    ]);
 }) (angular);
```

Well done, now we have implemented the `CategoryService`.

The `.service` function is a constructor to create a service instance, the `angular` acts under the hood. There is an injection on a constructor, for the service we need an `$http` service to make HTTP calls against our APIs. There are a couple of HTTP methods here. Pay attention to the correct method to keep the HTTP semantics.

Summary

In this chapter, we created our first Spring application. We saw Spring Initializr, the amazing tool that helps developers create the application skeleton.

We looked at how Spring works under the hood and how the framework got configured with a couple of annotations. Now, we have a basic knowledge of the Spring Bootstrap functions, and we can understand the Dependency Injection and component scan features present in the framework.

This knowledge is the basis for the next chapters, and now we are ready to start to work with more advanced features, such as persistence. Here we go. See you in the next chapter.

3
Persistence with Spring Data and Reactive Fashion

In the previous chapter, we created our **Content Management System (CMS)** application. We also introduced **REST (Representational State Transfer)** support in Spring, which enabled us to develop a simple web application. Also, we learned how dependency injection works in the Spring Framework, which is probably the most famous feature of the framework.

In this chapter, we will add more features to our application. Systems in the real world need to persist their data on a real database; this is an essential characteristic for a production-ready application. Also, based on our model, we need to choose the correct data structure to achieve performance and avoid the impedance mismatch.

In the first part of this chapter, we will use the traditional SQL database as a store for our application. We will deep dive on the Spring Data **JPA (Java Persistence API)** to achieve the persistence for our CMS application. We will understand how to enable transactions with this amazing Spring module.

After that, we will change to a more modern type of database called **NoSQL technologies**. In this field, we will use the famous database document model called **MongoDB** and then we will create the final solution for our CMS application.

MongoDB offers a fantastic solution for our application because it has support for a document storage model and enables us to store our objects in the form of JSON, which makes our data more readable. Also, MongoDB is schema-less, which is a fantastic feature because one collection can store different documents. It means records can have different fields, content, and sizes. The other important characteristic from MongoDB is the query model. It offers a document-based query that is easy to understand, and, based on JSON notations, our queries will be more readable than any other database can be.

Finally, we will add the most important feature present in Spring 5.0: support for Reactive Streams. Our application will be transformed into a modern web application which has some important requirements.

Here's an overview of what you will learn in this chapter:

- Implementing the Spring Data JPA
- Creating repositories with Spring Data Reactive MongoDB
- Learning the Reactive Spring
- Understand the Project Reactor

Learning the basics of Docker

We learned about Docker concepts in `Chapter 1`, *Journey to the Spring World*. Now, it is time to test our knowledge and put it into practice. In the first part of this chapter, we will start MongoDB and Postgres instances to serve as a database for our application. We will configure connection settings in the application.

In the last part of this chapter, we will introduce the Maven plugin which provides an easy way to create Docker images via `pom.xml` with a couple of configurations on file. Finally, we will run our application in a Docker container.

Preparing MongoDB

Let's create our MongoDB container. We will use the official image provided by the Docker Hub.

First, we need to pull the image:

```
docker pull mongo:3.4.10
```

Then, we will see the Docker Engine downloading the image contents.

To create an isolation from our containers, we will create a separated network for our application and database. The network should use the bridge driver to allow the container communications.

Let's create a `docker network`:

```
docker network create cms-application
```

The command output should be an ID of a created network. Your ID will probably be different compared to mine:

```
2 updates are security updates.

Last login: Wed Nov  1 00:13:53 2017 from 10.0.2.2
ubuntu@ubuntu-xenial:~$ docker network create cms-application
5a8485d8da42a4680347635e57041b35d2d09642ac9f5e1194c7334a5e4bfe92
ubuntu@ubuntu-xenial:~$
```

To check if the network was created successfully, the `docker network ls` command can help us.

We will start our MongoDB. The network should be `cms-application`, but we will map the database port to a host port. For debugging purposes, we will connect a client to a running database, but please don't do this in a non-development environment.

Exposing a port over host is not a best practice. Hence, we use a Docker container, which is one of the main advantages is process isolation. In this case, we will have no control over the network. Otherwise, we may cause some port conflicts.

To start, type the following command:

```
docker run -d --name mongodb --net cms-application -p 27017:27017
mongo:3.4.10
```

Also, we can stop the Docker MongoDB container using `docker stop mongodb` and start our container again by using the following command: `docker start mongodb`.

The output will be a hash which represents the ID of the container.

The parameter instructions are:

- `-d`: This instructs Docker to run the container in a background mode
- `--name`: The container name; it will be a kind of hostname in our network

- `--net`: The network where the container will be attached
- `-p`: The host port and container port, which will be mapped to a container on a host interface

Now, we have a pretty standard MongoDB instance running on our machines, and we can start to add a persistence in our CMS application. We will do that soon.

Preparing a PostgreSQL database

Like MongoDB, we will prepare a PostgreSQL instance for our CMS application. We will change our persistence layer to demonstrate how Spring Data abstracts it for developers. Then, we need to prepare a Docker Postgres instance for that.

We will use the version 9.6.6 of Postgres and use the `alpine` tag because it is smaller than other Postgres images. Let's pull our image. The command should be like this:

```
docker pull postgres:9.6.6-alpine
```

Then, wait until the download ends.

In the previous section, we created our Docker network called `cms-application`. Now, we will start our Postgres instance on that network as we did for MongoDB. The command to start the Postgres should be the following:

```
docker run -d --name postgres --net cms-application -p 5432:5432 -e
POSTGRES_PASSWORD=cms@springfive
postgres:9.6.6-alpine
```

The list of parameters is the same as we passed for MongoDB. We want to run it in background mode and attach it to our custom network. As we can see, there is one more new parameter in the `docker run` command. Let's understand it:

- `-e`: This enables us to pass environment variables for a container. In this case, we want to change the password value.

Good job. We have done our infrastructure requirements. Let's understand the persistence details right now.

Spring Data project

The Spring Data project is an umbrella project that offers a familiar way to create our data access layer on a wide range of database technologies. It means there are high-level abstractions to interact with different kinds of data structures, such as the document model, column family, key-value, and graphs. Also, the JPA specification is fully supported by the Spring Data JPA project.

These modules offer powerful object-mapping abstractions for our domain model.

There is support for different types of data structures and databases. There is a set of sub-modules to keep the framework modularity. Also, there are two categories of these sub-modules: the first one is a subset of projects supported by the Spring Framework Team and the second one is a subset of sub-modules provided by the community.

Projects supported by the Spring Team include:

- Spring Data Commons
- Spring Data JPA
- Spring Data MongoDB
- Spring Data Redis
- Spring Data for Apache Cassandra

Projects supported by the community include:

- Spring Data Aerospike
- Spring Data ElasticSearch
- Spring Data DynamoDB
- Spring Data Neo4J

The base of the repositories interfaces chain is the `Repository` interface. It is a marker interface, and the general purpose is to store the type information. The type will be used for other interfaces that extend it.

There is also a `CrudRepository` interface. It is the most important, and the name is self-explanatory; it provides a couple of methods to perform CRUD operations, and it provides some utility methods, such as `count()`, `exists()`, and `deleteAll()`. Those are the most important base interfaces for the repository implementations.

Spring Data JPA

The Spring Data JPA provides an easy way to implement a data access layer using the JPA specification from Java EE. Usually, these implementations had a lot of boilerplate and repetitive code and it was hard to maintain the changes in the database code. The Spring Data JPA is trying to resolve these issues and provides a comprehensible way to do that without boilerplate and repetitive code.

The JPA specification provides an abstraction layer to interact with different database vendors that have been implemented. Spring adds one more layer to the abstraction in a high-level mode. It means the Spring Data JPA will create a repositories implementation and encapsulate the whole JPA implementation details. We can build our persistence layer with a little knowledge of the JPA spec.

 The *JPA Specification* was created by the **JCP** (**Java Community Process**) to help developers to persist, access, and manage data between Java classes and relational databases. There are some vendors that implement this specification. The most famous implementation is Hibernate (`http://hibernate.org/orm/`), and by default, Spring Data JPA uses Hibernate as the JPA implementation.

Say goodbye to the **DAO** (**Data Access Object**) pattern and implementations. The Spring Data JPA aims to solve this problem with a well-tested framework and with some production-ready features.

Now, we have an idea of what the Spring Data JPA is. Let's put it into practice.

Configuring pom.xml for Spring Data JPA

Now, we need to put the correct dependencies to work with Spring Data JPA. There are a couple of dependencies to configure in our `pom.xml` file.

The first one is the Spring Data JPA Starter, which provides a lot of auto-configuration classes which permits us to bootstrap the application quickly. The last one is the PostgreSQL JDBC driver, and it is necessary because it contains the JDBC implementation classes to connect with the PostgreSQL database.

The new dependencies are:

```xml
<dependency>
  <groupId>org.springframework.boot</groupId>
  <artifactId>spring-boot-starter-data-jpa</artifactId>
</dependency>

<dependency>
  <groupId>org.postgresql</groupId>
  <artifactId>postgresql</artifactId>
  <version>42.1.4</version>
</dependency>
```

Simple and pretty easy.

Configuring the Postgres connections

To connect our application with our recently created database, we need to configure a couple of lines in the `application.yaml` file. Once again, thanks to Spring Data Starter, our connection will be configured automatically.

We can produce the connection objects using the `@Bean` annotations as well, but there are many objects to configure. We will go forward with the configuration file. It is more simple and straightforward to understand as well.

To configure the database connections, we need to provide the Spring Framework a couple of attributes, such as the database URL, database username, password, and also a driver class name to instruct the JPA framework about the full path of the JDBC class.

The `application.yaml` file should be like this:

```yaml
spring:
  datasource:
    url: jdbc:postgresql://localhost:5432/postgres
    username: postgres
    password: cms@springfive
    driver-class-name: org.postgresql.Driver
  jpa:
    show-sql: true
    generate-ddl: true
```

In the `datasource` section, we have configured the database credentials connections and database host as well.

The JPA section in `application.yaml` can be used to configure the JPA framework. In this part, we configured to log SQL instructions in the console. This is helpful to debug and perform troubleshooting. Also, we have configured the JPA framework to create our tables in a database when the application gets the startup process.

Awesome, the JPA infrastructure is configured. Well done! Now, we can map our models in the JPA style. Let's do that in the following section.

Mapping the models

We have configured the database connections successfully. Now, we are ready to map our models using the JPA annotations. Let's start with our `Category` model. It is a pretty simple class, which is good because we are interested in Spring Data JPA stuff.

Our first version of the `Category` model should be like this:

```
package springfive.cms.domain.models;

import javax.persistence.Entity;
import javax.persistence.GeneratedValue;
import javax.persistence.Id;
import javax.persistence.Table;
import lombok.Data;
import org.hibernate.annotations.GenericGenerator;

@Data
@Entity
@Table(name = "category")
public class Category {

  @Id
  @GeneratedValue(generator = "system-uuid")
  @GenericGenerator(name = "system-uuid", strategy = "uuid2")
  String id;

  String name;

}
```

We need to change some model classes to adapt to the JPA specification. We can find the model classes on GitHub at: `https://github.com/PacktPublishing/Spring-5.0-By-Example/tree/master/Chapter03/cms-postgres/src/main/java/springfive/cms/domain/models`.

There is some new stuff here. The `@Entity` annotation instructs the JPA framework that the annotated class is an entity, in our case, the `Category` class, and then the framework will correlate it with a database table. The `@Table` annotation is used to name the table in the database. These annotations are inserted on the class level, which means on top of the class declaration.

The `@Id` annotation instructs the JPA as to which annotated field is the primary key of the database table. It is not a good practice to generate IDs sequentially for entities, especially if you are creating the APIs. It helps hackers to understand the logic about the IDs and makes the attacks easier. So, we will generate UUIDs (Universally Unique IDentifiers) instead of simple sequentially IDs. The `@GenericGenerator` annotation instructs Hibernate, which is a JPA specification implementation vendor, to generate random UUIDs.

Adding the JPA repositories in the CMS application

Once the whole infrastructure and JPA mappings are done, we can add our repositories to our projects. In the Spring Data project, there are some abstractions, such as `Repository`, `CrudRepository`, and `JpaRepository`. We will use the `JpaRepository` because it supports the paging and sorting features.

Our repository will be pretty simple. There are a couple of standard methods, such as `save()`, `update()`, and `delete()`, and we will take a look at some DSL query methods which allow developers to create custom queries based on attribute names. We created an `AbstractRepository` to help us to store the objects in memory. It is not necessary anymore. We can remove it.

Let's create our first JPA repository:

```
package springfive.cms.domain.repository;

import java.util.List;
import org.springframework.data.jpa.repository.JpaRepository;
import springfive.cms.domain.models.Category;

public interface CategoryRepository extends JpaRepository<Category, String>
{
```

```
    List<Category> findByName(String name);

    List<Category> findByNameIgnoreCaseStartingWith(String name);

}
```

As we can see, the `JpaRepository` interface is typed with the desired entity and the type of ID of the entity as well. There is no secret to this part. This amazing thing happens to support the custom queries based on attribute names. In the `Category` model, there is an attribute called `name`. We can create custom methods in our `CategoryRepository` using the `Category` model attributes using the `By` instruction. As we can see, above `findByName(String name)`, **Spring Data Framework** will create the correct query to look up categories by name. It is fantastic.

There are many keywords supported by the custom query methods:

Logical Keyword	Logical Expressions
AND	And
OR	Or
AFTER	After, IsAfter
BEFORE	Before, IsBefore
CONTAINING	Containing, IsContaining, Contains
BETWEEN	Between, IsBetween
ENDING_WITH	EndingWith, IsEndingWith, EndsWith
EXISTS	Exists
FALSE	False, IsFalse
GREATER_THAN	GreaterThan, IsGreaterThan
GREATHER_THAN_EQUALS	GreaterThanEqual, IsGreaterThanEqual
IN	In, IsIn
IS	Is, Equals, (or no keyword)
IS_EMPTY	IsEmpty, Empty
IS_NOT_EMPTY	IsNotEmpty, NotEmpty
IS_NOT_NULL	NotNull, IsNotNull
IS_NULL	Null, IsNull
LESS_THAN	LessThan, IsLessThan
LESS_THAN_EQUAL	LessThanEqual, IsLessThanEqual
LIKE	Like, IsLike
NEAR	Near, IsNear
NOT	Not, IsNot
NOT_IN	NotIn, IsNotIn
NOT_LIKE	NotLike, IsNotLike
REGEX	Regex, MatchesRegex, Matches
STARTING_WITH	StartingWith, IsStartingWith, StartsWith
TRUE	True, IsTrue
WITHIN	Within, IsWithin

There are many ways to create a query based on attributes names. We can combine the keywords using keywords as well, such as `findByNameAndId`, for instance. The Spring Data JPA provides a consistent way to create queries.

Configuring transactions

When we use the JPA specification, most of the applications need to have support for transactions as well. Spring has excellent support for transactions even in other modules. This support is integrated with Spring Data JPA, and we can take advantage of it. Configuring transactions in Spring is a piece of cake; we need to insert the `@Transactional` annotation whenever needed. There are some different use cases to use it. We will use the `@Transactional` in our services layer and then we will put the annotation in our service classes. Let's see our `CategoryService` class:

```
package springfive.cms.domain.service;

import java.util.List;
import java.util.Optional;
import org.springframework.stereotype.Service;
import org.springframework.transaction.annotation.Transactional;
import springfive.cms.domain.exceptions.CategoryNotFoundException;
import springfive.cms.domain.models.Category;
import springfive.cms.domain.repository.CategoryRepository;
import springfive.cms.domain.vo.CategoryRequest;

@Service
@Transactional(readOnly = true)
public class CategoryService {

  private final CategoryRepository categoryRepository;

  public CategoryService(CategoryRepository categoryRepository) {
    this.categoryRepository = categoryRepository;
  }

  @Transactional
  public Category update(Category category) {
    return this.categoryRepository.save(category);
  }

  @Transactional
  public Category create(CategoryRequest request) {
    Category category = new Category();
    category.setName(request.getName());
    return this.categoryRepository.save(category);
```

```
  }

  @Transactional
  public void delete(String id) {
    final Optional<Category> category =
this.categoryRepository.findById(id);
    category.ifPresent(this.categoryRepository::delete);
  }

  public List<Category> findAll() {
    return this.categoryRepository.findAll();
  }

  public List<Category> findByName(String name) {
    return this.categoryRepository.findByName(name);
  }

  public List<Category> findByNameStartingWith(String name) {
    return this.categoryRepository.findByNameIgnoreCaseStartingWith(name);
  }

  public Category findOne(String id) {
    final Optional<Category> category =
this.categoryRepository.findById(id);
    if (category.isPresent()) {
      return category.get();
    } else {
      throw new CategoryNotFoundException(id);
    }
  }

}
```

There are many @Transactional annotations in the CategoryService class. The first annotation at class level instructs the framework to configure the readOnly for all methods present in those classes, except the methods configured with @Transactional. In this case, the class-level annotation will be overridden with readOnly=false. This is the default configuration when the value is omitted.

Installing and configuring pgAdmin3

To connect on our PostgreSQL instance, we will use pgAdmin 3, which is the free tool provided by the Postgres team.

To install pgAdmin 3, we can use the following command:

```
sudo apt-get install pgadmin3 -y
```

This will install pgAdmin 3 on our machine.

After installation, open pgAdmin 3 and then click on **Add a connection to a server**. The button looks like this:

Then, fill in the information, as shown in the following screenshot:

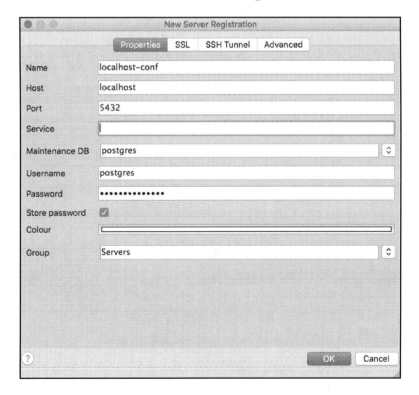

The password should be: cms@springfive.

Awesome, our pgAdmin 3 tool is configured.

Checking the data on the database structure

The whole application structure is ready. Now, we can check the database to get our persisted data. There are many open source Postgres clients. We will use pgAdmin 3, as previously configured.

The first time you open the application, you will be asked about the credentials and host. We must put the same information as we configured on the `application.yaml` file. Then, we are able to make instructions in the database.

Before checking the database, we can use Swagger to create some categories in our CMS system. We can use the instructions provided in `Chapter 2`, *Starting in the Spring World – The CMS Application,* to create some data.

After that, we can execute the following SQL instruction in the database:

```
select * from category;
```

And the result should be the categories created on Swagger calls. In my case, I have created two categories, `sports`, and `movies`. The result will be like the ones shown in the following screenshot:

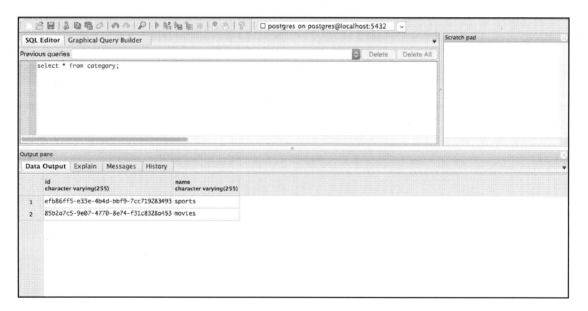

Awesome work, guys. The application is fully operational.

Now, we will create our final solution for the repositories. We have learned the basics of the Spring Data project and in the next section, we will change the persistence layer to a modern database.

Creating the final data access layer

We have played with the Spring Data JPA project, and we have seen how easy it can be. We learned how to configure the database connections to persist the real data on the Postgres database. Now, we will create the final solution for the data access layer for our application. The final solution will use MongoDB as a database and will use the Spring Data MongoDB project, which provides support for MongoDB repositories.

We will see some similarities with the Spring Data JPA projects. It is amazing because we can prove the power of Spring Data abstractions in practice. With a couple of changes, we can move to another database model.

Let's understand the new project and put it into practice in the following sections.

Spring Data MongoDB

The Spring Data MongoDB provides integration with our domain objects and the MongoDB document. With a couple of annotations, our entity class is ready to be persisted in the database. The mapping is based on a **POJO (Plain Old Java Object)** pattern, which is known by all Java developers.

There are two levels of abstraction supplied by the module. The first one is a high-level abstraction. It increases the developer productivity. This level provides a couple of annotations to instruct the framework to convert the domain objects in MongoDB documents and vice versa. The developer does not need to write any code about the persistence; it will be managed by the Spring Data MongoDB framework. There are more exciting things at this level, such as the rich mapping configurations provided by the Spring Conversion Service. The Spring Data projects provide a rich DSL to enable developers to create queries based on the attribute names.

The second level of abstraction is the low-level abstraction. At this level, behaviors are not automatically managed by the framework. The developers need to understand a little bit more about the Spring and MongoDB document model. The framework provides a couple of interfaces to enable developers to take control of the read and write instructions. This can be useful for scenarios where the high-level abstraction does not fit well. In this case, the control should be more granular in the entities mapping.

Again, Spring provides the power of choice for developers. The high-level abstraction improves the developer performance and the low-level permits developers to take more control.

Now, we will add mapping annotation to our model. Let's do it.

Removing the PostgreSQL and Spring Data JPA dependencies

We will convert our project to use the brand new Spring Data Reactive MongoDB repositories. After that, we will not use the Spring Data JPA and PostgreSQL drivers anymore. Let's remove these dependencies from our `pom.xml`:

```
<dependency>
  <groupId>org.springframework.boot</groupId>
  <artifactId>spring-boot-starter-data-jpa</artifactId>
</dependency>

<dependency>
  <groupId>org.postgresql</groupId>
  <artifactId>postgresql</artifactId>
  <version>42.1.4</version>
</dependency>
```

And then, we can add the following dependency:

```
<dependency>
  <groupId>org.springframework.boot</groupId>
  <artifactId>spring-boot-starter-data-mongodb-reactive</artifactId>
</dependency>
```

 The final version of `pom.xml` can be found on GitHub at `https://github.com/PacktPublishing/Spring-5.0-By-Example/blob/master/Chapter03/cms-mongo-non-reactive/pom.xml`.

Mapping the domain model

We will add mapping annotations on our domain model. The Spring Data MongoDB will use these annotations to persist our objects in the MongoDB collections. We will start with the `Category` entity, which should be like this:

```
package springfive.cms.domain.models;

import lombok.Data;
import org.springframework.data.annotation.Id;
import org.springframework.data.mongodb.core.mapping.Document;

@Data
@Document(collection = "category")
public class Category {

  @Id
  String id;

  String name;

}
```

We added two new annotations in the `Category` class. The `@Document` from Spring Data MongoDB enables us to configure the collection name. Collections in MongoDB are similar to tables in SQL databases.

The `@Id` annotation is from the Spring Data Commons project. It is interesting because, as we can see, it is not specific for MongoDB mappings. The field annotation with this will be converted in the `_id` field on MongoDB collection.

With these few annotations, the `Category` class is configured to be persisted on MongoDB. In the following section, we will create our repository classes.

We need to do the same task for our other entities. The `User` and `News` need to be configured in the same way as we did for the `Category` class. The full source code can be found on GitHub at: `https://github.com/PacktPublishing/Spring-5.0-By-Example/tree/master/Chapter03/cms-mongo-non-reactive/src/main/java/springfive/cms/domain/models`.

Configuring the database connection

Before we create our repositories, we will configure the MongoDB connection. The repository layer abstracts the driver implementation, but is necessary to configure the driver correctly.

On the resources directory, we will change the `application.yaml` file, previously configured for the Spring Data JPA. The Spring Framework supports the configuration through the YAML file. This kind of file is more readable for humans and has a kind of hierarchy. These features are the reason to choose this extension.

The `application.yaml` file should be like the following example:

```
spring:
  data:
    mongodb:
      database: cms
      host: localhost
      port: 27017
```

The `application.yaml` file for MongoDB can be found on GitHub (`https://github.com/PacktPublishing/Spring-5.0-By-Example/blob/master/Chapter03/cms-mongo-non-reactive/src/main/resources/application.yaml`).

The file is quite simple for now. There is a `database` tag for configuring the database name. The `host` and `port` tags are about the address that the MongoDB instance is running.

We also can configure the connections programmatically with a couple of objects, but it requires us to code a lot of boilerplate code. Spring Boot offers it out of the box for us. Let's enjoy it.

Excellent, the connection was configured successfully. The infrastructure requirements are solved. Let's go on to implement our repositories.

Spring Boot Framework supports profiles in `application.properties` or `application.yaml`. This means that if the application was configured in a properties file style, we could use `application-<profile>.properties`. Then, these properties will be applied to the required profile. In YAML style, we can use only one file with multiples profiles.

Adding the repository layer

Once the entities have been mapped, and the connections are done, it's time to create our repositories. The Spring Data Framework provides some interfaces that can be used in different use cases. We will use the specialization for the MongoDB database, which is `MongoRepository`. It extends the `PagingAndSortingRepository` and `QueryByExampleExecutor`. The first is about pagination and sorting features, and the other is about queries by example.

 In some cases, the database query result set can be very large. This can cause some application performance issues because we will fetch a lot of database records. We can limit the number of records fetched from the database and configure limits for that. This technique is called **Pagination**. We can find the full documentation at *Spring Data Commons Documentation* (`https://docs.spring.io/spring-data/commons/docs/current/reference/html/`).

This interface offers a lot of built-in methods for convenience. There are a couple of methods to insert one or more instances, methods for listing all instances of requested entities, methods to remove one or more instances, and many more features, such as ordering and paging.

It enables developers to create repositories without code or even without a deep knowledge of MongoDB. However, some knowledge of MongoDB is necessary to troubleshoot various errors.

We will start by creating the `CategoryRepository`. Change the type of `CategoryRepository` to an interface instead of a class. The code in this interface is not necessary. The Spring container will inject the correct implementation when the application starts.

Let's create our first concrete repository, which means the repository will persist the data on the MongoDB we previously configured. The `CategoryRepository` needs to be like this:

```
package springfive.cms.domain.repository;

import org.springframework.data.mongodb.repository.MongoRepository;
import springfive.cms.domain.models.Category;

public interface CategoryRepository extends
MongoRepository<Category,String> {}
```

The type is an `interface`. Repositories do not have any stereotypes anymore. The Spring container can identify the implementation because it extends the `MongoRepository` interface.

The `MongoRepository` interface should be parameterized. The first argument is the type of model that it represents. In our case, it represents a repository for the `Category` class. The second parameter is about the type of ID of the model. We will use the string type for that.

Now, we need to do the same for the other entities, `User`, and `News`. The code is quite similar to the preceding code. You can find the full source code on GitHub at: `https://github.com/PacktPublishing/Spring-5.0-By-Example/tree/master/Chapter03/cms-mongo-non-reactive/src/main/java/springfive/cms/domain/repository`.

In the next section, we will check the database to assert that the rows are persisted correctly.

Checking the persistence

Now, we can test the persistence and all layers of the application. We will provide the API documentation for that. Let's open the Swagger documentation and create some records in our CMS application.

Creating sample categories on Swagger:

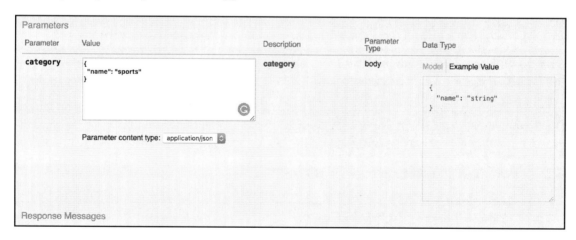

Fill in the category JSON, as shown in the preceding screenshot, and then click on **Try it out!**. It will invoke the Category API and persist the category on the database. Now, we can check it.

To connect to the MongoDB instance and check the collection, we will use the `mongo-express` tool. It is a web-based tool written in NodeJS to interact with our database instance.

The tool can be installed, but we will run the tool on a Docker container. The Docker tool will help us in this part. Let's start the container:

```
docker run -d --link mongodb:mongo--net cms-application -p 8081:8081 mongo-express
```

It instructs Docker to spin up a container with the `mongo-express` tool and connect to the desired instance. The `--link` argument instructs Docker to create a kind of *hostname* for our MongoDB instance. Remember the name of our instance is `mongodb`; we did it on the run command previously.

Good job. Go to `http://localhost:8081` and we will see this page:

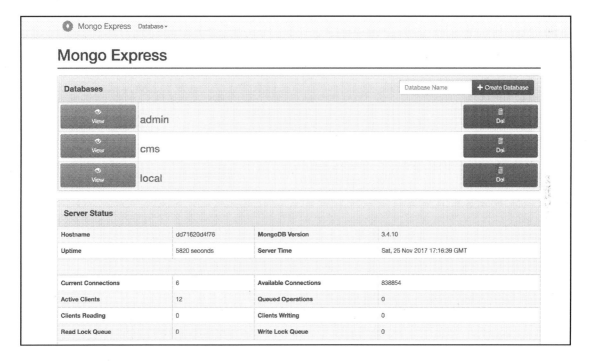

There are a couple of databases. We are interested in the CMS database. Click on the **View** button next to **cms**. Then, the tool will present the collections of the selected database; in our case, the CMS database. The view should be like this:

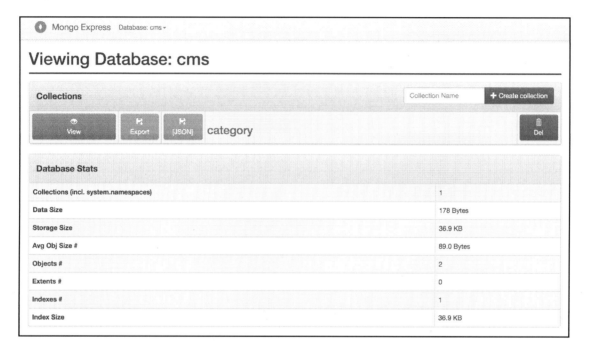

The category is presented as a collection. We can **View**, **Export**, and export as JSON, but for now, we are interested in checking if our CMS application persisted the data properly. So, click on the **View** button. We will use the MongoDB collection data like this:

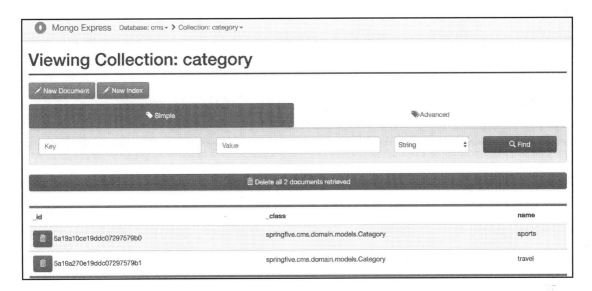

As we can see, the data was stored in MongoDB as expected. There are two categories in the database—**sports** and **travel**. There is a `_class` field that helps Spring Data to convert domain classes.

Awesome job, the CMS application is up and running, and also persisting the data in MongoDB. Now, our application is almost production ready, and the data is persisted outside in the amazing document datastore.

In the following section, we will create our Docker image, and then we will run the CMS application with Docker commands. It will be interesting.

Creating the Docker image for CMS

We are doing an awesome job. We created an application with the Spring Boot Framework. The application has been using the Spring REST, Spring Data, and Spring DI.

Now we will go a step forward and create our Docker image. It will be useful to help us to deliver our application for production. There are some advantages, and we can run the application on-premise or on any cloud providers because Docker abstracts the operating system layer. We do not need Java to be installed on the application host, and it also allows us to use different Java versions on the hosts. There are so many advantages involved in adopting Docker for delivery.

We are using Maven as a build tool. Maven has an excellent plugin to helps us to create Docker images. In the following section, we will learn how Maven can help us.

Configuring the docker-maven-plugin

There is an excellent Maven plugin provided by fabric8 (`https://github.com/fabric8io/docker-maven-plugin`). It is licensed under the Apache-2.0 license, which means we can use it without any worries.

We will configure our project to use it, and after image creation, we will push this image on Docker Hub. It is a public Docker registry.

The steps are:

1. Configure the plugin
2. Push the Docker image
3. Configure the Docker Spring profile

Then, it is show time. Let's go.

Adding the plugin on pom.xml

Let's configure the Maven plugin. It is necessary to add a plugin to the plugin section on our `pom.xml` and add some configurations. The plugin should be configured as follows:

```
<plugin>
    <groupId>io.fabric8</groupId>
    <artifactId>docker-maven-plugin</artifactId>
    <version>0.21.0</version>
    <configuration>
        <images>
            <image>
                <name>springfivebyexample/${project.build.finalName}</name>
                <build>
                    <from>openjdk:latest</from>
                    <entryPoint>java -Dspring.profiles.active=container -jar
/application/${project.build.finalName}.jar</entryPoint>
                    <assembly>
                        <basedir>/application</basedir>
                        <descriptorRef>artifact</descriptorRef>
                        <inline>
                            <id>assembly</id>
                            <files>
```

```
                       <file>
<source>target/${project.build.finalName}.jar</source>
                       </file>
                  </files>
               </inline>
            </assembly>
            <tags>
               <tag>latest</tag>
            </tags>
            <ports>
               <port>8080</port>
            </ports>
         </build>
         <run>
            <namingStrategy>alias</namingStrategy>
         </run>
         <alias>${project.build.finalName}</alias>
      </image>
   </images>
</configuration>
</plugin>
```

There are a couple of new configurations here. Let's start with the <name> tag—it configures the repository and Docker image name to push to Docker Hub. For this book, we will use springfivebyexample as a Docker ID. We can see there is a *slash* as a separator for the repository and image name. The image name for us will be the final project name. Then, we need to configure it.

 The Docker ID is free to use, which can be used to access some Docker services, such as Docker Store, Docker Cloud, and Docker Hub. We can find more information at Docker Page (https://docs.docker.com/docker-id/).

This configuration should be the same as shown in the following code snippet:

```
<build>
  <finalName>cms</finalName>
  ....
</build>
```

Another important tag is <entrypoint>. This is an exec system call instruction when we use the docker run command. In our case, we expected the application to run when the container bootstraps. We will execute java -jar passing the container as an active profile for Spring.

We need to pass the full path of the Java artifact. This path will be configured on the `<assembly>` tag with the `<basedir>` parameter. It can be any folder name. Also, there is a configuration to the Java artifact path. Usually, this is the target folder which is the result of the compilation. It can be configured in the `<source>` tag.

Finally, we have the `<port>` configuration. The port of the application will be exposed using this tag.

Now, we will create a Docker image by using the following instruction:

```
mvn clean install docker:build
```

It should be executed in the root folder of the project. The goal of the `docker:build` command is to build a Docker image for our project. After the build ends, we can check if the Docker image has been created successfully.

Then, type the following command:

```
docker images
```

The `springfivebyexample/cms` image should be present, as shown in the following screenshot:

REPOSITORY	TAG	IMAGE ID	CREATED	SIZE
springfivebyexample/cms	latest	94f297e9082f	29 minutes ago	773MB
mongo-express	latest	3fe03c9f9d40	2 weeks ago	246MB
mongo	latest	d22888af0ce0	3 weeks ago	361MB

Good. The image is ready. Let's push to the Docker Hub.

Pushing the image to Docker Hub

The Docker Hub is a public repository to store Docker images. It is free, and we will use it for this book. Now, we will push our image to the Docker Hub registry.

The command for that is pretty simple. Type:

```
docker push springfivebyexample/cms:latest
```

 I have used the `springfivebyexample` user that I have created. You can test the `docker push` command creating by your own user on Docker Hub and changing the user on the `docker push` command. You can create your Docker ID at Docker Hub (`https://cloud.docker.com/`).

Then, the image will be sent to the registry. That is it.

 We can find the image at Docker Hub (`https://store.docker.com/ community/images/springfivebyexample/cms`). If you have used your own user, the link will probably change.

Configuring the Docker Spring profile

Before we run our application in a Docker container, we need to create a YAML file to configure a container profile. The new YAML file should be named as `application-container.yaml` because we will use the container profile to run it. Remember, we configured the `entrypoint` on `pom.xml` in the previous section.

Let's create our new file. The file should be the same content as described in the following snippet:

```
spring:
  data:
    mongodb:
      database: cms
      host: mongodb
      port: 27017
```

The host must be changed for MongoDB. We have been running the MongoDB container with this name in the *Preparing a MongoDB* section. It is an important configuration, and we need to pay attention at this point. We cannot use localhost anymore because the application is running in the Docker container now. The localhost in that context means it is in the same container, and we do not have MongoDB in the CMS application container. We need to have one application per container and avoid multiple responsibilities for one container.

Done. In the following section, we will run our first application in the Docker container. It will be amazing. Let's do it.

Running the Dockerized CMS

In the previous section, we have created our file to configure the container profile properly. Now, it is time to run our container. The command is quite simple, but we need to pay attention to the arguments.

The instruction we run should be the same as the following code:

```
docker run -d --name cms --link mongodb:mongodb --net cms-application -p
8080:8080 springfivebyexample/cms:latest
```

We have been setting the link for the MongoDB container. Remember, we made this configuration in the YAML file, in the `host` property. During the bootstrapping phase, the application will look for MongoDB instance named `mongodb`. We solved this by using the link command. It will work perfectly.

We can check if our application is healthy by using the `docker ps` command. The output should be like this:

```
CONTAINER ID    IMAGE                           COMMAND             CREATED         STATUS          PORTS                       NAMES
4855a23b3ac1    springfivebyexample/cms:latest  "/bin/sh -c 'java ..."  22 minutes ago  Up 22 minutes   0.0.0.0:8080->8080/tcp      cms
e7ff58bc1a4b    mongo-express                   "tini -- node app"  19 hours ago    Up 19 hours     0.0.0.0:8081->8081/tcp      friendly_goodall
dd71620d4f76    mongo                           "docker-entrypoint..."  20 hours ago    Up 20 hours     0.0.0.0:27017->27017/tcp    mongo
```

In the first line, we have our application container. It is up and running.

Awesome work. Our application is fully containerized and ready to deploy anywhere we want.

Putting in Reactive fashion

We have been creating an amazing application with Spring Boot. The application was built on the traditional web stack present on Spring Framework. It means the application uses the web servers based on Servlet APIs.

The servlet specification was built with the blocking semantics or one-request-per-thread model. Sometimes, we need to change the application architecture because of non-functional requirements. For example, if the application was bought by a huge company, and that company wanted to create a plan to launch the application for the entire world, the volume of requests would probably increase a lot. So, we need to change the architecture to adapt the application structure for cloud environments.

Usually, in a cloud environment, the machines are smaller than traditional data centers. Instead of a big machine, it is popular to use many small machines and try to scale applications horizontally. In this scenario, the servlet spec can be switched to an architecture created upon Reactive Streams. This kind of architecture fits better than servlet for the cloud environments.

Spring Framework has been creating the Spring WebFlux to helps developers to create Reactive Web Applications. Let's change our application architecture to reactive and learn the pretty new Spring WebFlux component.

Reactive Spring

The Reactive Stream Spec is the specification that provides a standard for asynchronous programming for stream processing. It is becoming popular in the programming world nowadays, and Spring introduces it on the framework.

This style of programming is more efficient regarding resources usage and fits amazingly with the new generation of machines with multiple cores.

Spring reactive uses the Project Reactor as the implementation for the Reactive Streams. The Project Reactor is powered by Pivotal and has the very good implementation of the Reactive Streams Spec.

Now, we will deep dive in the reactive module for Spring Boot and create an amazing reactive API and try the new style of the Spring Framework.

Project Reactor

The Project Reactor was created by the Spring and Pivotal teams. This project is an implementation of Reactive Streams for JVM. It is a fully non-blocking foundation and helps developers to create a non-blocking application in the JVM ecosystem.

There is a restriction to using Reactor in our application. The project runs on Java 8 and above. It is important because we will use many lambda expressions in our examples and projects.

The Spring Framework internally uses the Project Reactor as an implementation of Reactive Streams.

Components

Let's look at the different components of the Project Reactor:

- **Publishers**: The publishers are responsible for pushing data elements to the stream. It notifies the subscribers that a new piece of data is coming to the stream. The publisher interface is defined in the following code snippet:

```
/**********************************************************************
******
 * Licensed under Public Domain (CC0)
 *
 *
 *
 * To the extent possible under law, the person who associated CC0
with   *
 * this code has waived all copyright and related or neighboring
 *
 * rights to this code.
 *
 *
 *
 * You should have received a copy of the CC0 legalcode along with
this   *
 * work. If not, see
<http://creativecommons.org/publicdomain/zero/1.0/>.*
 **********************************************************************
*****/

package org.reactivestreams;

/**
 * A {@link Publisher} is a provider of a potentially unbounded
number of sequenced elements, publishing them according to
 * the demand received from its {@link Subscriber}(s).
 * <p>
 * A {@link Publisher} can serve multiple {@link Subscriber}s
subscribed {@link #subscribe(Subscriber)} dynamically
 * at various points in time.
 *
 * @param <T> the type of element signaled.
 */
public interface Publisher<T> {

    public void subscribe(Subscriber<? super T> s);

}
```

- **Subscribers**: The subscribers are responsible for making the data flow in the stream. When the publisher starts to send the piece of data on the data flow, the piece of data will be collected by the `onNext(T instance)` method, which is the parametrized interface.

The subscriber interface is defined in the following code snippet:

```
/***************************************************************
******
 * Licensed under Public Domain (CC0)
 *
  *
 *
 * To the extent possible under law, the person who associated CC0
with  *
 * this code has waived all copyright and related or neighboring
 *
 * rights to this code.
 *
  *
 *
 * You should have received a copy of the CC0 legalcode along with
this  *
 * work. If not, see
<http://creativecommons.org/publicdomain/zero/1.0/>.*
 **************************************************************
*****/

package org.reactivestreams;

/**
 * Will receive call to {@link #onSubscribe(Subscription)} once
after passing an instance of {@link Subscriber} to {@link
Publisher#subscribe(Subscriber)}.
 * <p>
 * No further notifications will be received until {@link
Subscription#request(long)} is called.
 * <p>
 * After signaling demand:
 * <ul>
 * <li>One or more invocations of {@link #onNext(Object)} up to the
maximum number defined by {@link Subscription#request(long)}</li>
 * <li>Single invocation of {@link #onError(Throwable)} or {@link
Subscriber#onComplete()} which signals a terminal state after which
no further events will be sent.
 * </ul>
 * <p>
 * Demand can be signaled via {@link Subscription#request(long)}
```

```
     whenever the {@link Subscriber} instance is capable of handling
     more.
      *
      * @param <T> the type of element signaled.
      */
     public interface Subscriber<T> {
         public void onSubscribe(Subscription s);

         public void onNext(T t);

         public void onComplete();
     }
```

Hot and cold

There are two categories of reactive sequences—hot and cold. These functions affect the usage of the implementation directly. Hence, we need to understand them:

- **Cold**: The cold publishers start to generate data only if it receives a new subscription. If there are no subscriptions, the data never comes to the flow.
- **Hot**: The hot publishers do not need any subscribers to generate the data flow. When the new subscriber is registered, the subscriber will only get the new data elements emitted.

Reactive types

There are two reactive types which represent the reactive sequences. The `Mono` objects represent a single value or empty 0|1. The `Flux` objects represent a sequence of 0|N items.

We will find many references in our code. The Spring Data reactive repository uses these abstractions in their methods. The `findOne()` method returns the `Mono<T>` object and the `findAll()` returns a `Flux<T>`. The same behavior we will be found in our REST resources.

Let's play with the Reactor

To understand it better, let's play with the Reactor. We will implement and understand the difference between hot and cold publishers in practice.

Cold publishers do not produce any data until a new subscription arrives. In the following code, we will create a cold publisher and the `System.out:println` will never be executed because it does not have any subscribers. Let's test the behavior:

```
@Test
public void coldBehavior(){
   Category sports = new Category();
   sports.setName("sports");
   Category music = new Category();
   sports.setName("music");
   Flux.just(sports,music)
       .doOnNext(System.out::println);
}
```

As we can see, the method `subscribe()` is not present in this snippet. When we execute the code, we will not see any data on the standard print output.

We can execute the method on the IDE. We will able to see the output of this test. The output should be like this:

The process has finished, the test passed, and we will not be able to see the print. That is the cold publisher's behavior.

Now, we will subscribe the publisher and the data will be sent on the data flow. Let's try this.

We will insert the subscribe instruction after `doOnNext()`. Let's change our code:

```
@Test
 public void coldBehaviorWithSubscribe(){
   Category sports = new Category();
   sports.setId(UUID.randomUUID().toString());
   sports.setName("sports");
   Category music = new Category();
   music.setId(UUID.randomUUID().toString());
   music.setName("music");
   Flux.just(sports,music)
       .doOnNext(System.out::println)
      .subscribe();
 }
```

The output should be like this:

```
objc[4922]: Class JavaLaunchHelper is implemented in both /Library/Java/JavaVirtualMachines/jdk1.8
22:45:42.537 [main] DEBUG reactor.util.Loggers$LoggerFactory - Using Slf4j logging framework
Category(id=ce49b83b-2aee-47dd-8f68-e601eb1454da, name=sports)
Category(id=8fb25e99-a25b-4542-94be-ab35a1854104, name=music)

Process finished with exit code 0
```

In the preceding screenshot, we can see that the publisher pushes the data on the stream after the stream got subscribed. That is the cold publisher behavior after the subscription.

Hot publishers do not depend on any subscribers. The hot publisher will publish data, even if there is no subscriber to receive the data. Let's see an example:

```
@Test
public void testHotPublisher(){
  UnicastProcessor<String> hotSource = UnicastProcessor.create();
  Flux<Category> hotPublisher = hotSource.publish()
      .autoConnect().map((String t) -> Category.builder().name(t).build());
  hotPublisher.subscribe(category -> System.out.println("Subscriber 1: "+
category.getName()));
  hotSource.onNext("sports");
  hotSource.onNext("cars");
  hotPublisher.subscribe(category -> System.out.println("Subscriber 2:
"+category.getName()));
  hotSource.onNext("games");
  hotSource.onNext("electronics");
  hotSource.onComplete();
}
```

Let's understand what happens here. The `UnicastProcessor` is a processor that allows only one `Subscriber`.The processor replays notifications when the subscriber requests. It will emit some data on a stream. The first subscription will capture all the categories, as we will see, because it was registered before the event emissions. The second subscription will capture only the last events because it was registered before the last two emissions.

The output of the preceding code should be:

Awesome. This is the hot publisher's behavior.

Spring WebFlux

The traditional Java enterprise web applications are based on the servlet specification. The servlet specification before 3.1 is synchronous, which means it was created with blocking semantics. This model was good at the time because computers were big with a powerful CPU and hundreds of gigabytes of memory. Usually, the applications at the time were configured with a big thread pool with hundreds of threads because the computer was designed for this. The primary deployment model at that time was the replica. There are some machines with the same configuration and application deployments.

The developers have been creating applications like this for many years.

Nowadays, most of the applications are deployed in cloud vendors. There are no big machines anymore because the price is much higher. Instead of big machines, there are a number of small machines. It is much cheaper and these machines have a reasonable CPU power and memory.

In this new scenario, the application with the huge thread pools is not effective anymore, because the machine is small and it does not have the power to handle all these threads.

The Spring Team added the support for the Reactive Streams in the framework. This model of programming changes the application deployment and the way to build applications.

Instead of a thread-per-request model, the applications are created with the event-loop model. This model requires a small number of threads and is more efficient regarding resource usage.

Event-loop model

Popularized by the NodeJS language, this model is based on event-driven programming. There are two central concepts: the events which will be enqueued on a queue, and the handlers which keep track of and process these events.

There are some advantages of adopting this model. The first one is the ordering. The events are enqueued and dispatched in the same order in which the events are coming. In some uses cases, this is an important requirement.

The other one is the synchronization. The event-loop must be executed on only one thread. This makes the states easy to handle and avoids the shared state problems.

There is an important piece of advice here. The handlers must not be synchronous. Otherwise, the application will be blocked until the handlers end their workload.

Spring Data for Reactive Extensions

The Spring Data projects have some extensions to work with a reactive foundation. The project provides a couple of implementations based on asynchronous programming. It means the whole stack is asynchronous since database drivers are as well.

The Spring reactive repository supports Cassandra, MongoDB, and Redis as database stores. The repository implementations offer the same behaviors as the non-reactive implementation. There is a **DSL** (**Domain-Specific Language**) to create domain-specific query methods.

The module uses the Project Reactor as a reactive foundation implementation, but is possible to change the implementation to RxJava as well. Both libraries are production-ready and are adopted by the community. One point to be aware of is that if we change to RxJava, we need to ensure our method returns to `Observable` and `Single`.

Spring Data Reactive

The Spring Data Project has support for the reactive data access. Until now, Spring has support for MongoDB, Apache Cassandra, and Redis, all of which have reactive drivers.

In our CMS application, we will use the MongoDB reactive drivers to give the reactive characteristics for our repositories. We will use the new reactive interface provided by the Spring Data reactive. Also, we need to change the code a little bit. In this chapter, we will do that step by step. Let's start.

Reactive repositories in practice

Before we start, we can check out the full source code at GitHub, or we can perform the following steps.

Now, we are ready to build our new reactive repositories. The first thing that we need to do is add the Maven dependencies to our project. This can be done using `pom.xml`.

Let's configure our new dependency:

```
<dependency>
  <groupId>org.springframework.boot</groupId>
  <artifactId>spring-boot-starter-data-mongodb-reactive</artifactId>
</dependency>
```

Our project is ready to use reactive MongoDB repositories.

Creating the first Reactive repository

We have a couple of repositories in our CMS project. Now, we need to convert these repositories to reactive ones. The first thing we will do is remove the extension from `CrudRepository`, which is not necessary anymore. Now, we want the reactive version of that.

We will update the `ReactiveMongoRepository` interface. The parameters of the interface are the same as the ones we inserted before. The interface should be like this:

```
package springfive.cms.domain.repository;

import org.springframework.data.mongodb.repository.ReactiveMongoRepository;
import springfive.cms.domain.models.Category;

public interface CategoryRepository extends
ReactiveMongoRepository<Category, String> {
}
```

This is quite similar to the one we created before. We need to extend the new `ReactiveMongoRepository` interface, which contains methods for the CRUD operations and much more. The interface returns `Mono<Category>` or `Flux<Category>`. The methods do not return the entities anymore. It is a common way of programming when the Reactive Stream is adopted.

We need to change the other repositories as well. You can find the full source code on GitHub at: `https://github.com/PacktPublishing/Spring-5.0-By-Example/tree/master/Chapter03/cms-mongodb/src/main/java/springfive/cms/domain/repository`.

Now, we need to change the service layer. Let's do that.

Fixing the service layer

We need to change the service layer to adopt the new reactive programming style. We changed the repository layer, so now we need to fix the compilation problem result because of this change. The application needs to be reactive. Any point of the application can be blocked because we are using the event-loop model. If we do not do this, the application will be getting blocked.

Changing the CategoryService

Now, we will fix the `CategoryService` class. We will change the return type of a couple of methods. Before, we could return the model class, but now we need to change to return `Mono` or `Flux`, similar to what we did in the repository layer.

The new `CategoryService` should be like the implementation shown in the following code snippet:

```
package springfive.cms.domain.service;

import org.springframework.stereotype.Service;
import reactor.core.publisher.Flux;
import reactor.core.publisher.Mono;
import springfive.cms.domain.models.Category;
import springfive.cms.domain.repository.CategoryRepository;
import springfive.cms.domain.vo.CategoryRequest;

@Service
public class CategoryService {

  private final CategoryRepository categoryRepository;

  public CategoryService(CategoryRepository categoryRepository) {
    this.categoryRepository = categoryRepository;
  }

  public Mono<Category> update(String id,CategoryRequest category){
    return this.categoryRepository.findById(id).flatMap(categoryDatabase ->
```

```
{
        categoryDatabase.setName(category.getName());
        return this.categoryRepository.save(categoryDatabase);
    });
}

public Mono<Category> create(CategoryRequest request){
    Category category = new Category();
    category.setName(request.getName());
    return this.categoryRepository.save(category);
}

public void delete(String id){
    this.categoryRepository.deleteById(id);
}

public Flux<Category> findAll(){
    return this.categoryRepository.findAll();
}

public Mono<Category> findOne(String id){
    return this.categoryRepository.findById(id);
}

}
```

As we can see, the return types changed in the methods.

The important thing here is that we need to follow the reactive principles. When the method returns only one instance, we need to use Mono<Category>. When the method returns one or more instances, we should use Flux<Category>. This is essential to follow because developers and Spring containers can then interpret the code correctly.

The update() method has an interesting call: flatMap(). The project reactor allows us to use a kind of DSL to compose calls. It is very interesting and very useful as well. It helps developers to create code that is easier to understand than before. The flatMap() method is usually used to convert the data emitted by Mono or Flux. In this context, we need to set the new name of the category on the category retrieved from the database.

Changing the REST layer

We will make some fixes on the REST layer as well. We changed the service layer, and it caused some compilation problems in our resources classes.

We need to add the new dependency, `spring-web-reactive`. This supports the `@Controller` or `@RestController` annotations for the reactive non-blocking engine. The Spring MVC does not support the reactive extensions, and this module enables developers to use reactive paradigms, as they did before.

`spring-web-reactive` will change many contracts on the Spring MVC foundations, such as `HandlerMapping`, and `HandlerAdapter`, to enable reactive foundations on these components.

The following image can help us to better understand the Spring HTTP layers:

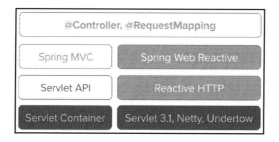

As we can see, `@Controller` and `@RequestMapping` can be used for different approaches in the Spring MVC traditional applications, or by using the Spring web reactive module.

Before we start to change our REST layer, we need to remove the Spring Fox dependencies and annotations in our project. At present, the Spring Fox has no support for reactive applications yet.

The dependencies to remove are:

```
<dependency>
  <groupId>io.springfox</groupId>
  <artifactId>springfox-swagger2</artifactId>
  <version>2.7.0</version>
</dependency>

<dependency>
  <groupId>io.springfox</groupId>
  <artifactId>springfox-swagger-ui</artifactId>
```

```
    <version>2.7.0</version>
  </dependency>
```

After that, we need to remove the annotations from the Swagger packages, such as `@Api` and `@ApiOperation`.

Now, let's adjust our REST layer.

Adding the Spring WebFlux dependency

Before we start to change our REST layer, we need to add the new dependency to our `pom.xml`.

First, we will remove the Spring MVC traditional dependencies. To do this, we need to remove the following dependency:

```
<dependency>
  <groupId>org.springframework.boot</groupId>
  <artifactId>spring-boot-starter-web</artifactId>
</dependency>
```

We do not need this dependency anymore. Our application will be reactive now. Then, we need to add the new dependencies described in the following code snippet:

```
<dependency>
  <groupId>io.netty</groupId>
  <artifactId>netty-transport-native-epoll</artifactId>
</dependency>

<dependency>
  <groupId>org.springframework.boot</groupId>
  <artifactId>spring-boot-starter-webflux</artifactId>
</dependency>
```

`spring-boot-starter-webflux` is a kind of syntax sugar for dependencies. It has the `spring-boot-starter-reactor-netty` dependency, which is the Reactor Netty, as embedded in the reactive HTTP server.

Awesome, our project is ready to convert the REST layer. Let's transform our application into a fully reactive application.

Changing the CategoryResource

We will change the `CategoryResource` class. The idea is pretty simple. We will convert our `ResponseEntity`, which is parametrized with the models class to `ResponseEntity` using `Mono` or `Flux`.

The new version of the `CategoryResource` should be like this:

```
package springfive.cms.domain.resources;

import org.springframework.http.HttpStatus;
import org.springframework.http.ResponseEntity;
import org.springframework.web.bind.annotation.DeleteMapping;
import org.springframework.web.bind.annotation.GetMapping;
import org.springframework.web.bind.annotation.PathVariable;
import org.springframework.web.bind.annotation.PostMapping;
import org.springframework.web.bind.annotation.PutMapping;
import org.springframework.web.bind.annotation.RequestBody;
import org.springframework.web.bind.annotation.RequestMapping;
import org.springframework.web.bind.annotation.ResponseStatus;
import org.springframework.web.bind.annotation.RestController;
import reactor.core.publisher.Flux;
import reactor.core.publisher.Mono;
import springfive.cms.domain.models.Category;
import springfive.cms.domain.service.CategoryService;
import springfive.cms.domain.vo.CategoryRequest;

@RestController
@RequestMapping("/api/category")
public class CategoryResource {

  private final CategoryService categoryService;

  public CategoryResource(CategoryService categoryService) {
    this.categoryService = categoryService;
  }

  @GetMapping(value = "/{id}")
  public ResponseEntity<Mono<Category>> findOne(@PathVariable("id") String
id){
    return ResponseEntity.ok(this.categoryService.findOne(id));
  }

  @GetMapping
  public ResponseEntity<Flux<Category>> findAll(){
    return ResponseEntity.ok(this.categoryService.findAll());
  }
```

```
@PostMapping
public ResponseEntity<Mono<Category>> newCategory(@RequestBody
CategoryRequest category){
    return new ResponseEntity<>(this.categoryService.create(category),
HttpStatus.CREATED);
}

@DeleteMapping("/{id}")
@ResponseStatus(HttpStatus.NO_CONTENT)
public void removeCategory(@PathVariable("id") String id){
    this.categoryService.delete(id);
}

@PutMapping("/{id}")
public ResponseEntity<Mono<Category>> updateCategory(@PathVariable("id")
String id,CategoryRequest category){
    return new ResponseEntity<>(this.categoryService.update(id,category),
HttpStatus.OK);
}

}
```

The code is quite similar to what we did before. We have used the `@RequestBody` annotation in the method argument; otherwise, the JSON converter will not work.

The other important characteristic here is the `return` method. It returns `Mono` or `Flux`, which are parameterized types for `ResponseEntity`.

We can test the reactive implementation by using the command line. It will persist the `Category` object on MongoDB. Type the following command on the Terminal:

```
curl -H "Content-Type: application/json" -X POST -d '{"name":"reactive"}'
http://localhost:8080/api/category
```

And then, we can use the following command to check the database. Using the browser, go to `http://localhost:8080/api/category`. The following result should be presented:

```
←  →  C   ⓘ localhost:8080/api/category

▼ [
  ▼ {
        "id": "5a86084b6e34490ec986468e",
        "name": "reactive"
    }
  ]
```

Awesome, our reactive implementation is working as expected. Well done!!!

Summary

In this chapter, we have learned a lot of Spring concepts. We have introduced you to Spring Data projects, which help developers to create data access layers as we have never seen before. We saw how easy it is to create repositories with this project.

Also, we presented some relatively new projects, such as Spring WebFlux, which permits developers to create modern web applications, applying the Reactive Streams foundations and reactive programming style in projects.

We have finished our CMS application. The application has the characteristics of a production-ready application, such as database connections, and services which have been well-designed with single responsibilities. Also, we introduced the `docker-maven-plugin`, which provides a reasonable way to create images using the `pom.xml` configurations.

In the next chapter, we will create a new application using the *Reactive Manifesto* based on message-driven applications. See you there.

4
Kotlin Basics and Spring Data Redis

Spring Boot allows developers to create different styles of application. In Chapter 2, *Starting in the Spring World – the CMS Application*, and Chapter 3, *Persistence with Spring Data and Reactive Fashion*, we have created a portal application, and now we will create an application based on message-driven architecture. It demonstrates how the Spring Framework fits well in a wide range of application architectures.

In this chapter, we will start to create an application which keeps the tracked hashtags on the Redis database. The application will get hashtags and put them in a couple of queues to our other projects, and consume and handle them appropriately.

As we have been doing in our previous projects, we will continue to use the Reactive Foundation to provide scalable characteristics in the application.

At the end of this chapter, we will have:

- Learned Kotlin basics
- Created the project structure
- Created the Reactive Redis repositories
- Applied some techniques in reactive programming, using the Reactive Redis Client

Let's start right now.

Learning Kotlin basics

The Kotlin language was released officially in February 2016. JetBrains created it and has been developing the language ever since. The company is the owner of the IntelliJ IDEA IDE.

In February 2012, JetBrains made the language open source under the Apache v2 license; the license allows developers to create applications.

The language is one option for **JVM (Java Virtual Machine)** languages such as Clojure and Scala, which means that the language can compile bytecode for JVM. As we will see, Kotlin has many similarities with Scala. Kotlin has the Scala language as a reference, but the JetBrains teams believe that Scala has problems with the compilation time.

Kotlin was becoming an adopted language in the Android world and because of this, in the Google I/O, 2017, the Google Team announced official support for the Android ecosystem. Since then, the language has been growing year by year and increasing in popularity.

Main characteristics of Kotlin

The Kotlin language was designed to maintain the interoperability with Java code. It means we can start to code with Java idioms in the Kotlin file.

The language is statically-typed, and it is an excellent attribute because it can help us find some problems at compilation time. Also, statically-typed languages are much faster than dynamic languages. The IDEs can help developers much better than dynamic languages, as well.

Syntax

The syntax is different from Java syntax. At first glance, it can be a problem but after some hours of playing with Kotlin, it is not a problem at all.

There are two interesting reserved words to understand the usage and concepts:

- `var`: This is a variable declaration. It indicates the variable is mutable and can be reassigned, as developers need.
- `val`: This is a variable declaration which indicates the variable is immutable and cannot be reassigned anymore. This definition is like a final declaration in the Java language.

The variable declarations have a name, and after the desired data type, the colon is necessary in the middle as a separator. If the variable is initialized, the type is not necessary because the compiler can infer the correct data type. Let's try it out to understand it better.

Here is a variable with the data type specified:

```
var bookName: String
```

In this case, we need to keep the data type because the variable is not initialized, then the compiler cannot infer the type. The variable, bookName, can be reassigned because of the modifier var.

Here is a variable without the data type:

```
val book = "Spring 5.0 by Example"
```

It is not a necessity to declare the data type because we have initialized the variable with the value, Spring 5.0 by Example. The compiler can infer the type is a kind of *syntactic sugar*. The variable cannot be reassigned because of the modifier val. If we try to reassign the instruction, we will get a compilation error.

The semicolons are optional in Kotlin, the compiler can detect the statement terminator. This is another point where Kotlin diverges from the Java programming language:

```
val book = "Spring 5.0 by Example"
var bookName: String
println("Hello, world!")
```

The semicolons were not provided, and the instructions were compiled.

 Immutable programming in the Kotlin language is recommended. It performs better on the multi-core environments. Also, it makes the developer's life easier to debug and troubleshoot scenarios.

Semantics

In Kotlin, there are classes and functions. However, there is no method anymore. The fun keyword should be used to declare a function.

Kotlin gets some concepts of the Scala language and brings some special classes such as Data classes and Object classes (which we will learn soon). Before that, we will understand how to declare a function in Kotlin. Let's do that!

Declaring functions in Kotlin

There are many variations in function declarations. We will create some declarations to understand the slight difference from Java methods.

Simple function with parameters and return type

This simple function has two parameters and a String as a return type. Take a look at a parameter declaration and observe the order, name and data type.

```
fun greetings(name:String,greeting:String):String{
   return greeting + name
}
```

As we can see, the type of argument which comes after the variable name is the same as on the variable declarations. The return type comes after the arguments list is separated with semicolons. The same function can be declared in the following way in Java:

```
public String greetings(String name,String greeting){
   return greeting + name;
}
```

There are some differences here. Firstly, there are semicolons in the Java code, and we can see the order of the methods and functions declarations.

Simple function without return

Let's understand how we can construct functions without a return value, the following function will not return any value:

```
fun printGreetings(name:String,greeting:String):Unit{
   println(greeting + name)
}
```

There is one difference, in this case, the Unit was introduced; this type of object corresponds to void in Java language. Then, in the preceding code, we have a function without a return. The Unit object can be removed if you want the compiler to understand the function has no return value.

Single expressions functions

When the function has a single expression we can remove the curly braces, the same as in Scala, and the function body should be specified after the = symbol. Let's refactor our first function, as follows:

```
fun greetings(name:String,greeting:String) = greeting + name
```

We can remove the return keyword, as well. Our function is pretty concise now. We removed return and the type of return as well. As we can see, the code is more readable now. If you want, the return type can be declared too.

Overriding a function

To override a function on Kotlin, it is necessary to put an override keyword on the function declaration, and the base function needs to have the open keyword as well.

Let's look at an example:

```
open class Greetings {
  open fun greeting() {}
}

class SuperGreeting() : Greetings() {
  override fun greeting() {
  // my super greeting
  }
}
```

This way is more explicit than Java, it increases the legibility of the code as well.

Data classes

Data classes are the right solution when we want to hold and transfer data between system layers. Like in Scala, these classes offer some built-in functionalities such as getters/setters, equals and hashCode, toString method and the copy function.

Let's create an example for that:

```
data class Book(val author:String,val name:String,val
description:String,val new:Boolean = false)
```

We have some interesting things in the code. The first thing we notice is that all of the attributes are immutable. It means there are no setters for all of them. The second is that in the class declaration, we can see a list of attributes. In this case, Kotlin will create a constructor with all attributes present in this class and because they are `val` it means final attributes.

In this case, there is no default constructor anymore.

Another interesting feature in Kotlin is that it enables developers to have default values on constructors, in our case the `new` attribute, if omitted, will assume the `false` value. We can get the same behavior in the parameters list in functions as well.

Finally, there is a fantastic way to copy objects. The `copy` method allows developers to copy objects with named parameters. This means we can change only attributes as we need. Let's take a look at an example:

```
fun main(args : Array<String>) {
  val springFiveOld = Book("Claudio E. de Oliveira","Spring 5.0 by
Example","Amazing example of Spring Boot Apps",false)
  val springFiveNew = springFiveOld.copy(new = true)
  println(springFiveOld)
  println(springFiveNew)
}
```

In the first object, we have created a book instance with `false` for the `new` attribute, then we copied a new object with `true` for the `new` attribute, and the other attributes are not changed. Goodbye to the complex clone logic and nice to meet the new way to copy objects.

The output of this code should look like the following:

```
Book(author=Claudio E. de Oliveira, name=Spring 5.0 by Example, description=Amazing example of Spring Boot Apps, new=false)
Book(author=Claudio E. de Oliveira, name=Spring 5.0 by Example, description=Amazing example of Spring Boot Apps, new=true)

Process finished with exit code 0
```

As we can see, only the `new` attribute is changed and the `toString` function was generated in good shape as well.

There are some restrictions on Data classes. They cannot be abstract, open, sealed, or inner.

Objects

The singleton pattern is commonly used in applications, and Kotlin provides an easy way to do that without much boilerplate code.

We can instruct Kotlin to create a singleton object using the `object` keyword. Once again, Kotlin used Scala as a reference because there are the same functionalities in the Scala language.

Let's try it:

```
object BookNameFormatter{
   fun format(book: Book):String = "The book name is" + book.name
}
```

We have created a formatter to return a message with the book name. Then, we try to use this function:

```
val springFiveOld = Book("Claudio E. de Oliveira","Spring 5.0 by
Example","Amazing example of Spring Boot Apps",false)
BookNameFormatter.format(springFiveOld)
```

The function format can be called in a static context. There is no instance to call the function because it is a singleton object.

Companion objects

A **companion object** is an object which is common for all instances of that class. It means there are many instances of a book, for example, but there is a single instance of their companion object. Usually, the developers use companion objects as a factory method. Let's create our first `companion object`:

```
data class Book(val author:String,val name:String,val
description:String,val new:Boolean = false{

   companion object {
     fun create(name:String,description: String,author: String):Book{
       return Book(author,name,description)
     }
   }

}
```

If the name of the `companion object` was omitted, the function could be called in a singleton way, without an instance, like this:

```
val myBookWithFactory = Book.create("Claudio E. de Oliveira","Spring 5.0 by
Example","Amazing example of Spring Boot Apps")
```

It is like an `object` behavior. We can call it in a static context.

Kotlin idioms

Koltin idioms are a kind of syntax sugar for Java programmers. It is a collection of pieces of code which help developers to create a concise code in Kotlin languages. Let's take a look at common Kotlin idioms.

String interpolation

Kotlin supports string interpolation, it is a little bit complex to do it in the Java language but it is not a problem for Kotlin. We do not require a lot of code to do this task as Kotlin supports it natively. It makes the code easier to read and understand. Let's create an example:

```
val bookName = "Spring 5.0"
val phrase = "The name of the book is $bookName"
```

As we can see, it is a piece of cake to interpolate strings in Kotlin. Goodbye `String.format()` with a lot of arguments. We can use `$bookName` to replace the `bookName` variable value. Also, we can access the functions present in objects, but for that, we need to put curly braces. Check the following code:

```
val springFiveOld = Book("Claudio E. de Oliveira","Spring 5.0 by
Example","Amazing example of Spring Boot Apps",false)
val phrase = "The name of the book is ${springFiveOld.name}"
```

Thanks, Kotlin we appreciate this feature.

Smart Casts

Kotlin supports the feature called Smart Casts which enables developers to use the cast operators automatically. After checking the variable type, in Java, the cast operator must be explicit. Let's check it out:

```
fun returnValue(instance: Any): String {
  if (instance is String) {
    return instance
  }
  throw IllegalArgumentException("Instance is not String")
}
```

As we can see, the cast operator is not present anymore. After checking the type, Kotlin can infer the expected type. Let's check the Java version for the same piece of code:

```java
public String returnValue(Object instance) {
  if (instance instanceof String) {
    String value = (String) instance;
     return value;
  }
  throw IllegalArgumentException("Instance is not String");
}
```

It makes the cast safer because we do not need to check and apply the cast operator.

Range expressions

Range expressions permit developers to work with ranges in `for` loops and `if` comparison. There are a lot of ways to work with ranges in Kotlin. We will take a look at most of the common ones here.

Simple case

Let's look at one simple case:

```kotlin
for ( i in 1..5){
  println(i)
}
```

It will iterate from 1 to 5 inclusive because we have used them in the `in` keyword.

The until case

We also can use the `until` keyword in `for` loops, in this case, the end element will be excluded from the interaction. Let's see an example:

```kotlin
for (i in 1 until 5) {
  println(i)
}
```

In this case, the 5 value will not be printed on the console, because the end element is not included in the interaction.

The downTo case

The `downTo` keyword enables developers to interact with the numbers in reverse order. The instruction is self-explanatory, as well. Let's see it in practice:

```
for (i in 5 downTo 1) {
  println(i)
}
```

It is pretty easy as well. The interaction will occur in the reverse order, in this case, the value `1` will be included. As we can see, the code is pretty easy to understand.

Step case

Sometimes we need to interact over values but with the arbitrary steps, not one by one, for example. Then we can use the `step` instruction. Let's practice:

```
for (i in 1..6 step 2) {
  print(i)
}
```

Here, we will see the following output: `135`, because the interaction will start on the `1` value and will be increased by two points.

Awesome. The Kotlin ranges can add more readability to our source code and help to increase the quality of code as well.

Null safety

Kotlin has amazing stuff to work with null references. The null reference is a nightmare for Java developers. The Java 8 has an `Optional` object, which helps developers work with nullable objects, but is not concise like in Kotlin.

Now, we will explore how Kotlin can help developers to avoid the `NullPointerException`. Let's understand.

The Kotlin type system makes a distinction between references which can hold null and those which cannot hold null. Due to this, the code is more concise and readable because it is a kind of advice for developers.

When the reference does not allow null, the declaration should be:

```
var myNonNullString:String = "my non null string"
```

The preceding variable cannot be assigned to a null reference, if we do this, we will get a compilation error. Look how easy the code is to understand.

Sometimes, we need to allow for a variable to have null references, in these cases, we can use the ? as an operator, such as follows:

```
var allowNull:String? = "permits null references"
```

Easy. Pay attention to a variable declaration on the ? operator, it makes the variable accept null references.

There are two different ways to avoid the `NullPointerReference` in Kotlin. The first one can be called **safe calls**, and the other can be called the **Elvis Operator**. Let's take a look at those.

Safe calls

The safe call can be written using the . ?. It can be called when the reference holds a non-null value when the value holds a null reference then the null value will be returned:

```
val hash:TrackedHashTag? = TrackedHashTag(hashTag="java",queue="java")
val queueString = hash?.queue
```

When the `hash?` holds null, the null value will be assigned to a `queueString` attribute. If the `hash?` has a valid reference, the queue attribute will be assigned to a `queueString` attribute.

Elvis operator

It can be used when developers expect to return a default value when the reference is null:

```
val hash:TrackedHashTag? = TrackedHashTag(hashTag="java",queue="java")
val queueString = hash?.queue ?: "unrecognized-queue"
```

When the value holds null, the default value will be returned.

Time to use Kotlin in the real world. Let's begin.

Wrapping it up

Now, we can use the basics of the Kotlin language. We saw some examples and practiced a little bit.

We looked at the main concepts of Kotlin. We have learned how data classes can help developers to transfer data between application layers. Also, we learned about singleton and companion objects. Now we can try to create a real project with the pretty new support from Spring Framework.

In the next sections, we will create a project using the Kotlin language, for now, we can forget about the Java language.

Creating the project

Now, we have a good idea about how we can use programming in Kotlin language. In this section, we will create the basic structure for our new project in which the main feature is consuming the Twitter stream. Let's do that.

Project use case

Before we start to code, we need to track the application requirements. The application is message-driven, we will use a broker to provide the messaging infrastructure. We choose the RabbitMQ broker because it provides reliability, high availability, and clustering options. Also, the RabbitMQ is a popular choice for the modern message-driven applications.

The software is powered by the Pivotal company, the same company which maintains Spring Framework. There is a huge community which supports the project.

We will have three projects. These three projects will collect the Twitter stream and send it to a recipient to show Tweets in a formatted way to the end user.

The first one, which will be created in this chapter, will be responsible for keeping the tracked hashtags on the Redis cache.

When the new hashtags are registered, it will send a message to the second project which will start to consume the Twitter stream and redirect it to the desired queue. This queue will be consumed by the other project which will format the Tweet, and finally, show them to the end user.

We will have three microservices. Let's create these things.

Creating the project with Spring Initializr

We have learned how to use the Spring Initializr page. We will go to the page and then select the following modules:

- `Reactive Web`

- `Reactive Redis`

The page content should look like this:

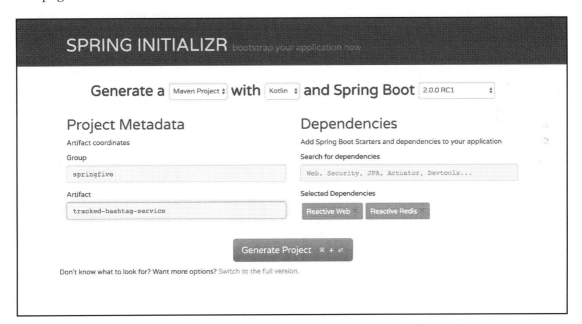

We can choose the group and artifact. There is no problem with using the different name. Then, we can click on **Generate Project** and wait until the download ends.

Adding Jackson for Kotlin

We need to add Jackson for Kotlin dependencies for Maven projects. In fact, we need a Kotlin standard library on our `pom.xml`. Also, we need to put `jackson-module-kotlin`, it allows us to work with JSON on Kotlin, there are some differences from Java in these parts.

This part is pretty simple, and we will add these following dependencies in the dependencies sections in `pom.xml`. The dependencies are as follows:

```xml
<dependency>
 <groupId>com.fasterxml.jackson.module</groupId>
 <artifactId>jackson-module-kotlin</artifactId>
 <version>${jackson.version}</version>
</dependency>
```

Now, we have the dependencies configured, and we can set the plugins to compile the Kotlin source code. In the next section, we will do that.

Looking for the Maven plugins for Kotlin

The project was created with Kotlin configured successfully. Now, we will take a look at the Maven plugin in our `pom.xml`. The configuration is necessary to instruct Maven on how to compile the Kotlin source code and add in the artifacts.

We will add the following plugins in the plugins section:

```xml
<plugin>
  <artifactId>kotlin-maven-plugin</artifactId>
  <groupId>org.jetbrains.kotlin</groupId>
  <version>${kotlin.version}</version>
  <configuration>
    <jvmTarget>1.8</jvmTarget>
  </configuration>
  <executions>
    <execution>
      <id>compile</id>
      <phase>process-sources</phase>
      <goals>
        <goal>compile</goal>
      </goals>
    </execution>
    <execution>
      <id>test-compile</id>
      <phase>process-test-sources</phase>
```

```
      <goals>
        <goal>test-compile</goal>
      </goals>
    </execution>
  </executions>
</plugin>
```

There is one more thing to do. Take a look how Maven configures the path for our Kotlin code. It is easy peasy. Look at the following:

```
<build>

<sourceDirectory>${project.basedir}/src/main/kotlin<
/sourceDirectory<testSourceDirectory>${project.basedir}/src/
test/kotlin</testSourceDirectory>

.....

</build>
```

We added our Kotlin folders in the source paths.

Awesome, the project structure is ready, and we can start coding!

Creating a Docker network for our application

To create isolation for our application, we will create a custom Docker network. This network was created using the bridge driver. Let's do that using the following command:

```
docker network create twitter
```

Good, now we can check the network list by typing the following command:

```
docker network list
```

The Twitter network should be on the list, like the following:

```
ubuntu@ubuntu-xenial:~$ docker network list
NETWORK ID      NAME            DRIVER      SCOPE
d2bb065f5d06    bridge          bridge      local
5a8485d8da42    cms-application bridge      local
1d4b5dc3ec8b    host            host        local
46b59abc89c2    none            null        local
fb27a7381539    twitter         bridge      local
```

The last one is our Twitter network. Let's pull the Redis image from the Docker Hub. Take a look at the next section.

Pulling the Redis image from the Docker Hub

The first thing we need to do is download the Redis image from the Docker Hub. To do that, it is necessary to execute the following command:

```
docker pull redis:4.0.6-alpine
```

We have used the alpine version from Redis because it is smaller than the others and has a reasonable security. While the image is downloaded, we can see the downloading status progress.

We can check the result using the following command:

```
docker images
```

The result should look like the following:

```
ubuntu@ubuntu-xenial:~$ docker images
REPOSITORY      TAG             IMAGE ID        CREATED         SIZE
redis           4.0.6-alpine    ed8544cc83de    5 days ago      26.9MB
postgres        9.6.6-alpine    e20de7998161    3 weeks ago     37.8MB
mongo           3.4.10          d22888af0ce0    5 weeks ago     361MB
```

Take a look at the images downloaded. The Redis must be on the list.

Awesome, now we will start the Redis instance.

Running the Redis instance

The image was downloaded, then we will start the Redis instance for our application. The command can be:

```
docker run -d --name redis --net twitter -p 6379:6379 redis:4.0.6-alpine
```

We have interesting attributes here. We named our Redis instance with `redis`, it will be useful for running our application in containers in the next chapters. Also, we exposed the Redis container ports to the host machine, the command argument used for that is `-p`. Finally, we attached the container to our Twitter network.

Good, the Redis instance is ready to use. Let's check out the Spring Data Reactive Redis stuff.

Configuring the redis-cli tool

There is an excellent tool to connect with the Redis instance which is called `redis-cli`. There are some Docker images for that, but we will install it on our Linux machine.

To install it, we can execute the following command:

```
sudo apt-get install redis-tools -y
```

Excellent, now we can connect and interact with our Redis container. The tool can perform the read and write instructions, then we need to be careful to avoid instructions unintentionally.

Let's connect. The default configuration is enough for us because we have exported the port `6379` on the `run` instruction. Type the following command in the Terminal:

```
redis-cli
```

Then we will connect with our running instance. The command line should display the Redis host and port, like the following screenshot:

```
ubuntu@ubuntu-xenial:~$ redis-cli
127.0.0.1:6379>
```

Excellent, the client is configured and tested.

Now, we will execute some Redis commands on our container.

Understanding Redis

Redis is an open source in-memory data structure. Redis fits well for a database cache and is not common, but it can be used as a message broker using the publish-subscribe feature, it can be useful to decouple applications.

There are some interesting features supported by Redis such as transactions, atomic operations, and support for time-to-live keys. Time-to-live is useful for giving a time for the key, the eviction strategy is always hard to implement, and Redis has a built-in solution for us.

Data types

There are a lot of supported data types by Redis. The most common ones are strings, hashes, lists, and sorted sets. We will understand each of these a little bit because it is important to help us to choose the correct data type for our use case.

Strings

Strings are the more basic data type of Redis. The string value can be at max 512 MB in length. We can store it as a JSON in the value of the key, or maybe as an image as well because the Redis is binary safe.

Main commands

Let's look at some important commands we would need:

- SET: It sets the key and holds the value. It is a simple and basic command of Redis. Here's an example:

  ```
  SET "user:id:10" "joe"
  ```

  The return of the command should be OK. It indicates the instruction has been executed with success.

- GET: This command gets the value of the requested key. Remember GET can only be used with a string data type:

  ```
  GET "user:id:10"
  ```

  As we can see, the return of that command should be joe.

- INCR: The INCR command increments the key by one. It can be useful to handle sequential numbers atomically in distributed systems. The number increment will be returned as a command output:

  ```
  SET "users" "0"
  INCR "users"
  GET "users"
  ```

  As we can see, the INCR command returned 1 as a command output and then we can check this using the GET and obtain the value.

- DECR: The DECR command is opposite of INCR, it will decrement the value atomically as well:

```
GET "users"
DECR "users"
GET "users"
```

The value of the users key was decremented by one and then transformed to 0.

- INCRBY: It will increment the value of the key by the argument. The new incremented value will be returned:

```
GET "users"
INCRBY "users" 2
GET "users"
```

The new value was returned as a command output.

Lists

Lists are simple lists of strings. They are ordered by the insertion order. Redis also offers instructions to add new elements at the head or tail of the list.

Lists can be useful for storing groups of things, groups of categories, for example, grouped by the categories key.

Main commands

LPUSH: Insert the new element at the head of the key. The command also supports multiple arguments, in this case, the values will be stored in the reverse order as we passed on the arguments.

Here are some command examples:

```
LPUSH "categories" "sports"
LPUSH "categories" "movies"
LRANGE "categories" 0 -1
```

Take a look at the LRANGE output, as we can see the value of the movie is the first one on the list because the LPUSH inserted the new element on the head.

RPUSH: Insert the new element at the tail of the key. The command supports multiple arguments as well, in this case, the values will respect the respective order.

Here are some command examples:

```
RPUSH "categories" "kitchen"
RPUSH "categories" "room"
LRANGE "categories" 0 -1
```

As we can see, in the LRANGE output, the new values are inserted at the tail of the values. It is the behavior of the RPUSH command.

LSET: It sets the element on the requested index.

Here are some command examples:

```
LSET "categories" 0 "series""
LRANGE "categories" 0 -1
```

The new value of the zero index is series. The LSET command does that for us.

LRANGE: It returns the specified elements of the key. The command arguments are the key, the start index, and finally the stop element. The -1 on the stop argument will return the whole list:

```
LRANGE "categories" 0 2
LRANGE "categories" 0 -1
```

As we can see, the first command will return three elements because the zero index will be grouped.

Sets

A **set** is a collection of strings. They have a property which does not allow repeated values. It means that if we add the pre-existing value on the sets, it will result in the same element, in this case, the advantage is not necessary to verify if the element exists on the set. Another important characteristic is that the sets are unordered. This behavior is different from the Redis lists. It can be useful in different use cases such as count the unique visitor, track the unique IPs, and much more.

Main commands

The following are the main commands listed with their usages:

- SADD: It adds the element in a requested key. Also, the return of this command is the number of the element added to the set:

```
SADD "unique-visitors" "joe"
SADD "unique-visitors" "mary"
```

As we can see, the command returned one because we added one user each time.

- SMEMBERS: It returns all the members of a requested key:

```
SMEMBERS "unique-visitors"
```

The command will return joe and mary because those are the values stored in the unique-visitors key.

- SCARD: It returns the numbers of elements of a requested key:

```
SCARD "unique-visitors"
```

The command will return the number of elements stored in the requested keys, in this case, the output will be 2.

Spring Data Reactive Redis

Spring Data Redis provides an easy way to interact with the Redis Server from Spring Boot Apps. The project is part of the Spring Data family and provides high-level and low-level abstractions for the developers.

The Jedis and Lettuce connectors are supported as a driver for this project.

The project offers a lot of features and facilities to interact with Redis. The Repository interfaces are supported as well. There is a CrudRepository for Redis like in other implementations, Spring Data JPA, for example.

The central class for this project is the `RedisTemplate` which provides a high-level API to perform Redis operations and serialization support. We will use this class to interact with set data structures on Redis.

The Reactive implementation is supported by this project, these are important characteristics for us because we are looking for Reactive implementations.

Configuring the ReactiveRedisConnectionFactory

To configure the `ReactiveRedisConnectionFactory`, we can use the `application.yaml file`, because it is easier to maintain and centralize our configuration.

The principle is the same as other Spring Data Projects, we should provide the host and port configurations in the `application.yaml` file, as follows:

```
spring:
  redis:
      host: localhost
      port: 6379
```

In the preceding configuration file, we point the Redis configuration to the `localhost`, as we can see. The configuration is pretty simple and easy to understand as well.

Done. The connection factory is configured. The next step is to provide a `RedisTemplate` to interact with our Redis instance. Take a look at the next section.

Providing a ReactiveRedisTemplate

The main class from Spring Data Redis is the `ReactiveRedisTemplate`, then we need to configure and provide an instance for the Spring container.

We need to provide an instance and configure the correct serializer for the desired `ReactiveRedisTemplate`. `Serializers` is the way Spring Data Redis uses to serialize and deserialize objects from raw bytes stored in Redis in the `Key` and `Value` fields.

We will use only the `StringRedisSerializer` because our `Key` and `Value` are simple strings and the Spring Data Redis has this serializer ready for us.

Let's produce our `ReactiveRedisTemplate`. The implementation should look like the following:

```
package springfive.twittertracked.infra.redis

import org.springframework.context.annotation.Bean
import org.springframework.context.annotation.Configuration
import
org.springframework.data.redis.connection.ReactiveRedisConnectionFactory
import org.springframework.data.redis.core.ReactiveRedisTemplate
import org.springframework.data.redis.serializer.RedisSerializationContext

@Configuration
open class RedisConfiguration {

  @Bean
  open fun
reactiveRedisTemplate(connectionFactory:ReactiveRedisConnectionFactory):
                          ReactiveRedisTemplate<String, String> {
      return ReactiveRedisTemplate(connectionFactory,
RedisSerializationContext.string())
  }

}
```

Awesome. That is our first code using Kotlin in the Spring Framework. The keyword `open` is the opposite of Java's `final` keyword. It means this function can be inherited from this class. By default, all classes in Kotlin are final. Spring Framework requires non-final functions on `@Bean` on the `@Configuration` class and then we need to insert `open`.

We received `ReactiveRedisConnectionFactory` as a parameter. Spring knows which we produced in the `application.yaml` file using the configurations for Redis. Then the container can inject the factory.

Finally, we declare `ReactiveRedisTemplate<String, String>` as a return value for our function.

Interesting work, we are ready to work with our Redis template. Now, we will implement our first repository for Redis. See you in the next section.

Creating Tracked Hashtag repository

We have created the `ReactiveRedisTemplate`, then we can use this object in our repository implementation. We will create a simple repository to interact with Redis, remember the repository should be reactive, it is an important characteristic of our application. Then we need to return `Mono` or `Flux` to make the repository Reactive. Let's look at our repository implementation:

```kotlin
package springfive.twittertracked.domain.repository

import org.springframework.data.redis.core.ReactiveRedisTemplate
import org.springframework.stereotype.Service
import reactor.core.publisher.Flux
import reactor.core.publisher.Mono
import springfive.twitterconsumer.domain.TrackedHashTag

@Service
class TrackedHashTagRepository(private val redisTemplate:
ReactiveRedisTemplate<String, String>){

  fun save(trackedHashTag: TrackedHashTag): Mono<TrackedHashTag>? {
    return this.redisTemplate
            .opsForSet().add("hash-tags",
"${trackedHashTag.hashTag}:${trackedHashTag.queue}")
            .flatMap { Mono.just(trackedHashTag) }
  }

  fun findAll(): Flux<TrackedHashTag> {
    return this.redisTemplate.opsForSet().members("hash-tags").flatMap
{ el ->
      val data = el.split(":")
      Flux.just(TrackedHashTag(hashTag = data[0],queue = data[1]))
    }
  }
}
```

We received the `ReactiveRedisTemplate<String, String>` as an injection on our class, the Spring Framework can detect the constructor and inject the correct implementation.

For now, we need these two functions. The first one is responsible for inserting our entity, `TrackedHashTag` on the set structure from Redis. We add the value of the `hash-tags` key on Redis. This function returns a `Mono` with the `TrackedHashTag` value. Pay attention to the `save` function. We have created a pattern for our value, the pattern follows the `hashtag, queue` where the hashtag is the value to gather Tweets and the queue we will use in the next sections to send to a RabbitMQ queue.

The second function returns all values from the `hash-tags` key, it means all tracked hashtags from our system. Moreover, we need to do some logic to create our model, `TrackedHashTag`, as well.

The repository is finished, now we can create our service layer to encapsulate the repository. Let's do that in the next section.

Creating the service layer

Our repository is ready to use, now we can create our service layer. This layer is responsible for orchestrating our repository calls. In our case, it is pretty simple but in some complex scenarios, it can help us to encapsulate the repository calls.

Our service will be called `TrackedHashTagService`, which will be responsible for interacting with our repository created previously. The implementation should look like the following:

```
package springfive.twittertracked.domain.service

import org.springframework.stereotype.Service
import springfive.twitterconsumer.domain.TrackedHashTag
import springfive.twitterconsumer.domain.repository.TrackedHashTagRepository

@Service
class TrackedHashTagService(private val repository:
TrackedHashTagRepository) {

  fun save(hashTag:TrackedHashTag) = this.repository.save(hashTag)

  fun all() = this.repository.findAll()

}
```

Well done. Here, there is basic stuff. We have the construct which injects our repository to interact with Redis. The interesting point here is the function declarations. There is not a body and return type because the Kotlin compiler can infer the return type, it helps the developer to avoid writing boilerplate code.

Exposing the REST resources

Now, we have created the repository and service layer, and we are ready to expose our service through HTTP endpoints:

```
package springfive.twittertracked.domain.resource

import org.springframework.web.bind.annotation.*
import springfive.twitterconsumer.domain.TrackedHashTag
import springfive.twitterconsumer.domain.service.TrackedHashTagService


@RestController
@RequestMapping("/api/tracked-hash-tag")
class TrackedHashTagResource(private val service:TrackedHashTagService)
{

  @GetMapping
  fun all() = this.service.all()

  @PostMapping
  fun save(@RequestBody hashTag:TrackedHashTag) =
this.service.save(hashTag)

}
```

The code is pretty concise and simple. Take a look at how concise this piece of code is. The preceding code is an example of how Kotlin helps developers to create readable codes. Thanks, Kotlin.

Creating a Twitter application

For this project, we will need to configure an application on the Twitter platform. It is necessary, because we will use Twitter's API to search Tweets, for example, and the Twitter account is the requirement for that. We will not explain how to create a Twitter account. There are plenty of articles about that on the internet.

After the Twitter account is created, we need to go to `https://apps.twitter.com/` and create a new app. The page is quite similar to the following screenshot:

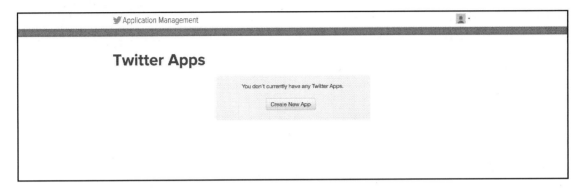

We will click on the **Create New App** button to start the creation process. When we click on that button, the following page will be displayed. We need to fill the required fields and accept the Twitter agreements:

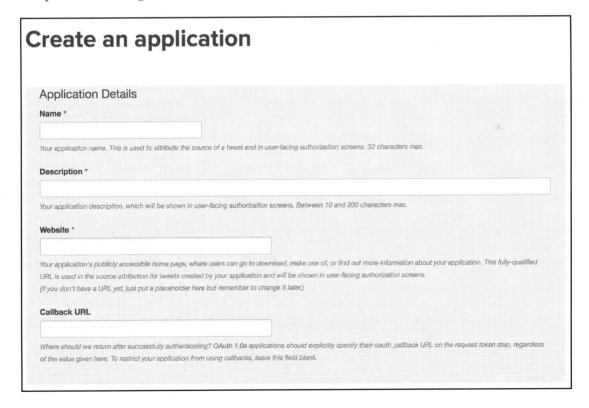

We can choose the application name, fill in the description, and website. These details are up to you.

Then, we need to accept the agreements and click on **Create your Twitter application**:

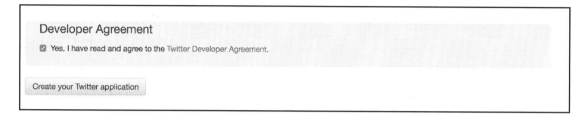

Awesome job. Our Twitter application is almost ready to use.

Now, we just need to configure the application for usage.

We need to check if our Keys and Access Tokens are correctly configured. Let's click on the **Keys and Access Tokens** tab and check the values, shown as follows:

As we can see, there are some important configurations in the preceding screenshot. The **Consumer Key** and **Consumer Secret** are mandatory to authenticate with Twitter APIs. Another important point here is the **Access Level**; be sure it is configured as read-only, as in the preceding screenshot, we will not do write actions on Twitter.

Let's Dockerize it.

Awesome. We have the system which keeps the tracked hashtags on the Redis instance. The application is fully Reactive and has no blocking threads.

Now, we will configure the Maven plugin to generate the Docker images. The configuration is quite similar to what we did in `Chapter 3`, *Persistence with Spring Data and Reactive Fashion*. However, now we will create a first container which we will run with the Kotlin language. Let's do that.

Configuring pom.xml

Now, we will configure our `pom.xml` to be able to generate our Docker image. The first thing we need to change is our final name artifact because Docker images do not allow the - character, then we need to configure properly.

The configuration is pretty simple, put the `<finalName>` tag on the `<build>` node. Let's do that:

```
<build>

  <finalName>tracked_hashtag</finalName>

  ....

</build>
```

Good. We have configured the final name properly to generate the Docker image correctly. Now, we will configure the Maven Docker plugin to generate the Docker image by the Maven goal.

In the plugins section inside the build node, we should put in the following plugin configuration:

```
<plugin>
  <groupId>io.fabric8</groupId>
  <artifactId>docker-maven-plugin</artifactId>
  <version>0.21.0</version>
  <configuration>
    <images>
      <image>
        <name>springfivebyexample/${project.build.finalName}</name>
        <build>
          <from>openjdk:latest</from>
          <entryPoint>java -Dspring.profiles.active=container -jar
      /application/${project.build.finalName}.jar</entryPoint>
```

```xml
                    <assembly>
                      <basedir>/application</basedir>
                      <descriptorRef>artifact</descriptorRef>
                      <inline>
                        <id>assembly</id>
                        <files>
                          <file>
                          <source>target/${project.build.finalName}.jar</source>
                          </file>
                        </files>
                      </inline>
                    </assembly>
                    <tags>
                      <tag>latest</tag>
                    </tags>
                    <ports>
                      <port>9090</port>
                    </ports>
                  </build>
                  <run>
                    <namingStrategy>alias</namingStrategy>
                  </run>
                  <alias>${project.build.finalName}</alias>
                </image>
              </images>
            </configuration>
          </plugin>
```

The configuration is pretty simple. We did this before. In the configuration section, we configured from the image, in our case the `openjdk:latest`, Docker entry point and exposed ports as well.

Let's create our Docker image in the next section.

Creating the image

Our project was previously configured with the Maven Docker plugin. We can generate the Docker image with the Maven Docker plugin using the `docker:build` goal. Then, it is time to generate our Docker image.

To generate the Docker image, type the following command:

```
mvn clean install docker:build
```

Now, we must wait for the Maven build and check if the Docker image was generated with success.

Check the Docker images and we should see the new image generated. To do this, we can use the `docker images` command:

```
docker images
```

Right, we should see the `springfivebyexample/tracked_hashtag:latest` on the image list, like the following screenshot:

```
REPOSITORY                              TAG          IMAGE ID       CREATED           SIZE
springfivebyexample/tracked_hashtag     latest       54d51eba299a   About an hour ago 766MB
redis                                   4.0.6-alpine ed8544cc83de   8 days ago        26.9MB
springfivebyexample/cms                 latest       a2609f25ded1   2 weeks ago       773MB
```

Awesome, our Docker image is ready to run with our first Spring Boot Application in the Kotlin language. Let's run it right now.

Running the container

Let's run our container. Before that, we need to keep in mind some things. The container should be run on the Twitter network to be able to connect to our Redis instance which is running on the Twitter network as well. Remember the `localhost` address for Redis does not work anymore when running in the containers infrastructure.

To run our container, we can execute the following command:

```
docker run –d ––name hashtag-tracker ––net twitter –p 9090:9090
springfivebyexample/tracked_hashtag
```

Congratulations, our application is running in the Docker container and connected to our Redis instance. Let's create and test our APIs to check the desired behaviors.

Testing APIs

Our container is running. Now, we can try to call the APIs to check the behaviors. In this part, we will use the `curl` command line. The `curl` allows us to call APIs by the command line on Linux. Also, we will use `jq` to make the JSON readable on the command line, if you do not have these, look at the Tip Box to install these tools.

Let's call our create API, remember to create we can use the `POST` method in the base path of API. Then type the following command:

```
curl -H "Content-Type: application/json" -X POST -d
'{"hashTag":"java","queue":"java"}' \
 http://localhost:9090/api/tracked-hash-tag
```

There are interesting things here. The `-H` argument instructs `curl` to put it in the request headers and `-d` indicates the request body. Moreover, finally, we have the server address.

We have created the new `tracked-hash-tag`. Let's check our `GET` API to obtain this data:

```
curl 'http://localhost:9090/api/tracked-hash-tag' | jq '.'
```

Awesome, we called the `curl` tool and printed the JSON value with the `jq` tool. The command output should look like the following screenshot:

```
  % Total    % Received % Xferd  Average Speed   Time    Time     Time  Current
                                 Dload  Upload   Total   Spent    Left  Speed
100    35    0    35    0     0   1415      0 --:--:-- --:--:-- --:--:--  1458
[
  {
    "hashTag": "java",
    "queue": "java"
  }
]
```

> To install `curl` on Ubuntu, we can use `sudo apt-get install curl -y`. Moreover, to install `jq`, we can use `sudo apt-get install jq -y`.

Summary

In this chapter, we have been introduced to the Kotlin language, which is the most prominent language for the JVM, because it has a super-fast compiler, if we compare it to Scala, for example. It also brings the simplicity of code and helps developers to create more concise and readable code.

We have also created our first application in the Spring Framework using Kotlin as the basic concepts of the language, and we saw how Kotlin helps the developers in a practical way.

We have introduced Redis as a cache and Spring Data Reactive Redis, which supports Redis in a Reactive paradigm.

In the last part of the chapter, we learned how to create a Twitter application which required us to create our next application, and start to consume the Twitter API in reactive programming with a Reactive Rest Client.

Let's jump to the next chapter and learn more about Spring Reactive.

5
Reactive Web Clients

Until now, we have created the whole project infrastructure to consume the Twitter stream. We have created an application which stores the tracked hashtags.

In this chapter, we will learn how to use the Spring Reactive Web Client and make HTTP calls using the reactive paradigm, which is one of the most anticipated features of Spring 5.0. We will call the Twitter REST APIs asynchronously and use the Project Reactor to provide an elegant way to work with streams.

We will be introduced to Spring Messaging for the RabbitMQ. We will interact with the RabbitMQ broker using the Spring Messaging API and see how Spring helps developers use the high-level abstractions for that.

At the end of this chapter, we will wrap up the application and create a docker image.

In this chapter, we will learn about:

- Reactive web clients
- Spring Messaging for RabbitMQ
- RabbitMQ Docker usage
- Spring Actuator

Creating the Twitter Gathering project

We learned how to create Spring Boot projects with the amazing Spring Initializr. In this chapter, we will create a project in a different way, to show you an alternative way of creating a Spring Boot project.

Create the `tweet-gathering` folder, in any directory. We can use the following command:

```
mkdir tweet-gathering
```

Then, we can access the folder created previously and copy the `pom.xml` file located at GitHub: `https://github.com/PacktPublishing/Spring-5.0-By-Example/blob/master/Chapter05/tweet-gathering/pom.xml`.

Open the `pom.xml` on IDE.

There are some interesting dependencies here. The `jackson-module-kotlin` helps to work with JSON in Kotlin language. Another interesting dependency is `kotlin-stdlib`, which provides the Kotlin standard libraries in our classpath.

In the plugin sections, the most important plugin is the `kotlin-maven-plugin`, which permits and configures the build for our Kotlin code.

In the next section, we will create a folder structure to start the code.

Let's do it.

Project structure

The project structure follows the maven suggested pattern. We will code the project in the Kotlin language, then we will create a `kotlin` folder to store our code.

We made that configuration on the `pom.xml` created before, so it will work fine. Let's take a look at the correct folder structure for the project:

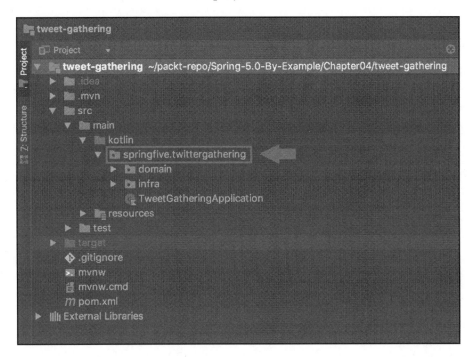

As we can see, the base package is the `springfive.twittergathering` package. Then, we will start to create sub-packages in this package as soon.

Let's create our infrastructure for the microservice.

> The full source code can be found at GitHub: `https://github.com/` `PacktPublishing/Spring-5.0-By-Example/tree/master/Chapter05/` `tweet-gathering`.

Starting the RabbitMQ server with Docker

We can use Docker to spin up the RabbitMQ server. We do not want to install the server on our developer machines as it can create library conflicts and a lot of files. Let's understand how to start RabbitMQ in a Docker container.

Let's do that in the next couple of sections.

Pulling the RabbitMQ image from Docker Hub

We need to pull the RabbitMQ image from Docker Hub. We will use the image from the official repository as it is more safe and reliable.

To get the image, we need to use the following command:

```
docker pull rabbitmq:3.7.0-management-alpine
```

Wait for the download to end and then we can move forward to the next section. In the next section, we will learn how to set up the RabbitMQ server.

Starting the RabbitMQ server

To start the RabbitMQ server, we will run the Docker command. There are some considerations which we need to pay attention to; we will run this container on the Twitter Docker network created previously, but we will expose some ports on the host, as it makes it easier to interact with the broker.

Also, we will use the management image because it provides a page which enables us to manage and see the RabbitMQ information on something similar to a control panel.

Let's run:

```
docker run -d --name rabbitmq --net twitter -p 5672:5672 -p 15672:15672
rabbitmq:3.7.0-management-alpine
```

Wait for a few seconds so that RabbitMQ establishes the connections and then we can connect to the management page. To do that, go to `http://localhost:15672` and log on to the system. The default user is **guest**, and the password is `guest` as well. The control panel looks like this:

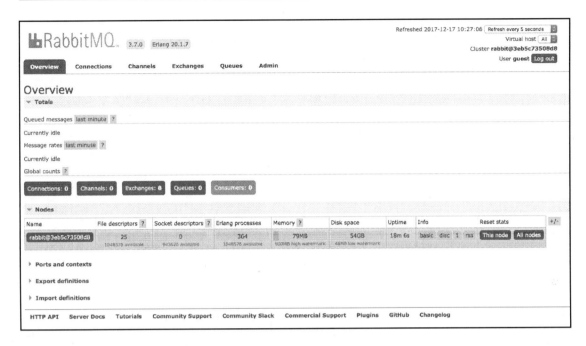

There is a lot of interesting information on the panel, but for now, we are going to explore the channels and some interesting parts.

Awesome. Our RabbitMQ server is up and running. We will use the infrastructure soon.

Spring Messaging AMQP

This project supports the AMQP-based messaging solutions. There is a high-level API to interact with desired brokers. These interactions can send and receive messages from a broker.

Like in the other Spring projects, these facilities are provided by the *template* classes, which expose the core features provided by the broker and implemented by the Spring Module.

This project has two parts: `spring-amqp` is the base abstraction, and `spring-rabbit` is the RabbitMQ implementation for RabbitMQ. We will use `spring-rabbit` because we are using the RabbitMQ broker.

Adding Spring AMQP in our pom.xml

Let's add the `spring-amqp` jars to our project. `spring-amqp` has a starter dependency which configures some common things for us, such as `ConnectionFactory` and `RabbitTemplate`, so we will use that. To add this dependency, we will configure our `pom.xml` follows:

```
<dependency>
  <groupId>org.springframework.boot</groupId>
  <artifactId>spring-boot-starter-amqp</artifactId>
</dependency>
```

The next step is to configure the connections; we will use the `application.yaml` file because we are using the starter. In the next section, we will do the configuration.

Integrating Spring Application and RabbitMQ

We have configured the `spring-amqp` dependencies in our project. Now, it is time to configure the RabbitMQ connections properly. We will use the `RabbitMQTemplate` to send messages to the broker; this has some converters which help us convert our domain models into JSON and vice versa.

Let's configure our RabbitMQ connections. The configurations should be in the `application.yaml` file and should look like this:

```
spring:
  rabbitmq:
    host: localhost
    username: guest
    password: guest
    port: 5672
```

As we can see, some Spring configurations are quite similar to others, the same style, and the node in `yaml` is the name of the technology followed by a couple of attributes.

We are using the default credentials for the RabbitMQ. The host and port are related to the RabbitMQ Broker address. The configuration is quite simple but does a lot of things for us such as `ConnectionFactory`.

Understanding RabbitMQ exchanges, queues, and bindings

We are doing some interesting things with RabbitMQ. We configured connections successfully. There are some other things that we have not done yet, such as configuring the exchanges, queue, and bindings, but before we do that, let's understand a little bit more about these terms.

Exchanges

Exchanges are RabbitMQ entities where the messages are sent. We can make an analogy with a river where the water is flowing; the river is the course of the messages. There are four different kinds of exchanges which we will understand in the following sections.

Direct exchanges

The direct exchanges allow for route messages based on the routing key. The name is self-explanatory, it permits to send the messages directly to the specified customer, who is the one listening to the exchange. Remember, it uses the routing key as the argument to route the message to the customers.

Fanout exchanges

The fanout exchanges route the messages for all the queues bound independently of the routing key. All the bound queues will receive the message sent to fanout exchanges. They can be used to have the topic behavior or distributed listings.

Topic exchanges

The topic exchanges are similar to direct exchanges, but topic exchanges enable us to use pattern matching as compared to the direct exchanges, which permit only the exact routing key. We will use this exchange in our project.

Header exchanges

Header exchanges are self-explanatory, the behavior is like the topic exchange, but instead of using the routing key, it uses the header attributes to match the correct queue.

Queues

Queues are the buffer where the exchanges will write the messages respecting the routing key. Queues are the place where consumers get the messages which are published to exchanges. Messages are routed to queues depending on the exchange type.

Bindings

Binding can be thought of as a link between exchanges and queues. We can say that it is a kind of traffic cop which instructs the messages where they should be redirected based on the configuration, in this case, links.

Configuring exchanges, queues, and bindings on Spring AMQP

The Spring AMQP project has abstractions for all the RabbitMQ entities listed previously, and we need to configure it to interact with the broker. As we did in other projects, we need a @Configuration class, which will declare the beans for the Spring container.

Declaring exchanges, queues, and bindings in yaml

We need to configure the entity names to instruct the framework to connect with the broker entities. We will use the application.yaml file to store these names, since it is easier to maintain and is the correct way to store application infrastructure data.

The section with the entity names should look like this snippet:

```
queue:
  twitter: twitter-stream
exchange:
  twitter: twitter-exchange
routing_key:
  track: track.*
```

The properties are self-explanatory, the exchange node has the name of the exchange, the queue node has the queue name, and finally, the routing_key node has the routing argument.

Awesome. The properties are configured, and now we will create our @Configuration class. Let's do that in the next section. We are almost ready to interact with the RabbitMQ broker.

Declaring Spring beans for RabbitMQ

Now, let's create our configuration class. The class is pretty simple and as we will see with the Spring abstraction, they are easy to understand too, especially because the class names allude to the RabbitMQ entities.

Let's create our class:

```
package springfive.twittergathering.infra.rabbitmq

import com.fasterxml.jackson.databind.ObjectMapper
import com.fasterxml.jackson.module.kotlin.KotlinModule
import org.springframework.amqp.core.Binding
import org.springframework.amqp.core.BindingBuilder
import org.springframework.amqp.core.Queue
import org.springframework.amqp.core.TopicExchange
import org.springframework.amqp.support.converter.Jackson2JsonMessageConverter
import org.springframework.beans.factory.annotation.Value
import org.springframework.context.annotation.Bean
import org.springframework.context.annotation.Configuration

@Configuration
open class RabbitMQConfiguration(@Value("\${queue.twitter}") private val queue:String,
                                 @Value("\${exchange.twitter}") private val exchange:String,
                                 @Value("\${routing_key.track}") private val routingKey:String){

    @Bean
    open fun queue():Queue{
        return Queue(this.queue,false)
    }

    @Bean
    open fun exchange():TopicExchange{
        return TopicExchange(this.exchange)
    }

    @Bean
```

```
    open fun binding(queue: Queue, exchange: TopicExchange): Binding {
        return
BindingBuilder.bind(queue).to(exchange).with(this.routingKey)
    }

    @Bean
    open fun converter(): Jackson2JsonMessageConverter {
        return
Jackson2JsonMessageConverter(ObjectMapper().registerModule(KotlinModule()))
    }

}
```

There are interesting things to pay attention to here. In the `RabbitMQConfiguration` constructor, we injected the values configured in the `application.yaml` file to name the entities. After that, we started to configure the Spring beans for the container to allow it to inject them into the Spring-managed classes. The key point here is that if they do not exist in the RabbitMQ broker, Spring will create them. Thanks, Spring, we appreciate that and love how helpful that is.

We can see the DSL to declare `Binding`, it makes the developer's life easier and prevents errors in the code.

On the last part of the class, we declared the `Jackson2JsonMessageConverter`. These converters are used to convert the domain models in JSON and vice versa. It enables us to receive the domain object on Listener instead of an array of bytes or strings. The same behavior can be used in the `Producers`, we are able to send the domain object instead of JSON.

We need to supply the `ObjectMapper` to `Jackson2JsonMessageConverter`, and we have used the Kotlin module because of the way Kotlin handles data classes, which do not have no-args constructors.

Excellent job! Our infrastructure is fully configured. Let's code the producers and consumers right now!

Consuming messages with Spring Messaging

Spring AMQP provides the `@RabbitListener` annotation; it will configure the subscriber for the desired queue, it removes a lot of infrastructure code, such as connect to `RabbitListenerConnectionFactory`, and creates a consumer programmatically. It makes the creation of queue consumers really easy.

The `spring-boot-starter-amqp` provides some automatic configurations for us. When we use this module, Spring will automatically create a `RabbitListenerConnectionFactory` for us and configure the Spring converters to convert JSON to domain classes automatically.

Pretty simple. Spring AMQP really provides a super high-level abstraction for developers.

Let's see an example which will be used in our application soon:

```
@RabbitListener(queues = ["twitter-track-hashtag"])
fun receive(hashTag:TrackedHashTag) {
...
}
```

 The full source code can be found at GitHub: `https://github.com/PacktPublishing/Spring-5.0-By-Example/blob/master/Chapter05/tweet-gathering/src/main/kotlin/springfive/twittergathering/domain/service/TwitterGatherRunner.kt.`

A piece of cake. The code is really easy to understand and it makes it possible to pay attention only to the business rules. The infrastructure is not a good thing to maintain because this does not bring real value to the business, as it is only a piece of technology. Spring tries to abstract the whole infrastructure code to help developers write business code. It is a real asset provided by the Spring Framework.

Thanks, Spring Team.

Producing messages with Spring Messaging

The `spring-amqp` module provides a `RabbitTemplate` class, which abstracts high-level RabbitMQ driver classes. It improves the developer performance and makes the application void of bugs because the Spring modules are a very well-tested set of codes. We will use the `convertAndSend()` function which permits to pass exchange, the routing key, and the message object as parameters. Remember this function uses Spring converters to convert our model class into a JSON string.

There are a lot of overloaded functions for `convertAndSend()`, and depending on the use case, others could be more appropriate. We will use the simple one as we saw before.

Let's see the piece of code which sends the message to the broker:

```
this.rabbitTemplate.convertAndSend("twitter-
exchange","track.${hashTag.queue}",it)
```

Good. The first parameter is the `Exchange` name, and the second is the `RoutingKey`. Finally, we have the message object, which will be converted into a JSON string.

We will see the code in action soon.

Enabling Twitter in our application

In this section, we will enable the use of Twitter APIs on our Twitter Gathering application. This application should get Tweets based on the query specified by the user. This query was registered on the previous microservice that we created in the previous chapter.

When the user calls the API to register `TrackedHashTag`, the microservice will store the `TrackedHashTag` on the Redis database and send the message through the RabbitMQ. Then, this project will start to gather Tweets based on that. This is the data flow. In the next chapter, we will do a reactive stream and dispatch Tweets through our Reactive API. It will be amazing.

However, for now, we need to configure the Twitter credentials; we will do that using Spring beans – let's implement it.

Producing Twitter credentials

We will use the `@Configuration` class to provide our Twitter configuration objects. The `@Configuration` class is really good to provide infrastructure beans, if we do not have starter projects for the required module.

Also, we will use the `application.yaml` file to store the Twitter credentials. This kind of configuration should not be kept in the source code repository because it is sensitive data and should not be shared with others. Then, the Spring Framework enables us to declare properties in the `yaml` file and configures the environment variables to fill these properties at runtime. It is an excellent way to keep sensitive data out of the source code repository.

Configuring Twitter credentials in application.yaml

To start configuring the Twitter API in our application, we must provide the credentials. We will use the `yaml` file for this. Let's add credentials in our `application.yaml`:

```
twitter:
  consumer-key: ${consumer-key}
  consumer-secret: ${consumer-secret}
  access-token: ${access-token}
  access-token-secret: ${access-token-secret}
```

Easy peasy. The properties have been declared and then we used the `$` to instruct the Spring Framework that this value will be received as an environment variable. Remember, we configured the Twitter account in the previous chapter.

Modelling objects to represent Twitter settings

We must create abstractions and an amazing data model for our applications. This will create some models which make the developer's life easier to understand and code. Let's create our Twitter settings models.

Twittertoken

This class represents the application token previously configured in Twitter. The token can be used for the application authentication only. Our model should look like this:

```
data class TwitterToken(val accessToken: String, val
accessTokenSecret: String)
```

I love the Kotlin way to declare data classes—totally immutable and without boilerplate.

TwitterAppSettings

`TwitterAppSettings` represents the consumer key and consumer secret. It is a kind of identity for our application, from Twitter's perspective. Our model is pretty simple and must look like this:

```
data class TwitterAppSettings(val consumerKey: String, val
consumerSecret: String)
```

Good job, our models are ready. It is time to produce the objects for the Spring Container. We will do that in the next section.

Declaring Twitter credentials for the Spring container

Let's produce our Twitter configuration objects. As a pattern we have been using, we will use the @Configuration class for that. The class should be as follows:

```
package springfive.twittergathering.infra.twitter

import org.springframework.beans.factory.annotation.Value
import org.springframework.context.annotation.Bean
import org.springframework.context.annotation.Configuration


@Configuration
open class TwitterConfiguration(@Value("\${twitter.consumer-key}") private
val consumerKey: String,
                               @Value("\${twitter.consumer-secret}")
private val consumerSecret: String,
                               @Value("\${twitter.access-token}") private
val accessToken: String,
                               @Value("\${twitter.access-token-secret}")
private val accessTokenSecret: String) {

    @Bean
    open fun twitterAppSettings(): TwitterAppSettings {
        return TwitterAppSettings(consumerKey, consumerSecret)
    }

    @Bean
    open fun twitterToken(): TwitterToken {
        return TwitterToken(accessToken, accessTokenSecret)
    }

}
```

Pretty simple and a Spring way to declare beans. We are improving how we use Spring step by step. Well done!

Now, we are done with Twitter configurations. We will consume the Twitter API using the WebClient from the Spring WebFlux, which supports the reactive programming paradigm. Let's understand something before we run the code.

Spring reactive web clients

This is a pretty new feature which was added in Spring Framework 5. It enables us to interact with HTTP services, using the reactive paradigm.

It is not a replacement for a `RestTemplate` provided by Spring, however, it is an addition to working with reactive applications. Do not worry, the `RestTemplate` is an excellent and tested implementation for interaction with HTTP services in traditional applications.

Also, the `WebClient` implementation supports the `text/event-stream` mime type which can enable us to consume server events.

Producing WebClient in a Spring Way

Before we start to call the Twitter APIs, we want to create an instance of `WebClient` in a Spring way. It means we are looking for a way to inject the instance, using the Dependency Injection Pattern.

To achieve this, we can use the `@Configuration` annotation and create a `WebClient` instance, using the `@Bean` annotation to declare the bean for the Spring container. Let's do that:

```
package springfive.twittergathering.infra.web

import org.springframework.context.annotation.Bean
import org.springframework.context.annotation.Configuration
import org.springframework.web.reactive.function.client.WebClient

@Configuration
open class WebClientProducer {

    @Bean
    open fun webClient(): WebClient? {
        return WebClient.create()
    }

}
```

There are a couple of known annotations in this class; this is a pretty standard way to declare bean instances in a Spring way. It makes it possible to inject an instance of `WebClient` in other Spring-managed classes.

Creating the models to gather Tweets

If we want to consume the Twitter APIs asynchronously and reactively, then we should create the API client. Before we code the client, we need to create our classes for modeling, according to our requirements.

We do not need all Tweets' attributes. We expect the following attributes:

- id
- text
- createdAt
- user

Then, we will model our class based on the attributes listed.

Let's start with the user attribute. This attribute is a JSON attribute, and we will create a separated class for that. The class should look like this:

```
@JsonIgnoreProperties(ignoreUnknown = true)
data class TwitterUser(val id:String,val name:String)
```

We have used the Kotlin `data class`, it fits our use case well, and we want to use that as a data container. Also, we need to put in `@JsonIgnoreProperties(ignoreUnknown = true)` because this annotation instructs the Spring converters to ignore the attribute when it is missing in the JSON response. That is the important part of this portion of code.

We have created the `TwitterUser` class, which represents the user who created the Tweet. Now, we will create the `Tweet` class which represents the Tweet. Let's create our class:

```
@JsonIgnoreProperties(ignoreUnknown = true)
data class Tweet(val id:String, val text:String,
@JsonProperty("created_at")val createdAt:String, val
user:TwitterUser)
```

There are some common things for us and one that's new. The `@JsonProperty` permits developers to customize the attribute name on the class which has a different attribute name in JSON; this is common for Java developers because they usually use *CamelCase* as a way to name attributes, and in JSON notation, people usually use *SnakeCase*. This annotation can help us to solve this mismatch between the programming language and JSON.

We can find a more detailed explanation of snake case here: https://en.wikipedia.org/wiki/Snake_case. Also, we can find a full explanation of camel case here: https://en.wikipedia.org/wiki/Camel_case.

Good. Our API objects are ready. With these objects, we are enabled to interact with the APIs. We will create a service to collect the Tweets. We will do that in the next section.

Authentication with Twitter APIs

With our objects ready, we need to create a class to help us handle the Twitter authentication. We will use the Twitter Application Only Auth authentication model. This kind of authentication should be used for backend applications.

The application using this kind of authentication can:

- Pull user timelines
- Access friends and followers of any account
- Access lists and resources
- Search in Tweets
- Retrieve any user information

As we can see, the application is a read-only Twitter API consumer.

We can use the Twitter documentation to understand this kind of authentication in detail. The documentation can be found here: https://developer.twitter.com/en/docs/basics/authentication/guides/authorizing-a-request.

We will follow the Twitter documentation to authorize our request, which is a kind of cooking recipe, so we must follow all the steps. The final class should look like this:

```
package springfive.twittergathering.infra.twitter

import org.springframework.util.StringUtils
import
springfive.twittergathering.infra.twitter.EncodeUtils.computeSignature
import springfive.twittergathering.infra.twitter.EncodeUtils.encode
import java.util.*

object Twitter {
```

```kotlin
    private val SIGNATURE_METHOD = "HMAC-SHA1"

    private val AUTHORIZATION_VERIFY_CREDENTIALS = "OAuth " +
            "oauth_consumer_key=\"{key}\", " +
            "oauth_signature_method=\"" + SIGNATURE_METHOD + "\", " +
            "oauth_timestamp=\"{ts}\", " +
            "oauth_nonce=\"{nonce}\", " +
            "oauth_version=\"1.0\", " +
            "oauth_signature=\"{signature}\", " +
            "oauth_token=\"{token}\""

fun buildAuthHeader(appSettings: TwitterAppSettings, twitterToken:
TwitterToken, method: String, url: String, query: String):String{
        val ts = "" + Date().time / 1000
        val nounce = UUID.randomUUID().toString().replace("-".toRegex(),
"")
        val parameters =
"oauth_consumer_key=${appSettings.consumerKey}&oauth_nonce=$nounce&oauth_si
gnature_method=$SIGNATURE_METHOD&oauth_timestamp=$ts&oauth_token=${encode(t
witterToken.accessToken)}&oauth_version=1.0&track=${encode(query)}"
        val signature = "$method&" + encode(url) + "&" + encode(parameters)
        var result = AUTHORIZATION_VERIFY_CREDENTIALS
        result = StringUtils.replace(result, "{nonce}", nounce)
        result = StringUtils.replace(result, "{ts}", "" + ts)
        result = StringUtils.replace(result, "{key}",
appSettings.consumerKey)
        result = StringUtils.replace(result, "{signature}",
encode(computeSignature(signature,
"${appSettings.consumerSecret}&${encode(twitterToken.accessTokenSecret)}"))
)
        result = StringUtils.replace(result, "{token}",
encode(twitterToken.accessToken))
        return result
    }

}

data class TwitterToken(val accessToken: String,val accessTokenSecret:
String)

data class TwitterAppSettings(val consumerKey: String,val consumerSecret:
String)
```

It is a recipe. The function, `buildAuthHeader`, will create the authorization header using the rules to authorize the request. We have signed some request headers combined with a request body. Moreover, replace the template values with our Twitter credentials objects.

Some words about server-sent events (SSE)

Server-sent events (SSE) is a technology where the server sends events to the client, instead of the client polling the server to check the information availability. The message flow will not get interrupted until the client or server closes the stream.

The most important thing to understand here is the direction of the information flow. The server decides when to send data to a client.

It is very important to handle resource load and bandwidth usage. The client will receive the chunk of data instead to apply load on the server through the polling techniques.

Twitter has a stream API and the Spring Framework WebClient supports SSE. It is time to consume the Twitter stream.

Creating the gather service

The `TweetGatherService` will be responsible for interacting with Twitter APIs and collecting the request tweets according to the requested hashtag. The service will be a Spring bean with some inject attributes. The class should look like this:

```
package springfive.twittergathering.domain.service

import com.fasterxml.jackson.annotation.JsonIgnoreProperties
import com.fasterxml.jackson.annotation.JsonProperty
import org.springframework.http.MediaType
import org.springframework.stereotype.Service
import org.springframework.web.reactive.function.BodyInserters
import org.springframework.web.reactive.function.client.WebClient
import reactor.core.publisher.Flux
import springfive.twittergathering.infra.twitter.Twitter
import springfive.twittergathering.infra.twitter.TwitterAppSettings
import springfive.twittergathering.infra.twitter.TwitterToken


@Service
class TweetGatherService(private val twitterAppSettings:
TwitterAppSettings,
                    private val twitterToken: TwitterToken,
                    private val webClient: WebClient) {

    fun streamFrom(query: String): Flux<Tweet> {
        val url = "https://stream.twitter.com/1.1/statuses/filter.json"
        return this.webClient.mutate().baseUrl(url).build()
```

```
                    .post()
                    .body(BodyInserters.fromFormData("track", query))
                    .header("Authorization",
   Twitter.buildAuthHeader(twitterAppSettings, twitterToken, "POST", url,
   query))
                    .accept(MediaType.TEXT_EVENT_STREAM)
                    .retrieve().bodyToFlux(Tweet::class.java)
       }

   }

   @JsonIgnoreProperties(ignoreUnknown = true)
   data class Tweet(val id: String = "", val text: String = "",
   @JsonProperty("created_at") val createdAt: String = "", val user:
   TwitterUser = TwitterUser("", ""))

   @JsonIgnoreProperties(ignoreUnknown = true)
   data class TwitterUser(val id: String, val name: String)
```

There are some important points here. The first is the function declaration; take a look at
`Flux<Tweet>`, it means the data can never get interrupted because it represents the N
values. In our case, we will consume the Twitter stream until the client or server interrupts
the data flow.

After that, we configured the HTTP request body with our desired track to get events. After
that, we configured the Accept HTTP header; it is essential to instruct the WebClient what
kind of mime type it needs to consume.

Finally, we have used our `Twitter.buildAuthHeader` function to configure the Twitter
authentication.

Awesome, we are ready to start to consume the Twitter API, and we only need to code the
trigger to use that function. We will do that in the next section.

Listening to the Rabbit Queue and consuming the Twitter API

We will consume the Twitter API, but when?

We need to start to get Tweets when the request for tracking the hashtags comes to our
application. To reach that goal, we will implement the RabbitMQ Listener when the
`TrackedHashTag` gets registered on our microservice. The application will send the
message to the broker to start consuming the Twitter stream.

Let's take a look at the code and step by step understand the behaviors; the final code should look like this:

```
package springfive.twittergathering.domain.service

import org.springframework.amqp.rabbit.annotation.RabbitListener
import org.springframework.amqp.rabbit.core.RabbitTemplate
import org.springframework.stereotype.Service
import reactor.core.publisher.Mono
import reactor.core.scheduler.Schedulers
import springfive.twittergathering.domain.TrackedHashTag
import java.util.concurrent.CompletableFuture
import java.util.concurrent.TimeUnit

@Service
class TwitterGatherRunner(private val twitterGatherService:
TweetGatherService,private val rabbitTemplate: RabbitTemplate) {

    @RabbitListener(queues = ["twitter-track-hashtag"])
    fun receive(hashTag:TrackedHashTag) {
        val streamFrom =
this.twitterGatherService.streamFrom(hashTag.hashTag).filter({
            return@filter it.id.isNotEmpty() && it.text.isNotEmpty() &&
             it.createdAt.isNotEmpty()
        })
        val subscribe = streamFrom.subscribe({
            println(it.text)
            Mono.fromFuture(CompletableFuture.runAsync {
                this.rabbitTemplate.convertAndSend("twitter-
                exchange","track.${hashTag.queue}",it)
            })
        })
        Schedulers.elastic().schedule({ subscribe.dispose()
},10L,TimeUnit.SECONDS)
    }

}
```

Keep calm. We will cover the whole code. In the @RabbitListener, we configured the name of the queue we want to consume. The Spring AMQP module will configure our listener automatically for us and start to consume the desired queue. As we can see, we received the TrackedHashTag object; remember the converters on the previous sections.

The first instruction will start to consume the Twitter stream. The stream returns a flux and can have a lot of data events there. After the consumer, we want to filter the data on the flow. We want `Tweet` in which the `id`, `text`, and `createdAt` are not null.

Then, we subscribe this stream and start to receive the data in the flow. Also, the `subscribes` function returns the disposable object which will be helpful in the next steps. We have created an anonymous function which will print the `Tweet` on the console and send the Tweet to the RabbitMQ queue, to be consumed in another microservice.

Finally, we use the schedulers to stop the data flow and consume the data for 10 seconds.

Before you test the Twitter stream, we need to change the Tracked Hashtag Service to send the messages through the RabbitMQ. We will do that in the next sections. The changes are small ones and we will do them quickly.

Changing the Tracked Hashtag Service

To run the whole solution, we need to make some changes to the Tracked Hashtag Service project. The changes are simple and basic; configure the RabbitMQ connection and change the service to send the messages to the broker.

Let's do that.

Adding the Spring Starter RabbitMQ dependency

As we did before in the Twitter Gathering project, we need to add `spring-boot-starter-amqp` to provide some auto-configuration for us. To do that, we need to add the following snippet to our `pom.xml`:

```xml
<dependency>
  <groupId>org.springframework.boot</groupId>
  <artifactId>spring-boot-starter-amqp</artifactId>
</dependency>
```

Right. Now, it is time to configure the RabbitMQ connections. We will do this in the next section.

Configuring the RabbitMQ connections

We will use the `application.yaml` to configure the RabbitMQ connections. Then, we need to create a couple of properties in it and the Spring AMQP module will use that provided configuration to start the connection factory.

It is pretty simple to configure it. The final `yaml` file for Tracked Hashtag should look like this:

```yaml
spring:
  rabbitmq:
    host: localhost
    username: guest
    password: guest
    port: 5672
  redis:
    host: 127.0.0.1
    port: 6379

server:
  port: 9090

queue:
  twitter: twitter-track-hashtag
exchange:
  twitter: twitter-track-exchange
routing_key:
  track: "*"
---
spring:
  profiles: docker
  rabbitmq:
    host: rabbitmq
    username: guest
    password: guest
    port: 5672
  redis:
    host: redis
    port: 6379

server:
  port: 9090

queue:
  twitter: twitter-track-hashtag
exchange:
  twitter: twitter-track-exchange
```

```
        routing_key:
           track: "*"
```

There are two profiles in this yaml. Take a look at the different host for the RabbitMQ. In the default profile, we are able to connect the localhost because we exposed the RabbitMQ ports on the host. But on the Docker profile, we are not able to connect the localhost, we need to connect to the `rabbitmq` host, which is the host for the Twitter network.

Our RabbitMQ connection is ready to use. Let's try it in the next section. Let's go.

Creating exchanges, queues, and bindings for the Twitter Hashtag Service

Let's declare our RabbitMQ entities for the Tracked Hashtag usage. We will do that using the `@Configuration` class.

The RabbitMQ connection should look like this:

```
package springfive.twittertracked.infra.rabbitmq

import com.fasterxml.jackson.databind.ObjectMapper
import com.fasterxml.jackson.module.kotlin.KotlinModule
import org.springframework.amqp.core.Binding
import org.springframework.amqp.core.BindingBuilder
import org.springframework.amqp.core.Queue
import org.springframework.amqp.core.TopicExchange
import org.springframework.amqp.support.converter.Jackson2JsonMessageConverter
import org.springframework.beans.factory.annotation.Value
import org.springframework.context.annotation.Bean
import org.springframework.context.annotation.Configuration

@Configuration
open class RabbitMQConfiguration(@Value("\${queue.twitter}") private val
queue:String,
                                 @Value("\${exchange.twitter}") private val
exchange:String,
                                 @Value("\${routing_key.track}") private
val routingKey:String){

    @Bean
    open fun queue():Queue{
        return Queue(this.queue,false)
    }
```

```
    @Bean
    open fun exchange():TopicExchange{
        return TopicExchange(this.exchange)
    }

    @Bean
    open fun binding(queue: Queue, exchange: TopicExchange): Binding {
        return
BindingBuilder.bind(queue).to(exchange).with(this.routingKey)
    }

    @Bean
    open fun converter(): Jackson2JsonMessageConverter {
        return
Jackson2JsonMessageConverter(ObjectMapper().registerModule(KotlinModule()))
    }

}
```

Pretty straightforward. We declared one exchange, queue, and binding, as we did before.

Sending the messages to the broker

This is the most interesting part now. When we want to save the `TrackedHashTag`, we must send the pretty new entity to the RabbitMQ. This process will send the message, and then the Twitter Gathering microservice will start to consume the stream in ten seconds.

We need to change the `TrackedHashTagService` a little bit; the final version should look like this:

```
package springfive.twittertracked.domain.service

import org.springframework.amqp.rabbit.core.RabbitTemplate
import org.springframework.beans.factory.annotation.Value
import org.springframework.stereotype.Service
import reactor.core.publisher.Mono
import springfive.twittertracked.domain.TrackedHashTag
import springfive.twittertracked.domain.repository.TrackedHashTagRepository
import java.util.concurrent.CompletableFuture

@Service
class TrackedHashTagService(private val repository:
TrackedHashTagRepository,
                            private val rabbitTemplate: RabbitTemplate,
                            @Value("\${exchange.twitter}") private val
```

```
exchange: String,
                              @Value("\${routing_key.track}") private val
routingKey: String) {

    fun save(hashTag: TrackedHashTag) {
        this.repository.save(hashTag).subscribe { data ->
            Mono.fromFuture(CompletableFuture.runAsync {
                this.rabbitTemplate.convertAndSend(this.exchange,
this.routingKey,
                hashTag)
            })
        }
    }

    fun all() = this.repository.findAll()

}
```

Awesome job. When the new entity comes, it will be sent to the broker. We have finished our changes on the Tracked Hashtag Service.

Finally, we are able to test the whole flow. Let's start to play and perceive the real power of our built application.

It's showtime!!!

Testing the microservice's integrations

Now, we are ready to test the whole solution. Before you start, we need to check the following infrastructure items:

- Redis
- RabbitMQ

If the items are up and running, we can jump to the next section.

 We can use the `docker ps` command, and the command should list the Redis and RabbitMQ containers in running mode.

Running Tracked Hashtag Service

There is no special thing to run this application. It includes the infrastructure connections which are configured in the default profile in `application.yaml`.

Run the main function present on the `TrackedHashTagApplication`. We can use the IDE or command line to do that.

Check the console output; the output will be presented on the IDE or command line. We want to find the following line:

```
[          main] o.s.c.support.DefaultLifecycleProcessor  : Starting beans in phase 2147483647
[ctor-http-nio-1] r.ipc.netty.tcp.BlockingNettyContext     : Started HttpServer on /0:0:0:0:0:0:0:0:9090
[          main] o.s.b.web.embedded.netty.NettyWebServer  : Netty started on port(s): 9090
[          main] s.t.TrackedHashTagApplication$Companion  : Started TrackedHashTagApplication.Companion in 4.179 seconds (JVM running for 5.059)
```

It means the first application is fully operational and we are able to run Twitter Gathering. Please keep the application running as it is required.

Let's run Twitter Gathering!!!

Running the Twitter Gathering

This application is a little bit more complicated to run. We need to configure some environment variables for that. It is required because we do not want the Twitter application credentials in our repository.

It is pretty simple to do in the IDE. To do that, we can configure the run configuration. Let's do it:

1. Click on the **Edit Configurations...** like in the following image:

Then, we are able to see the **Environment variables** like this:

2. We need to click on **...**, as highlighted in the proceeding image.
3. The next screen will be shown and we can configure the **Environment Variable**:

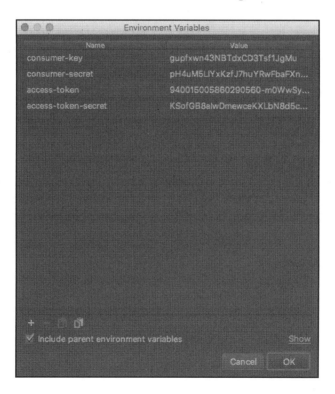

4. We need to configure the following environment variables:
   - **consumer-key**
   - **consumer-secret**
   - **access-token**
   - **access-token-secret**

These values should be filled with the **Twitter Application Management** values.

Then, we can run the application. Run it!!

Now, we should see the following lines in the console, which means the application is running:

```
2017-12-23 15:58:46.362  INFO 1635 --- [ctor-http-nio-1] r.ipc.netty.tcp.BlockingNettyContext      : Started HttpServer on /0:0:0:0:0:0:0:8081
2017-12-23 15:58:46.363  INFO 1635 --- [           main] o.s.b.web.embedded.netty.NettyWebServer   : Netty started on port(s): 8081
2017-12-23 15:58:46.369  INFO 1635 --- [           main] s.t.TweetGatheringApplications$Companion  : Started TweetGatheringApplication.Companion in 7.012 seconds (JVM running for 7.645)
```

Awesome, our two microservices are running. Let's trigger the Twitter stream. We will do that in the next section.

 There are other ways to run the application, for example, with the maven Spring Boot goals or Java command line. If you prefer to run in the Java command line, keep in mind the -D argument to pass environment variables.

Testing stuff

We are excited to test the full integration. We can use the `curl` tool to send request data to the Tracked Hashtag Service. We want to track the `"bitcoin"` from Twitter.

We can execute the following command line:

```
curl -H "Content-Type: application/json" -X POST -d
'{"hashTag":"bitcoin","queue":"bitcoin"}' \
http://localhost:9090/api/tracked-hash-tag
```

Check the HTTP status code; it should be HTTP status 200. After that, we can check the console from the Twitter Gathering project, and there should be a lot of Tweets logged.

Take a look at the log, the log must have Tweets like this:

```
RT @PayperExnet: Bitcoin is going down? GOOD! buy PAX and join the last days of the sale! buy PAX TOKEN NOW!!! @PayperExnet  @Bitcoin https...
RT @AttWorldNews: Bitcoin Goes on Wild Journey and it Could Solely Get Crazier #Bitcoin #Blockchain #LengthyIslandIcedTeaCorp https://t.co/...
@BKBrianKelly #Listen to #Bitcoin #audio #voxpop  #BitcoinMadness #LetMeAsk @AmaroufmediaAsk #YouTube... https://t.co/IhqC9HKbdW
The blockchain that wouldn't die #crypto https://t.co/dYXPwm86fi
RT @rajneeshchhabra: No Place Like Home: The Internet Of Things And Its Promise For Consumers https://t.co/vAwghGoECa #IoT #InternetOfThing...
RT @ItsHooverr: +gets one dollar profit with bitcoin+ https://t.co/PE8OvP7ydc
3 Cryptocurrencies to Consider Buying Over Bitcoin @themotleyfool #stocks $SAN, $IBM, $AXP, $BP https://t.co/qf1AVE87wo.
So in order to buy 1 bit you'll need to pay 3500 bits in fees. That sounds like fun! That's what the Core developer... https://t.co/um5QrfwWwc
RT @lifeinvestasset: #CryptocurrencyLifeInvest (Change 24h):
→#Bitcoin $15.584,80 (-7,82%).
→#BitcoinCash $3.212,84 (-16,70%).
→#Ether $809...
RT @HealthRanger: What do you think: Do #China and #Russia really have this much control over #Bitcoin ? https://t.co/yjKPxOGQsW
RT @ToshiDesk: Guys - Next #ICO to watch out for!

https://t.co/Vfol8rWYcm

They already have 10+ courses up on their Educational Site...
RT @AlexanderHaxton: One of my favorite ICOs right now: Trade.io is revolutionising the banking industry. Many #ICO's will be launched on T...
RT @VahapErenTR: Dear @Poloniex !
My friend's account @gurselkaraaslan has been frozen for 10 days.Please respond the #580589 ticket which...
@krios_io Bitcoin Diamond ($BCD) successfully launch mainnet and 28 global exchanges start trades! If you have bala... https://t.co/P6uHaCVEY1
Zum ständigen auf und ab der #Bitcoin ein sehr lesenswerter Artikel von @SPIEGELONLINE - danke für das Interview,... https://t.co/iY2xhRikc8
RT @JamesGRickards: OK, let's make this simple. Bitcoin is a multiplayer game dressed up as a real world experience. Enjoy! https://t.co/1w...
RT @rajneeshchhabra: No Place Like Home: The Internet Of Things And Its Promise For Consumers https://t.co/vAwghGoECa #IoT #InternetOfThing...
Bitcoin value tumbles by 30 per cent as investors face 'reality check' https://t.co/td8kaTEZrv
Uh what? 😱😱 guess he forgot to show where the Nasdaq is today 🤣🤣🤣 https://t.co/mChT4uRkqN
```

Awesome!

Great work guys, we have the full application integrated with RabbitMQ and the Twitter stream.

Spring Actuator

The Spring Boot Actuator is a kind of helper when the application is running in production. The project provides built-in information of a deployed application.

In the microservices world, monitoring instances of applications are the key point to getting success. In these environments, there are usually many applications calling the other applications over the network protocols such as HTTP. The network is an unstable environment and sometimes it will fail; we need to track these incidents to make sure the application is up and fully operational.

The Spring Boot Actuator helps developers in these situations. The project exposes a couple of HTTP APIs with application information, such as the memory usage, CPU usage, application health check, and the infrastructure components of the application, such as a connection with databases and message brokers, as well.

One of the most important points is that the information is exposed over HTTP. It helps integrations with external monitor applications such as Nagios and Zabbix, for instance. There is no specific protocol for exposing this information.

Let's add it to our project and try a couple of endpoints.

Adding Spring Boot Actuator in our pom.xml

Spring Boot Actuator is pretty simple to configure in our `pom.xml`. We extended the parent pom of Spring Boot, so it is not necessary to specify the version of the dependency.

Let's configure our new dependency:

```
<dependencies>
  <dependency>
    <groupId>org.springframework.boot</groupId>
    <artifactId>spring-boot-starter-actuator</artifactId>
  </dependency>
</dependencies>
```

Awesome, really easy. Let's understand a little bit more before we test.

Actuator Endpoints

The projects have a lot of built-in endpoints and they will be up when the application started. Remember, we have used the starter project, which is the one that configures it automatically for us.

There are several endpoints for different requirements, and we will take a look at the most used in production microservices.

- `/health`: The most known actuator endpoint; it shows the application's health, and usually, there is a `status` attribute
- `/configprops`: Displays a collapse `@ConfigurationProperties`
- `/env`: Exposes properties from the Spring `ConfigurableEnvironment`
- `/dump`: Shows the thread dump
- `/info`: We can put some arbitrary information at this endpoint
- `/metrics`: Metrics from the running application
- `/mappings`: `@RequestMappings` endpoints from the current application

There is another important endpoint to show the application logs over the HTTP interface. The /logfile endpoint can help us visualize logfiles.

 The list of endpoints created by the Spring Boot Actuator can be found at: https://docs.spring.io/spring-boot/docs/current/reference/html/production-ready-endpoints.html.

Application custom information

There is one particular endpoint which we can use to expose custom information from our application. This information will be exposed to /info endpoint.

To configure that, we can use the application.yaml file and put the desired information respecting the pattern, as follows:

```
info:
    project: "twitter-gathering"
    kotlin: @kotlin.version@
```

Thr desired properties must be preceded by the info. *. Then, we can test our first actuator endpoint and check our /info resource.

Let's try to access the http://localhost:8081/info. The information filled on application.yaml should be displayed, as shown here:

```
←  →  C  ⓘ localhost:8081/actuator/info

▼ {
    "project": "twitter-gathering",
    "kotlin": "1.2.0"
  }
```

As we can see, the properties are exposed from the HTTP endpoint. We can use that to put the application version, for instance.

Testing endpoints

In version 2 of Spring Boot, the Spring Actuator management endpoints are disabled by default, because these endpoints can have sensitive data of a running application. Then, we need to configure to enable these endpoints properly.

There is a special point to pay attention to. If the application is exposed publicly, you should protect these endpoints.

Let's enable our management endpoints:

```
management:
  endpoints:
    web:
      expose: "*"
```

In the preceding configuration, we enabled all the management endpoints, and then we can start to test some endpoints.

Let's test some endpoints. First, we will test the metrics endpoints. This endpoint shows the metrics available for the running application. Go to `http://localhost:8081/actuator/metrics` and check the result:

```
← → C   ① localhost:8081/actuator/metrics
{
  "names": [
    "jvm.buffer.memory.used",
    "jvm.memory.used",
    "jvm.buffer.count",
    "logback.events",
    "process.uptime",
    "jvm.memory.committed",
    "system.load.average.1m",
    "http.server.requests",
    "jvm.buffer.total.capacity",
    "jvm.memory.max",
    "system.cpu.count",
    "process.start.time"
  ]
}
```

We are using port 8081 because we configured the property
server.port in application.yaml. The port can be changed as you
desire.

There are a lot of metrics configured automatically for us. That endpoint exposes only the
available metrics. To check the metric value, we need to use another endpoint. Let's check
the value of the http.server.request.

The base endpoint to check the value
is: http://localhost:8081/actuator/metrics/{metricName}. Then, we need to go
to: http://localhost:8081/actuator/metrics/http.server.requests. The result
should be:

```
←  →  C  ⓘ localhost:8081/actuator/metrics/http.server.requests

▼ {
      "name": "http.server.requests",
    ▼ "measurements": [
      ▼ {
            "statistic": "Count",
            "value": 8
        },
      ▼ {
            "statistic": "TotalTime",
            "value": 281213374
        },
      ▼ {
            "statistic": "Max",
            "value": 281213374
        }
    ],
    ▶ "availableTags": [ … ] // 4 items
  }
```

As you can see, the server received eight calls. Try to hit a few more times to see the metrics
changing.

Awesome job. Our microservice is ready for production. We have the docker image and
endpoints for monitoring our services.

Summary

In this chapter, we learned and put into practice a lot of Spring Advanced concepts, such as RabbitMQ integration.

We have created a fully reactive WebClient and took advantage of the reactive paradigm; it enables resource computational optimization and increases performance for the application.

Also, we have integrated two microservices through the RabbitMQ broker. This is an excellent solution to integrating applications because it decouples the applications and also permits you to scale the application horizontally really easily. Message-driven is one of the required characteristics to build a reactive application; it can be found at Reactive Manifesto (`https://www.reactivemanifesto.org/en`).

In the next chapter, we will improve our solution and create a new microservice to stream the filtered Tweets for our clients. We will use RabbitMQ one more time.

6
Playing with Server-Sent Events

In `Chapter 4`, Kotlin Basics and Spring Data Redis and `Chapter 5`, *Reactive Web Clients*, we created two microservices. The first one is responsible for keeping tracked data on Redis and triggering the second microservice which one will consume the Twitter stream. This process happens asynchronously.

In this chapter, we will create another microservice which will consume the data produced by Twitter Gathering and expose it via a REST API. It will be possible to filter Tweets by text content.

We have consumed the Twitter stream using the **Server-Sent Events** (**SSE**); we created a reactive REST client to consume that. Now, it is time to create our implementation for SSE. We will consume the RabbitMQ queue and push the data to our connected clients.

We will take a look at the SSE and understand why this solution fits well for our couple of microservices.

At the end of the chapter, we will be confident about using SSE in the Spring ecosystem.

In this chapter, we will learn the following:

- Implementation of SSE endpoints with the Spring Framework
- Consuming RabbitMQ using the Reactor Rabbit client

Creating the Tweet Dispatcher project

Now, we will create our last microservice. It will push the Tweets filtered by Twitter Gathering for our connected clients, in this case, consumers.

In this chapter, we will use the Spring Initializr page to help us create our pretty new project. Let's create.

Using Spring Initializr once again

As you can see, the Spring Initializr page is a kind of partner for creating Spring projects. Let's use it one more time and create a project:

Go to `https://start.spring.io` and fill in the data using the following screenshot:

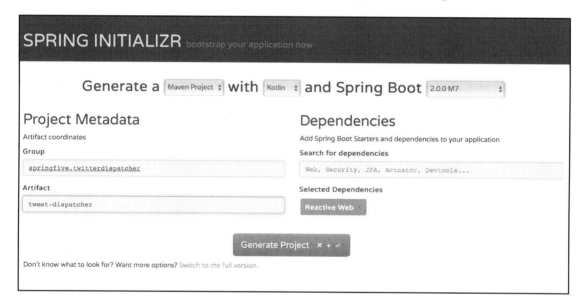

We have selected the **Reactive Web** dependencies; we will also keep using Kotlin as a programming language. Finally, click on the **Generate Project** button. Good, it is enough for us.

There are some missing dependencies which are not displayed in the Spring Initializr. We need to set these dependencies manually. We will do that task in the next section. Let's go there.

Additional dependencies

We need to use the Jackson Kotlin Module as a dependency to handle JSON properly in our new microservice. Also, we will use the Reactor RabbitMQ dependency, which allows us to interact in the reactive paradigm with the RabbitMQ Broker.

To add these dependencies, we need to add the following snippet to `pom.xml`:

```xml
<dependency>
  <groupId>com.fasterxml.jackson.module</groupId>
  <artifactId>jackson-module-kotlin</artifactId>
  <version>${jackson.version}</version>
</dependency>

<dependency>
  <groupId>io.projectreactor</groupId>
  <artifactId>reactor-test</artifactId>
  <scope>test</scope>
</dependency>

<dependency>
  <groupId>io.projectreactor.rabbitmq</groupId>
  <artifactId>reactor-rabbitmq</artifactId>
  <version>1.0.0.M1</version>
</dependency>
```

Awesome. Our dependencies are configured. Our project is ready to start.

Before we start, we need to understand, in depth, the concept of SSE. We will learn this in the next section.

Server-Sent Events

Server-Sent Events (SSE) is a standard way to send data streams from a server to clients. In this next section, we will learn how to implement it using the Spring Framework.

Also, we will understand the main differences between SSE and WebSockets.

A few words about the HTTP protocol

HTTP is an application layer protocol in the OSI model. The application layer is the last layer represented in the OSI model. It means this layer is closer to the user interface. The main purpose of this layer is to send and receive the data input by the user. In general, it happens by the user interface, also known as applications, such as file transfer and sending an email.

There are several protocols on the application layer such as Domain Name Service (DNS), which translates the domain names to IP address, or SMTP, whose main purpose is to deliver an email to a mail manager application.

The application layer interacts directly with software such as email clients, for instance; there are no interactions with the hardware parts. It is the last layer of the OSI model and the closest to the end user as well.

All these layers deal with software, which means there are no concerns about the physical parts represented in the OSI model.

 A more detailed explanation of the OSI model can be found at: `https://support.microsoft.com/en-us/help/103884/the-osi-model-s-seven-layers-defined-and-functions-explained`.

The following is an OSI model representation:

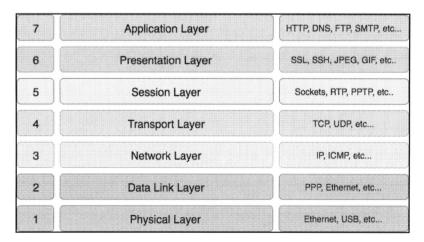

7	Application Layer	HTTP, DNS, FTP, SMTP, etc...
6	Presentation Layer	SSL, SSH, JPEG, GIF, etc..
5	Session Layer	Sockets, RTP, PPTP, etc..
4	Transport Layer	TCP, UDP, etc...
3	Network Layer	IP, ICMP, etc...
2	Data Link Layer	PPP, Ethernet, etc...
1	Physical Layer	Ethernet, USB, etc...

The HTTP protocol uses the TCP protocol as a transportation channel. Then, it will establish a connection and start to flow the data on the channel.

The TCP protocol is a stream protocol and a full duplex channel. This means the server and clients can send data across the connection.

HTTP and persistent connections

The HTTP protocol is a request-response model, where the client submits the message (HTTP Request) and the server processes this message and sends the response (HTTP Response) to the client. The connection will be closed after the response is sent.

Look at the following diagram:

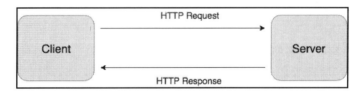

It's pretty simple to understand. The client will send the request, and in this case, the connection will be opened. After that, the server will receive the request to process something and it will send the answer to the client. The connection will be closed after the whole process. If the client needs to send a new request, the connection should be opened again and the flow happens in the same order.

There is a perceived drawback here, the clients need to open the new connection per-request. From the server's eyes, the server needs to process a lot of new connections simultaneously. This consumes a lot of CPU and memory.

On HTTP's 1.0 version, the connections are not persistent. To enable it, the `keep-alive` header should be included on the request. The header should look like this:

```
Connection: keep-alive
```

This is the only way to make an HTTP connection persistent on the 1.0 version, as described previously; when it happens, the connection will not be dropped by the server and the client is able to reuse the opened connection.

On HTTP 1.1, the connections are persistent by default; in this case, as opposed to the first version, the connection is kept opened and the client can use it normally.

There is a perceived improvement here and it can bring some advantages. The server needs to manage fewer connections, and it reduces a lot of CPU time. The HTTP Requests and Responses can be pipelined in the same connection.

As we know, *there is no such thing as a free lunch*. There are some disadvantages to this as well; the server needs to keep the connection opened and the server will reserve the required connection for the client. This may cause server unavailability in some scenarios.

Persistent connections can be useful to maintain a stream between the server and clients.

WebSockets

In the HTTP protocol, the communication supports full-duplex, which means the client and server can send data through the channel. The standard way to support this kind of communication is WebSockets. In this specification, both client and server can send data to each other in the persistent connection. Look at the following diagram:

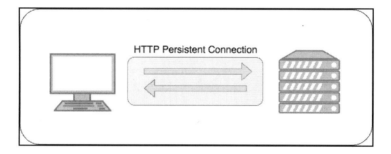

As we can see, the data can be sent and received by the two actors, client, and server—this is how WebSockets works.

In our case, we do not need to send any data to the server during the connection. Because of this characteristic, we will choose SSE. We will learn about them in the following section.

Server-Sent Events

As opposed to the full-duplex communication implemented by WebSockets, the SSE uses a half-duplex communication.

The client sends a request to the server, and when necessary, the server will push the data to the client. Remember the active actor here is the server; the data can be sent only by the server. This is a half-duplex behavior. Look at the following diagram:

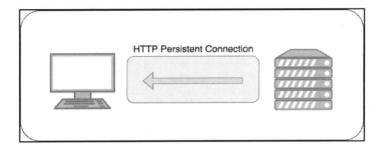

A piece of cake. It is the base of the SSE technology. SSE is self-explanatory. We will use it with the Spring Framework. However, before we do that, let's look at a Reactor RabbitMQ project.

Reactor RabbitMQ

Our solution is fully reactive, so we need to use Reactor RabbitMQ, which allows us to interact with the RabbitMQ broker using the reactive paradigm.

On this new microservice, we do not need to send messages through the message broker. Our solution will listen to the RabbitMQ queues and push the received Tweets for the connected clients.

Understanding the Reactor RabbitMQ

The Reactor RabbitMQ tries to provide a reactive library to interact with the RabbitMQ rboker. It enables developers to create non-blocking applications based on the reactive stream, using RabbitMQ as a message-broker solution.

As we learned before, this kind of solution, in general, does not use a lot of memory. The project was based on the RabbitMQ Java client and has similar functionalities, if we compare it to the blocking solution.

We are not using the `spring-amqp-starter`, so the magic will not happen. We will need to code the beans declarations for the Spring context and we will do that in the following section.

Configuring RabbitMQ Reactor beans

In this section, we will configure the RabbitMQ infrastructure classes in the Spring context. We will use a @Configuration class to declare it.

The configuration class should look like the following:

```
package springfive.twitterdispatcher.infra.rabbitmq

import com.fasterxml.jackson.databind.ObjectMapper
import com.fasterxml.jackson.module.kotlin.KotlinModule
import com.rabbitmq.client.ConnectionFactory
import org.springframework.beans.factory.annotation.Value
import org.springframework.context.annotation.Bean
import org.springframework.context.annotation.Configuration
import reactor.rabbitmq.ReactorRabbitMq
import reactor.rabbitmq.Receiver
import reactor.rabbitmq.ReceiverOptions

@Configuration
class RabbitMQConfiguration(private @Value("\${spring.rabbitmq.host}")
val host:String,
                           private @Value("\${spring.rabbitmq.port}")
val port:Int,
                           private
@Value("\${spring.rabbitmq.username}")  val username:String,
                           private
@Value("\${spring.rabbitmq.password}")  val password:String){

  @Bean
  fun mapper(): ObjectMapper =
ObjectMapper().registerModule(KotlinModule())

  @Bean
  fun connectionFactory():ConnectionFactory{
    val connectionFactory = ConnectionFactory()
    connectionFactory.username = this.username
    connectionFactory.password = this.password
    connectionFactory.host = this.host
    connectionFactory.port = this.port
    connectionFactory.useNio()
    return connectionFactory
  }

  @Bean
  fun receiver(connectionFactory: ConnectionFactory):Receiver{
      val options = ReceiverOptions()
```

```
        options.connectionFactory(connectionFactory)
        return ReactorRabbitMq.createReceiver(options)
    }

}
```

There are two important things here. The first one is that we configured the Jackson support for Kotlin. It allows us to inject the `ObjectMapper` into our Spring beans. The next important thing is related to the RabbitMQ connections' configuration.

We have declared a `ConnectionFactory` bean for the Spring Context. We injected the configurations with `@Value` annotations and received the values on the constructor. We can set the value directly in the attributes, in the Kotlin language; look at the `ConnectionFactory` attributes assignments.

After the `ConnectionFactory` configuration, we are able to declare a receiver, which is a `Reactive` abstraction to consume the queues, using reactive programming. We receive the `ConnectionFactory` previously created and set it as the `ReceiverOptions`.

That is all for the Reactor RabbitMQ configuration.

Consuming the RabbitMQ queues reactively

Now, we will consume the RabbitMQ queues. The implementation is quite similar to what we have seen in the blocking implementation, and the names of the functions are similar as well.

We have consumed some RabbitMQ messages in the previous chapters, but this solution is quite different. Now, we will use the Reactive RabbitMQ implementation. The main idea here is to consume the stream of events; these events represent the messages that have arrived in the broker. These messages arrive and the Reactor RabbitMQ converts these messages to Flux, to enable us to consume in the reactive paradigm.

In the reactive paradigm, the representation of a stream of events (we can think of messages in the queue), is the `Flux`.

Then our function, which is listening to the RabbitMQ, should return `Flux`, an infinite representation of events. The Receiver implementation returns the `Flux` of messages, which is enough for us and fits well with our needs.

Our implementation should look like the following:

```kotlin
package springfive.twitterdispatcher.domain.service

import com.fasterxml.jackson.annotation.JsonIgnoreProperties
import com.fasterxml.jackson.annotation.JsonProperty
import com.fasterxml.jackson.databind.ObjectMapper
import com.fasterxml.jackson.module.kotlin.readValue
import org.springframework.beans.factory.annotation.Value
import org.springframework.stereotype.Service
import reactor.core.publisher.Flux
import reactor.core.publisher.Mono
import reactor.rabbitmq.Receiver

@Service
class TwitterDispatcher(private @Value("\${queue.twitter}") val queue:
String,
        private val receiver: Receiver,
        private val mapper: ObjectMapper) {

    fun dispatch(): Flux<Tweet> {
        return this.receiver.consumeAutoAck(this.queue).flatMap {
message ->
            Mono.just(mapper.readValue<Tweet>(String(message.body)))
        }
    }

}

@JsonIgnoreProperties(ignoreUnknown = true)
data class Tweet(val id: String = "",
    val text: String = "", @JsonProperty("created_at")
    val createdAt: String = "", val user: TwitterUser = TwitterUser("",
""))

@JsonIgnoreProperties(ignoreUnknown = true)
data class TwitterUser(val id: String, val name: String)
```

Let's understand a little bit more. We received the `Receiver` as an injection in our
constructor. When someone invokes the `dispatch()` function, the `Receiver` will start to
consume the queue, which was injected in the constructor as well.

The `Receiver` produces `Flux<Delivery>`. Now, we need to convert the instance of `Flux<Delivery>`, which represents a message abstraction, to our domain model Tweet. The `flatMap()` function can do it for us, but first, we will convert the `message.body` to string and then we have used Jackson to read JSON and convert to our Tweet domain model.

Take a look at how simple the code is to read; the API is fluent and really readable.

The consumer will not terminate until the connected client disconnects. We will be able to see this behavior soon.

Filtering streams

We are receiving the messages from RabbitMQ. Now, we need to return the messages to the connected customer.

For that, we will use SSE with Spring WebFlux. The solution is a good fit for us because we will produce a `Flux<Tweet>` and start to push the Tweets for our clients. The clients will send a query to filter the desired Tweets.

The application will be fully reactive. Let's take a look at our code:

```
package springfive.twitterdispatcher.domain.controller

import org.springframework.http.MediaType
import org.springframework.web.bind.annotation.GetMapping
import org.springframework.web.bind.annotation.RequestMapping
import org.springframework.web.bind.annotation.RequestParam
import org.springframework.web.bind.annotation.RestController
import reactor.core.publisher.Flux
import springfive.twitterdispatcher.domain.service.Tweet
import springfive.twitterdispatcher.domain.service.TwitterDispatcher

@RestController
@RequestMapping("/tweets")
class TweetResource(private val dispatcher: TwitterDispatcher) {

  @GetMapping(produces = [MediaType.TEXT_EVENT_STREAM_VALUE])
  fun tweets(@RequestParam("q")query:String):Flux<Tweet>{
    return dispatcher.dispatch()
        .filter({ tweet: Tweet? -> tweet!!.text.contains(query,ignoreCase =
true) })
    }
}
```

Pretty easy and simple to understand. We have declared the `tweets()` function; this function is mapped to a GET HTTP Request and produces a `MediaType.TEXT_EVENT_STREAM_VALUE`. When the client connects to the endpoint, the server will start to send Tweets accordingly with the desired argument.

When the client disconnects, the Reactor RabbitMQ will close the requested RabbitMQ connection.

Dockerizing the whole solution

Now, it is time to wrap the whole solution and create a Docker image for all projects. It is useful to run the projects anywhere we want.

We will configure all the projects step by step and then run the solution in Docker containers. As a challenge, we can use `docker-compose` to orchestrate the whole solution in a single `yaml` file.

For the Tracked Hashtag Service, we have created the docker image. Then, we will start to configure the Tweet Gathering, and the last one is Tweet Dispatcher. Let's do that right now.

 You can find more `docker-compose` project details at: `https://docs.docker.com/compose/`. Also, in the new versions, `docker-compose` supports Docker Swarm to orchestrate the stack between cluster nodes. It can be really useful to deploy Docker containers in production.

Tweet Gathering

Let's configure our `pom.xml` for the Tweet Gathering project.

The build node should look like the following:

```
<plugin>
  <groupId>io.fabric8</groupId>
  <artifactId>docker-maven-plugin</artifactId>
  <version>0.21.0</version>
  <configuration>
    <images>
      <image>
        <name>springfivebyexample/${project.build.finalName}</name>
        <build>
```

```xml
            <from>openjdk:latest</from>
            <entryPoint>java -Dspring.profiles.active=container -jar
                /application/${project.build.finalName}.jar</entryPoint>
            <assembly>
              <basedir>/application</basedir>
              <descriptorRef>artifact</descriptorRef>
              <inline>
                <id>assembly</id>
                <files>
                  <file>
          <source>target/${project.build.finalName}.jar</source>
                  </file>
                </files>
              </inline>
            </assembly>
            <tags>
              <tag>latest</tag>
            </tags>
            <ports>
              <port>8081</port>
            </ports>
          </build>
          <run>
            <namingStrategy>alias</namingStrategy>
          </run>
          <alias>${project.build.finalName}</alias>
        </image>
      </images>
    </configuration>
  </plugin>
```

Take a look at the port configuration; it should be the same as what we have configured in the `application.yaml`. The configuration is done, so let's create our Docker image:

```
mvn clean install docker:build
```

The command output should look like the following screenshot:

```
[INFO] DOCKER> [springfivebyexample/tweet_gathering:latest] "tweet_gathering": Created docker-build.tar in 196 milliseconds
[INFO] DOCKER> [springfivebyexample/tweet_gathering:latest] "tweet_gathering": Built image sha256:e1973
[INFO] DOCKER> [springfivebyexample/tweet_gathering:latest] "tweet_gathering": Tag with latest
[INFO] ------------------------------------------------------------------------
[INFO] BUILD SUCCESS
[INFO] ------------------------------------------------------------------------
[INFO] Total time: 13.714 s
[INFO] Finished at: 2018-01-04T22:51:58-02:00
[INFO] Final Memory: 65M/524M
```

There is an image recently created and tagged as a latest; the image is ready to run. Let's do the same thing for our Tweet Dispatcher project.

Tweet Dispatcher

Our new plugin entry should look like this:

```
<plugin>
  <groupId>io.fabric8</groupId>
  <artifactId>docker-maven-plugin</artifactId>
  <version>0.21.0</version>
  <configuration>
    <images>
      <image>
        <name>springfivebyexample/${project.build.finalName}</name>
        <build>
          <from>openjdk:latest</from>
          <entryPoint>java -Dspring.profiles.active=container -jar
          /application/${project.build.finalName}.jar</entryPoint>
          <assembly>
            <basedir>/application</basedir>
            <descriptorRef>artifact</descriptorRef>
            <inline>
              <id>assembly</id>
              <files>
                <file>
          <source>target/${project.build.finalName}.jar</source>
                </file>
              </files>
            </inline>
          </assembly>
          <tags>
            <tag>latest</tag>
          </tags>
          <ports>
            <port>9099</port>
          </ports>
        </build>
        <run>
          <namingStrategy>alias</namingStrategy>
        </run>
        <alias>${project.build.finalName}</alias>
      </image>
    </images>
  </configuration>
</plugin>
```

Take a look at the port configuration, one more time. It will be used by Docker to expose the correct port. Now, we can run the image creation command:

```
mvn clean install docker:build
```

Then, we can see the command's output, as shown in the following screenshot:

```
[INFO] DOCKER> [springfivebyexample/tweet_dispatcher:latest] "tweet_dispatcher": Created docker-build.tar in 164 milliseconds
[INFO] DOCKER> [springfivebyexample/tweet_dispatcher:latest] "tweet_dispatcher": Built image sha256:19317
[INFO] DOCKER> [springfivebyexample/tweet_dispatcher:latest] "tweet_dispatcher": Tag with latest
[INFO] ------------------------------------------------------------
[INFO] BUILD SUCCESS
[INFO] ------------------------------------------------------------
[INFO] Total time: 14.020 s
[INFO] Finished at: 2018-01-04T23:07:29-02:00
[INFO] Final Memory: 61M/528M
[INFO] ------------------------------------------------------------
```

Awesome, all images are ready. Let's run it.

> We need to create Docker images for all the projects. The process is the same; configure the maven Docker plugin and then use `mvn clean install docker:build` on the project. The full source code can be found at GitHub. The Tracked Hashtag Service can be found here (`https://github.com/PacktPublishing/Spring-5.0-By-Example/tree/master/Chapter04`), the Tweet Gathering can be found here (`https://github.com/PacktPublishing/Spring-5.0-By-Example/tree/master/Chapter05`) and finally, the Tweet Dispatcher can be found here (`https://github.com/PacktPublishing/Spring-5.0-By-Example/tree/master/Chapter06`).

Running the containerized solution

We are ready to run the solution in Docker containers. We have been running the solution with the IDE or command line, but now we will spin up some container and test the solution and Spring profiles as well.

Before that, let's do a quick recap of the solution:

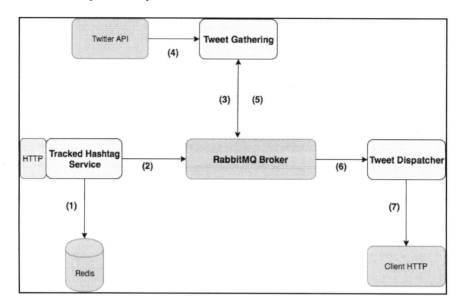

1. The first operation, the **Tracked Hashtag Service**, will persist the hashtag in the **Redis** database.
2. After that, the **Tracked Hashtag Service** will send the newly tracked hashtag to a queue in the **RabbitMQ** Broker.
3. **Tweet Gathering** is listening to the queue to track Tweets and trigger the event and starts by listening to the **Twitter stream**.
4. **Tweet Gathering** starts to get Tweets from the **Twitter stream.**
5. **Tweet Gathering** publishes Tweets to a queue in the **RabbitMQ broker**.
6. **Tweet Dispatcher** consumes the message.
7. **Tweet Dispatcher** sends the message to the **Client** using SSE.

Now that we have understood the solution, let's starts the containers.

Running the Tracked Hashtag Service container

The image has been created in the previous section, so now we are able to spin up the container. The command to start the container should look like this:

```
docker run -d --name tracked --net twitter -p 9090:9090
springfivebyexample/tracked_hashtag
```

Let's explain the instruction. -d tells the Docker engine to run the container in background mode or detached. The other important parameter is --net, which attaches the container to the desired network.

We can use the following command to tail the container logs at runtime:

```
docker logs tracked -f
```

This command is like the `tail -f` command on Linux, which looks at the last part of the log stream. We can remove the flag -f to see the last lines of the log.

The output of docker logs should look like this:

```
  .   ____          _            __ _ _
 /\\ / ___'_ __ _ _(_)_ __  __ _ \ \ \ \
( ( )\___ | '_ | '_| | '_ \/ _` | \ \ \ \
 \\/  ___)| |_)| | | | | || (_| |  ) ) ) )
  '  |____| .__|_| |_|_| |_\__, | / / / /
 =========|_|==============|___/=/_/_/_/
 :: Spring Boot ::        (v2.0.0.M7)

2018-01-15 23:54:12.282  INFO 5 --- [           main] s.t.TrackedHashTagApplication$Companion  : Starting TrackedHashTagApplication.Companion v0.0.1
-SNAPSHOT on c79e1bad3528 with PID 5 (/application/tracked_hashtag.jar started by root in /)
2018-01-15 23:54:12.326  INFO 5 --- [           main] s.t.TrackedHashTagApplication$Companion  : The following profiles are active: docker
```

Look at the profile selected, in the logs:

```
INFO 7 --- [                main] s.t.TrackedHashTagApplication$Companion    : The
following profiles are active: docker
```

Remember, we have parameterized it in the `pom.xml` file from the Tracked Hash Tag Service. Let's look at the following snippet:

```
<entryPoint>java -Dspring.profiles.active=docker -jar
/application/${project.build.finalName}.jar</entryPoint>
```

Awesome job. Our first service is running properly. Let's run Tweet Gathering; there is some interesting configuration here.

 We have created the Twitter network in chapter 4, *Kotlin Basics and Spring Data Redis*, and we need to use this network to enable the containers to see each other by container name in our custom network.

Running the Tweet Gathering container

To run the **Tweet Gathering** application is slightly different. This container needs environment variables which are used to interact with the Twitter API. We can use the `-e` argument on the `docker run` command. Let's do that:

```
docker run -d --name gathering --net twitter -e
CONSUMER_KEY=gupfxwn43NBTdxCD3Tsf1JgMu \
-e CONSUMER_SECRET=pH4uM5LlYxKzfJ7huYRwFbaFXn7ooK01LmqCP69QV9a9kZrHw5 \
-e ACCESS_TOKEN=940015005860290560-m0WwSyxGvp5ufff9KW2zm5LGXLaFLov \
-e ACCESS_TOKEN_SECRET=KSofGB8aIwDmewceKXLbN8d5chvZkZyB31VZa09pNBhLo \
-p 8081:8081 springfivebyexample/tweet_gathering
```

Take a look at the environment variables we have configured in the `application.yaml` file. The Docker run command will inject these variables into the system and then we can use them in our Java application.

Let's inspect our container logs. We can do that using the following command:

```
2018-01-15 23:54:29.084  INFO 6 --- [cTaskExecutor-1] o.s.a.r.c.CachingConnectionFactory       : Created new connection: rabbitConnectionFactory#57d
7f8ca:0/SimpleConnection@50ecfb4a [delegate=amqp://guest@172.19.0.6:5672/, localPort= 48016]
2018-01-15 23:54:29.088  INFO 6 --- [cTaskExecutor-1] o.s.amqp.rabbit.core.RabbitAdmin         : Auto-declaring a non-durable, auto-delete, or exclu
sive Queue (twitter-stream) durable:false, auto-delete:false, exclusive:false. It will be redeclared if the broker stops and is restarted while the
connection factory is alive, but all messages will be lost.
2018-01-15 23:54:29.088  INFO 6 --- [cTaskExecutor-1] o.s.amqp.rabbit.core.RabbitAdmin         : Auto-declaring a non-durable, auto-delete, or exclu
sive Queue (twitter-track-hashtag) durable:false, auto-delete:false, exclusive:false. It will be redeclared if the broker stops and is restarted whi
le the connection factory is alive, but all messages will be lost.
2018-01-15 23:54:29.235  INFO 6 --- [           main] r.ipc.netty.tcp.BlockingNettyContext     : Started HttpServer on /0.0.0.0:8081
2018-01-15 23:54:29.242  INFO 6 --- [           main] o.s.b.web.embedded.netty.NettyWebServer  : Netty started on port(s): 8081
2018-01-15 23:54:29.246  INFO 6 --- [           main] s.t.TweetGatheringApplication$Companion  : Started TweetGatheringApplication.Companion in 20.5
99 seconds (JVM running for 21.708)
```

Awesome, our application is up and running. As you can see, the application is connected to the RabbitMQ Broker.

> **RabbitMQ** and **Redis** should be running to enable you to run Tweet Gathering. We can check it using the `docker ps` command; it will list the running containers, RabbitMQ and Redis need to be on this list.

Now, we can run the Dispatcher application to complete the whole solution. Let's do that.

Running the Tweet Dispatcher container

There is no secret to running the Tweet Dispatcher container. We can use the following command to run it:

```
docker run -d --name dispatcher --net twitter -p 9099:9099
springfivebyexample/tweet_dispatcher
```

It will spin up the container, it is a good idea to name the container during the run. It can help us manage the container with command-line tools, such as `docker container ls` or `docker ps`, because it shows the container name in the last column. Then, let's check if our container is running, so type the following command:

```
docker container ls
```

Or, you can run the following command:

```
docker ps
```

We should be able to see the Gathering container running, like in the following output:

There are five containers, three applications, and two infrastructure services, **RabbitMQ** and **Redis**.

At any time, we can stop the desired container using the following command:

```
docker stop gathering
```

The `docker stop` will only stop the container; the information will be kept in the container volume. We can use the container name or container ID as well, we named it before. It is easy for us. If we use the `docker ps` command, the image recently stopped will never appear on the list. To show all the containers, we can use `docker ps -a` or `docker container ls -a`.

Now, we will start the container again; the command is self-explanatory:

```
docker start gathering
```

The container is running again. We have practiced more with Docker.

Awesome job, guys. The whole application is containerized. Well done.

 We can use the Linux instruction and execute some batch instructions. For instance, we can use `docker stop $(docker ps -q)` — it will stop all containers running. The `docker ps -q` command will bring only the container's IDs.

The docker-compose tool

In the microservices architectural style, the whole solution is decoupled in small and well-defined services. Usually, when we adopt these styles, we have more than one artifact to deploy.

Let's analyze our solution; we have three components to deploy. We have used the Docker containers and we have run these containers using the `docker run` command. One by one, we have used `docker run` three times. It is quite complex and very hard to do in the development routine.

`docker-compose` can help us in this scenario. It is a tool which helps to orchestrate Docker containers in complex scenarios like ours.

Let's imagine our application is growing fast and we need to build four more microservices to achieve the desired business case, it will implicate on four more `docker run` commands and will probably be painful to maintain, especially during the development life cycle. Sometimes, we need to promote the artifacts to test the environment and we probably need to modify our command line to achieve this.

`docker-compose` enables us to deploy multiple containers with a single `yaml` file. This `yaml` file has a defined structure which allows us to define and configure several containers in the same file. Moreover, we can run the solution configured in this `yaml` file with a single command, it makes development life easy.

The tool can work on the local machine or we can integrate it with the Docker Swarm tool which can manage clusters of Docker hosts.

Docker Swarm is a native tool to manage docker clusters. It makes it easy to deploy a container on the Docker cluster. In the new version, `docker-compose` is fully integrated with Docker Swarm. We can define it from Docker Swarm properties in `docker-compose.yaml`. The Docker Swarm documentation can be found at: `https://docs.docker.com/engine/swarm/`.

The `docker-compose yaml` has a defined structure to follow; the documentation can be found here: `https://docs.docker.com/compose/compose-file/#compose-and-docker-compatibility-matrix`. We will create a simple file to understand the `docker-compose` behaviors. Let's create our simple `yaml`— the `yaml` should look like this:

```
version: '3'
services:
  rabbitmq:
    image: rabbitmq:3.7.0-management-alpine
    ports:
      - "5672:5672"
      - "15672:15672"
  redis:
    image: "redis:alpine"
    ports:
      - "6379:6379"
```

The `yaml` in the preceding code will create the structure detailed in the following diagram:

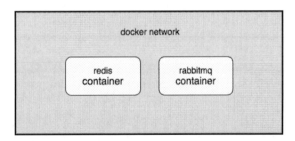

It simplifies the development time. Now, we will learn how to install `docker-compose`.

Installing docker-compose

The `docker-compose` installation is pretty simple and well-documented. We are using Linux, so we will use the Linux instructions.

Open the terminal and use the following command:

```
sudo curl -L
https://github.com/docker/compose/releases/download/1.18.0/docker-compose-`
uname -s`-`uname -m` -o /usr/local/bin/docker-compose
```

Wait for the download and then we can execute the following instructions to give executable permissions for the program. Let's do this by executing the following command:

```
sudo chmod +x /usr/local/bin/docker-compose
```

As you may know, you may be asked for the administrator password. Our `docker-compose` is now installed. Let's check it:

```
docker-compose --version
```

The prompt will display the installed version, like the following screenshot:

```
docker-compose version 1.18.0, build 8dd22a9
```

`docker-compose` is up and running, so let's jump to the next section and start to create our `yaml` file and deploy the whole stack with one single command.

 For different operating systems, the instructions can be found here: `https://docs.docker.com/compose/install/#install-compose`. Then, you can navigate around the instructions and click on the desired operating system.

Creating a docker-compose file

Now, we have `docker-compose` installed and we can try to work with the tool. We want to run the whole stack with a single command. We will create the `yaml` file to represent the stack. Our `yaml` file should have the Redis container, the RabbitMQ container, the Tracked Hashtag application, the Gathering application, and finally, the Dispatcher application.

We can create a `docker-compose.yaml` file wherever we want, there is no restriction for that.

Our `docker-compose.yaml` file should look like the following:

```yaml
version: '3'
services:
  rabbitmq:
    image: rabbitmq:3.7.0-management-alpine
    hostname: rabbitmq
    ports:
      - "5672:5672"
      - "15672:15672"
    networks:
      - solution
  redis:
    image: "redis:4.0.6-alpine"
    hostname: redis
    ports:
      - "6379:6379"
    networks:
      - solution
  tracked:
    image: springfivebyexample/tracked_hashtag
    ports:
      - "9090:9090"
    networks:
      - solution
  gathering:
    image: springfivebyexample/tweet_gathering
    ports:
      - "8081:8081"
    networks:
      - solution
    environment:
      - CONSUMER_KEY=gupfxwn43NBTdxCD3Tsf1JgMu
      -
CONSUMER_SECRET=pH4uM5LlYxKzfJ7huYRwFbaFXn7ooK01LmqCP69QV9a9kZrHw5
      - ACCESS_TOKEN=940015005860290560-m0WwSyxGvp5ufff9KW2zm5LGXLaFLov
      -
ACCESS_TOKEN_SECRET=KSofGB8aIwDmewceKXLbN8d5chvZkZyB31VZa09pNBhLo
  dispatcher:
    image: springfivebyexample/tweet_dispatcher
    ports:
      - "9099:9099"
    networks:
      - solution
networks:
  solution:
    driver: bridge
```

As you can see, we have defined the whole stack in the `yaml`. Something to note is that we can find some similarities with the `docker run` command, in fact, it will use the Docker engine to run. The `environment` node in yaml has the same behavior as `-e` in the Docker run command.

We have defined the application ports, docker images, and have also connected the containers to the same network. This is really important because when we use the `docker-compose` file name on the network, it can find that the container name has a kind of DNS behavior.

For instance, inside the defined network `solution`, the container can find the Redis container instance by the name `redis`.

Running the solution

`docker-compose` simplifies the process to run the whole stack. Our `yaml` file was configured and defined properly.

Let's start the solution. Run the following command:

```
docker-compose up -d
```

The command is pretty simple, the `-d` parameter instructs Docker to run the command in the background. As we did on the Docker run command.

The output of this command should be the following:

```
Creating network "compose_solution" with driver "bridge"
Creating compose_gathering_1  ... done
Creating compose_redis_1      ... done
Creating compose_tracked_1    ... done
Creating compose_rabbitmq_1   ... done
Creating compose_dispatcher_1 ... done
```

Take a look, `docker-compose` has created a network for our stack. In our case, the network driver is a bridge, after the network creation, the containers are started.

Testing the network

Let's test it, find the Gathering container – the container name in `docker-compose` is prefixed by the folder name, where `docker-compose` was started.

For instance, I have started my `docker-compose` stack in the compose folder. My container name will be `compose_gathering_1` because of the folder name.

Then, we will connect the Gathering container. It can be achieved using the following command:

```
docker exec -it compose_gathering_1  /bin/bash
```

The `docker exec` command allows us to execute something inside the container. In our case, we will execute the `/bin/bash` program.

The command structure is like this:

```
docker exec -it <container name or container id> <program or instruction>
```

Awesome, pay attention to the command line. It should be changed because now we are in the container command line:

```
root@cc6520b2bdc5:/# ls -l
total 68
drwxr-xr-x    2 root root 4096 Jan 11 00:11 application
drwxr-xr-x    1 root root 4096 Sep 14 04:18 bin
```

We are not connected as a root on our host, but now we are a root on the container. This container is on the same network as the Redis container instance, which is called `redis`.

Let's test with the `ping` command; we should be able to find the `redis` container by the name `redis`, let's do it. Type the following:

```
ping redis
```

The command output should be the following:

```
root@cc6520b2bdc5:/# ping redis
PING redis (172.19.0.2): 56 data bytes
64 bytes from 172.19.0.2: icmp_seq=0 ttl=64 time=0.280 ms
64 bytes from 172.19.0.2: icmp_seq=1 ttl=64 time=0.368 ms
64 bytes from 172.19.0.2: icmp_seq=2 ttl=64 time=0.221 ms
64 bytes from 172.19.0.2: icmp_seq=3 ttl=64 time=0.255 ms
64 bytes from 172.19.0.2: icmp_seq=4 ttl=64 time=0.310 ms
^C--- redis ping statistics ---
5 packets transmitted, 5 packets received, 0% packet loss
round-trip min/avg/max/stddev = 0.221/0.287/0.368/0.050 ms
```

Awesome, our container can find the Redis container by the name. The `yaml` file is fully working.

Summary

In this chapter, we completed our second solution. We were introduced to the RabbitMQ Reactor library, which enables us to connect to RabbitMQ, using the reactive paradigm.

We have prepared the whole solution in Docker containers and connected it to the same network to enable the applications to talk to each other.

We also learned the important pattern for pushing data from server to client through the HTTP persistent connection, and we learned the difference between WebSockets and Server-Sent Events, as well.

Finally, we learned how `docker-compose` helps us to create the stack and run the whole solution with a couple of commands.

In the following chapters, we will build a fully microservice solution, using some important patterns such as Service Discovery, API Gateway, Circuit Breakers, and much more.

7
Airline Ticket System

Our last projects—Twitter Consumers, Twitter Gathering, and Twitter Dispatcher—were excellent. We learned several exciting features, and they were implemented using the new features present in Spring 5.0. All of them are implemented in Reactive Streams and use Kotlin as the programming language. They are the hottest features in Spring 5.0; it was an impressive progression.

However, there are notably missing parts on these projects; we have microservice needs in mind. There are no infrastructure services such as service discovery, distributed configurations, API Gateway, distributed tracing, and monitoring. These kinds of services are mandatory in distributed systems such as microservice architectures.

There are several reasons for that. Firstly, we can think of the configuration management. Let's imagine the following scenario – in the development cycle, we have three environments: DEV, TST, and PROD. This is a pretty simple standard found in companies. Also, we have an application decoupled in 4 microservices, then with the minimum infrastructure, we have 12 instances of services; remember, this is a good scenario because in a real situation, we will probably have several instances of microservice applications.

In the earlier scenario, we will maintain at least three configuration files per microservice, remember there are three environments for which we need to keep the configurations. Then, we will have 12 *versions* of settings. It is a hard task to maintain the configurations, to keep the files synchronized and updated. These files probably contain sensitive information, such as database passwords and message brokers' configurations, and it is not recommended that you put these files on the host machines.

In this case, the distributed configuration can solve our problems easily. We will learn about configuration servers in this chapter, and other infrastructure services as well.

Let's summarize what we will learn in this chapter:

- How to create a Config Server
- Implementing a service discovery with Eureka
- Monitoring applications with Spring Cloud Zipkin
- Exposing the applications with the Spring Cloud Gateway

The Airline Ticket System

In these last few chapters, we will work on the Airline Ticket System. The solution is quite complex and involves a lot of HTTP integrations and message-based solutions. We will explore what we have learned from the book journey.

We will use Spring Messaging, Spring WebFlux, and Spring Data components to create the solution. The application will split up into several microservices to guarantee the scalability, elasticity, and fault tolerance for the system.

Also, we will have some infrastructure services to help us deliver an efficient system. Some new patterns will be introduced, such as circuit breakers and OAuth. In the infrastructure layer, we will use the Netflix OSS components integrated with the Spring Framework ecosystem.

The main purpose of our application is to sell airline tickets, but to achieve this task, we need to build an entire ecosystem. We will build a microservice which will manage the seats and planes' characteristics. There will also be a microservice to manage available company flights; the basic idea is to manage flight dates and routes. Of course, we will have a microservice to manage passengers, fares, bookings, and payments. Finally, we will have an e-commerce API with which end users will buy airline tickets.

Airline functionalities

We will create some microservices to compose the solution and then we will decompose the solution into small pieces, that is, microservices. For that, we will use the Bounded Context pattern which is an essential part of the **Domain-Driven Design (DDD)**.

Let's look at the following diagram to have an idea about what we will build:

Microservice	Functionalities		
Ecommerce	Search Flights	Buy Tickets	Passenger Registration
Bookings	Seat Reservation	Generate Boarding Pass	Cancel Boarding Pass
Passengers	Passengers Data Management		
Flights	Create Flights	Search Flights	
Planes	Planes Data Management		
Payments	Process Payments		
Fare	Fare Calculations		

It is a summary of what we will do in these few chapters; we have defined the basic functionalities for each microservice.

Now, we will take a look at components; let's go to the next section.

Solution diagram

The following diagram illustrates the whole solution, which we will implement in the following chapters:

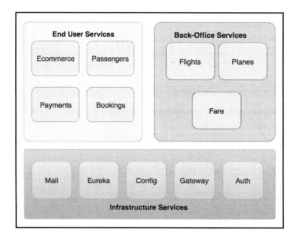

As we can see, there are different kinds of components. Some components will be exposed through the **Gateway** for end users, in our case, our customers. There is a category which the company users will use to register flights, for instance, where these microservices will be exposed on **Gateway** as well.

The infrastructure category will not be exposed over the internet, except the **Gateway** service. These services help the solution infrastructure and should be not exposed because there is sensitive data in there.

There a lot of things to do; let's get on with the show.

 DDD enables us to deal easily with microservices. Some DDD patterns fit well for the microservices architectural style. There are many interesting books in the Packt catalog.

Spring Cloud Config Server

When we adopt the microservices architectural style, there are some challenges to solve. One of the first problems to solve is how to manage the microservices configurations in the cluster, and how to make them easy and distributed, as well?

Spring Cloud Config provides a Spring way, based on annotations and Spring beans. It is an easy way to solve this problem in a production-ready module. There are three main components in this module, the Configuration Repository, that is, version control system, the Config Server, which will provide the configurations, and finally, the Configuration Client, which will consume the configuration from the Config Server.

This module supplies the configuration files over an HTTP interface. It is the main feature provided by this project and it acts as a central repository for configuration in our architecture.

We want to remove the `application.yaml` file from our classpath; we do not need this file in classpath anymore, and so we will use the Config Server to serve this file for our application.

Now, our microservices will not have the configuration file, that is, `application.yaml`. During the application bootstrap, the application will look at the Config Server to get the correct configuration, and after that, the application will finish the bootstrap to get them up and into running status.

The following diagram explains the **Config Server** and Config Client:

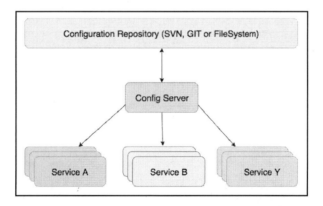

As we can see, the basic idea here is to try to distribute the configuration through the **Config Server**. There are some advantages to using this approach. The first one keeps the configuration in the central repository. It makes the configuration easy to maintain. The second one is that the configurations are served with a standard protocol, such as HTTP. Most of the developers know the protocol and make the interaction easy to understand. Finally, and most importantly, when the properties change, it can reflect immediately in other microservices.

Time to implement it. Let's go there.

 The Config Server is usually maintained on private networks, if we are deploying in cloud environments, although the Spring Cloud Config supports encrypt and decrypt based on symmetric or asymmetric keys. Keep in the mind that the microservices configurations should not be published on public networks.

Creating the Config Server project

Let's create our project with Spring Initializr. Go to Spring Initializr (`https://start.spring.io/`) and follow the image instructions:

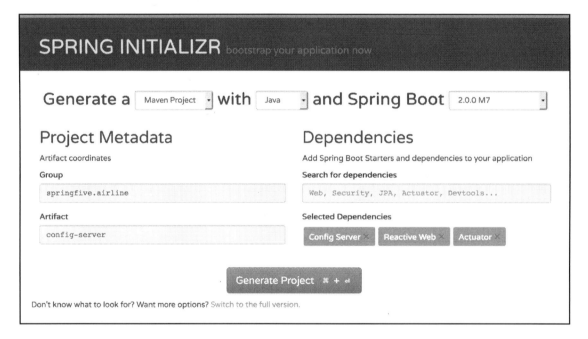

Click on **Generate Project** and then we can open the project on the IDE.

Enabling Spring Cloud Config Server

We will use the Git repository as a property source, and then we need to create a repository to keep these files. However, before that, let's navigate to the pom.xml file and see some interesting stuff. We can find the following dependency:

```
<dependency>
  <groupId>org.springframework.cloud</groupId>
  <artifactId>spring-cloud-config-server</artifactId>
</dependency>
```

It is a Config Server dependency. It enables us to use the Config Server in our application. Remember, we need to put this into the pom.xml file to achieve the required Config Server.

Using GitHub as a repository

The Spring Cloud Config Server enables us to use different datastore technologies to work as a properties repository. There are some options such as Git repository, filesystem, or SVN and others, provided by the community.

We will choose the Git repository, and use GitHub as a host.

> We will use the Git repository that has the source code of the book. The repository is located at: `https://GitHub.com/PacktPublishing/Spring-5.0-By-Example/tree/master/config-files`.
> The Spring Cloud Config Server also supports private repositories. For that purpose, we need to supply the private/public keys.

Configuring the Spring Boot application

It's a piece of cake to enable and run the Config Server and provide our configuration HTTP protocol. To achieve it, we need to put the following annotation in our Spring Boot starter class. The implementation is as follows:

```
package springfive.airline.configserver;

import org.springframework.boot.SpringApplication;
import
org.springframework.boot.autoconfigure.SpringBootApplication;
import org.springframework.cloud.config.server.EnableConfigServer;

@EnableConfigServer
@SpringBootApplication
```

```
public class ConfigServerApplication {

  public static void main(String[] args) {
    SpringApplication.run(ConfigServerApplication.class, args);
  }

}
```

Awesome. `@EnableConfigServer` does the magic for us. It will stand up the Config Server and make the application ready to connect.

Configuring the Git repository as a properties source

Our Config Server needs to be configured. For that purpose, we will use the `application.yaml` file. This file should be simple and with minimal configurations as well. The configuration file should look like this:

```
server:
  port: 5000

spring:
  cloud:
    config:
      name: configserver
      server:
        git:
          uri:
https://github.com/PacktPublishing/Spring-5.0-By-Example
          search-paths: config-files*
```

We have configured the application port, which is a common task. We named our Config Server, and the most important part is the `server.git.uri` configuration property which instructs the Spring Framework to get the configurations files.

Another configuration is `search-paths`; it allows us to search the configuration in `git` repository folders, instead of a root address in the repository.

Running the Config Server

Awesome job; our configuration server is ready to use. Then let's run it. We can use the JAR file, or through IDE as well, it is up to you to choose the desired way.

We can use the Java command line or IDE to run it. I prefer to use IDE because it enables us to debug and make some code changes.

Run it.

The output should look like this:

Tomcat started successfully; our Config Server is up and running. We can find some different endpoints in our Config Server. These endpoints are exposed to serve the configuration file.

The Spring Cloud Config Server supports profiles as well, providing different configurations for different environments is important.

The pattern supported by the Config Server is as follows:

```
<application-name>-<profile>.<properties|yaml>
```

It is really important to keep this in mind. Also, it makes it mandatory to declare the `application.name` property in our microservices, to identify the application.

We can find the endpoints provided by the Spring Cloud Config Server on the application bootstrap. Take a look at the log:

Remember the Config Server supports environments; because of this, there is a kind of regex on endpoints. Look at the `"/{name}-{profiles}.yml"` endpoint.

Testing our Config Server

We are able to test our Config Server over the REST API.

Let's create a simple `yaml` file to create the test; the file should be called `dummy.yaml`:

```
info:
  message: "Testing my Config Server"
  status: "It worked"
```

Push it to GitHub – if you are using the GitHub book, this step is unnecessary. Then, we can call the Config Server API using the following command:

```
curl http://localhost:5000/dummy/default | jq
```

The command looks for the `dummy` configuration in the profile `default`; the URL is self-explanatory. The following output should be displayed:

```
% Total    % Received % Xferd  Average Speed   Time    Time     Time  Current
                                 Dload  Upload   Total   Spent    Left  Speed
100   309    0   309    0     0    261      0 --:--:--  0:00:01 --:--:--   261
{
  "name": "dummy",
  "profiles": [
    "default"
  ],
  "label": null,
  "version": "bca0b9ad5fdd1f853744d7dc2abf92411423e2b1",
  "state": null,
  "propertySources": [
    {
      "name": "https://github.com/PacktPublishing/Spring-5.0-By-Example/config-files/dummy.yaml",
      "source": {
        "info.message": "Testing my Config Server",
        "info.status": "It worked"
      }
    }
  ]
}
```

Our Config Server is fully operational. Now, we will configure our service discovery using Netflix Eureka.

Spring Cloud service discovery

The service discovery is one of the key points of the microservices architecture. The basis of the microservices architecture is to decouple the monolithic application into smaller pieces of software which have well-defined boundaries.

This impacts our system design in the monolithic application. In general, the application logic stays in a single place with regards to the code. It means the procedure or methods calls are invoked in the same context when the application is running.

When we adopt the microservices architectural style, these invocations are typically external, in other words, they will invoke the service through HTTP calls, for example, in another application context or web server.

Then, the services need to call other services through HTTP, for instance, but how do the services call the others if the instances of these services change with a considerable frequency? Remember, we are creating distributed and scalable systems, where the instances of services can be increased according to the system usage.

The services need to know where the other services are running to be able to call them. Let's imagine that we are considering putting the services IPs in the configuration; it will be hard to manage and impossible to track the machine changes during that time.

The service discovery pattern addresses this challenge. In general, the solution involves a Service Registry, which knows the locations of all the running services. The client then needs to have a kind of Service Registry Client to be able to query this Service Registry to obtain the valid address for the desired service; the Service Registry will then return a healthy address, and finally, the client can invoke the desired service.

Let's look at the following diagram:

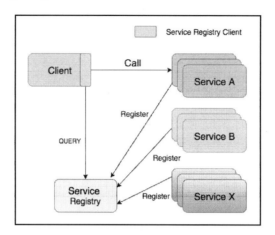

 The full documentation of this pattern can be found at `http://microservices.io/patterns/client-side-discovery.html` and `https://www.nginx.com/blog/service-discovery-in-a-microservices-architecture/`. There are so many implementations for that pattern.

The Spring Cloud service discovery supports some service discovery implementations, such as Hashicorp Consul provided by the Spring Cloud Consul, and Apache Zookeeper provided by the Spring Cloud Zookeeper.

We are using the Netflix OSS stack where we will use the Eureka server, which was provided by the Spring Netflix OSS. It enables us to use the Eureka server as a managed Spring bean.

The Spring Eureka Client provides a client aware of the Service Registry, and it can be done with a couple of annotations and some configurations – we will do that soon.

We will start to create and configure the Eureka server in the following sections. Let's do that.

 The full documentation for the Spring Cloud Consul can be found at: `https://cloud.spring.io/spring-cloud-consul`, and the Spring Cloud Zookeeper can be found at: `https://cloud.spring.io/spring-cloud-zookeeper`.

Creating Spring Cloud Eureka

To enable service discovery in our infrastructure, we need to create an instance of a service which will act as a service discovery. The Spring Cloud Eureka server enables us to achieve this task. Let's create our project. Go to Spring Initializr and fill in the information, as shown in the following screenshot:

Take a look at the required dependencies. The Eureka server is the dependency which allows us to spin up a service discovery server.

Let's open the project on IDE and start to configure it. We will do this in the following section.

Creating the Eureka server main class

Before we start the configuration, we will create the `main` class. This class will start the Spring Boot application. The Eureka server is embedded in the application. It is a pretty standard Spring Boot application with a single annotation.

The `main` application class should look like this:

```
package springfive.airline.eureka;

import org.springframework.boot.SpringApplication;
import
org.springframework.boot.autoconfigure.SpringBootApplication;
import
org.springframework.cloud.netflix.eureka.server.EnableEurekaServer;

@EnableEurekaServer
@SpringBootApplication
public class EurekaApplication {

  public static void main(String[] args) {
    SpringApplication.run(EurekaApplication.class, args);
  }


}
```

The `@EnableEurekaServer` annotation will start the embedded Eureka server in our application and make it ready to use. It will enable the service registry in our application as well.

Configuring the Spring Cloud Eureka server

Our Eureka server needs to be configured using the Spring Cloud Server configured in the previous sections. Then, we need to keep the `application.yaml` off our project, to use the Config Server properly. Instead of the `application.yaml`, we need to put the `bootstrap.yaml` and put the Config Server address on it.

Then, we need to:

- Create `discovery.yaml` on GitHub
- Create `bootstrap.yaml` file in the classpath project

Let's start with the `discovery.yaml` file. The file should look like this:

```
server:
  port: 8761

eureka:
  instance:
    hostname: localhost
```

```
        health-check-url-path: /actuator/health
        status-page-url-path: /actuator/info
    client:
      registerWithEureka: false
      fetchRegistry: false
logging:
  level:
    com.netflix.discovery: 'ON'
    org.springframework.cloud: 'DEBUG'
```

There are some interesting things to explore. We are using the localhost as `hostname` because we are running on the developer machine. There are a couple of configurations about the URLs health check and status page – pay attention to the configurations that are related to the server. They are placed below the `eureka.instance` YAML node. The configurations are `health-check-url-path` and `status-page-url-path`. We can use the default values as well, but the new Spring Boot Actuator changes the URL for those two features, so we need to configure them properly.

The `eureka.client` YAML node is about the client configuration; in our case, we set `registerWithEureka` to false. We do not want the Eureka server to act as a client as well. The same is true for the `fetchRegistry` configuration, it is a client configuration and it will cache the Eureka registry's information.

The `logging` node is about logging configuration.

Awesome – our `gateway.yaml` is ready.

Let's create our `bootstrap.yaml` file in the Eureka server project classpath. The file should look like this:

```
spring:
  application:
    name: discovery
  cloud:
    config:
      uri: http://localhost:5000
      label: master
```

Easy peasy – we have configured `spring.cloud.config`. It instructs Spring of the Config Server address. Also, we have configured the `label`, which is the branch when we are using the **version control system** (**VCS**) as a repository.

Well done. The configuration is ready. Time to run it. Let's do it in the following section.

Running the Spring Cloud Eureka server

The Eureka server is ready to use. We will start the Spring Boot application and put our Eureka server online. We can use the Java command line or IDE to run it. I prefer to use IDE because it enables us to debug and make some code changes.

> The Config Server needs to be running because the discovery will find the configuration file to bootstrap the server properly.

Run it!

We should see the following lines in the application bootstrap logs:

```
2018-01-07 14:42:42.602 INFO 11191 --- [           main] o.s.c.support.DefaultLifecycleProcessor : Starting beans in phase 0
2018-01-07 14:43:42.602 INFO 11191 --- [           main] o.s.c.n.e.s.EurekaServiceRegistry      : Registering application discovery with eureka with status UP
2018-01-07 14:42:42.605 DEBUG 11191 --- [           main] s.c.c.d.h.DiscoveryClientHealthIndicator : Discovery Client has been initialized
2018-01-07 14:42:42.608 INFO 11191 --- [   Thread-32] o.s.c.n.e.server.EurekaServerBootstrap  : Setting the eureka configuration..
2018-01-07 14:42:42.610 INFO 11191 --- [   Thread-32] o.s.c.n.e.server.EurekaServerBootstrap  : Eureka data center value eureka.datacenter is not set, defaulting to default
2018-01-07 14:42:42.611 INFO 11191 --- [   Thread-32] o.s.c.n.e.server.EurekaServerBootstrap  : Eureka environment value eureka.environment is not set, defaulting to test
2018-01-07 14:42:42.620 INFO 11191 --- [   Thread-32] o.s.c.n.e.server.EurekaServerBootstrap  : isAws returned false
2018-01-07 14:42:42.622 INFO 11191 --- [   Thread-32] o.s.c.n.e.server.EurekaServerBootstrap  : Initialized server context
2018-01-07 14:42:42.622 INFO 11191 --- [   Thread-32] c.n.e.r.PeerAwareInstanceRegistryImpl   : Got 1 instances from neighboring DS node
2018-01-07 14:42:42.623 INFO 11191 --- [   Thread-32] c.n.e.r.PeerAwareInstanceRegistryImpl   : Renew threshold is: 1
2018-01-07 14:42:42.623 INFO 11191 --- [   Thread-32] c.n.e.r.PeerAwareInstanceRegistryImpl   : Changing status to UP
2018-01-07 14:42:42.636 INFO 11191 --- [   Thread-32] e.s.EurekaServerInitializerConfiguration : Started Eureka Server
2018-01-07 14:42:42.696 INFO 11191 --- [           main] o.s.b.w.embedded.tomcat.TomcatWebServer : Tomcat started on port(s): 8761 (http) with context path ''
2018-01-07 14:42:42.697 INFO 11191 --- [           main] .s.c.n.e.s.EurekaAutoServiceRegistration : Updating port to 8761
2018-01-07 14:42:42.702 INFO 11191 --- [           main] s.airline.eureka.EurekaApplication      : Started EurekaApplication in 10.862 seconds (JVM running for 11.719)
2018-01-07 14:42:43.067 INFO 11191 --- [on(8)-127.0.0.1] c.c.c.ConfigServicePropertySourceLocator : Fetching config from server at: http://localhost:5000
```

Awesome. Look at the following line of the log:

```
2018-01-07 14:42:42.636  INFO 11191 --- [     Thread-32]
e.s.EurekaServerInitializerConfiguration : Started Eureka Server
```

It means our Eureka server is ready to use. To check the solution, we can go to the Eureka server home page. Go to `http://localhost:8761/` and the following page will be displayed:

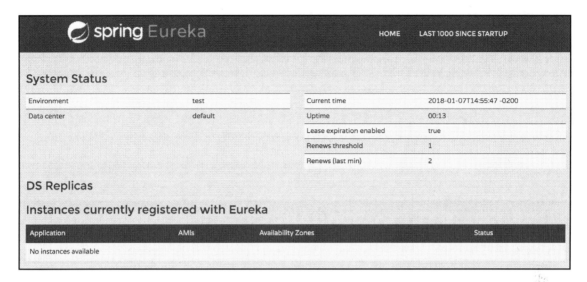

As we can see, there is no instance of service available yet. We can find some relevant information such as the server **Uptime**, the current **Data center**, and the **Current time**. There is some information in the **General Info** section, information regarding the server where the Eureka server is running.

Good job. Our service discovery service is running. We will use this infrastructure soon.

Spring Cloud Zipkin server and Sleuth

Our solution involves some microservices; it makes our solution easy to deploy and easy to write code. Each solution has a particular repository and codebase.

In the monolith solution, the whole problem is solved in the same artifact to be deployed. Usually, in Java, these artifacts are `.jar`, `.war`, or `.ear`, if the application was written in the Java EE 5/6 specifications.

The logging strategies for these kinds of applications is quite easy to work with (hence problems can be solved easily) because everything happens in the same context; the requests are received from the same application server or web server, which have the business components. Now, if we go to the logs, we will probably find the log entries we want. It makes the trace application easier to find errors and debug.

In the microservices solution, the application behaviors are split in the distributed systems; it increases the trace tasks substantially because the request probably arrives in the API Gateway and comes into microservices. They log the information in different sources. In this scenario, we need a kind of log aggregator and a way to identify the whole transaction between services.

For this purpose, the Spring Cloud Sleuth and Spring Cloud Zipkin can help us and make the trace features more comfortable for developers.

In this section, we will look at and understand how it works under the hood.

Infrastructure for the Zipkin server

Before we start to work, we need to configure a service which the Zipkin server needs. By default, the Zipkin server uses in-memory databases, but it is not recommended for production; usually, developers use this feature to demonstrate Zipkin features.

We will use MySQL as a data store. The Zipkin server also supports different sources, such as Cassandra and Elasticsearch.

Spring Cloud Sleuth supports synchronous and asynchronous operations. The synchronous operations are over the HTTP protocol and asynchronous can be done by RabbitMQ or Apache Kafka.

To use the HTTP, that is, REST API, we should use `@EnableZipkinServer`, it will delegate the persistence for REST tier through the `SpanStore` interface.

We will choose the asynchronous solution, since it fits well for our project, and we do not want the trace collector to cause some performance issues. The asynchronous solution uses the Spring Cloud Stream binder to store the `Spans`. We choose the RabbitMQ message broker to do that. It can be achieved using the `@EnableZipkinStreamServer` annotations which configure Spring Sleuth to use streams for store `Spans`.

Let's create our `docker-compose-min.yaml` to bootstrap our RabbitMQ and MySQL containers. The file should look like this:

```
version: '3'
services:

  rabbitmq:
    hostname: rabbitmq
    image: rabbitmq:3.7.0-management-alpine
    ports:
```

```
      - "5672:5672"
      - "15672:15672"
    networks:
      - airline

  mysql:
    hostname: mysql
    image: mysql:5.7.21
    ports:
      - "3306:3306"
    environment:
      - MYSQL_ROOT_PASSWORD=root
      - MYSQL_DATABASE=zipkin
    networks:
      - airline

  mongo:
    hostname: mongo
    image: mongo
    ports:
      - "27017:27017"
    networks:
      - airline

  redis:
    hostname: redis
    image: redis:3.2-alpine
    ports:
      - "6379:6379"
    networks:
      - airline

networks:
  airline:
    driver: bridge
```

The `docker-compose-min.yaml` file can be found at `GitHub`, there is a MongoDB and Redis – they will be used in the next chapter.

There is nothing special here. We have declared two containers—RabbitMQ and MySQL—and exposed the ports on the host machine. Also, we have created the `airline` network; we will use this network to attach our infrastructure microservices.

Now, we can create our Zipkin server, which we will do in the next section.

Creating the Spring Cloud Zipkin server

We will create our Zipkin panel structure in Spring Initializr, and then we need to follow
the instructions:

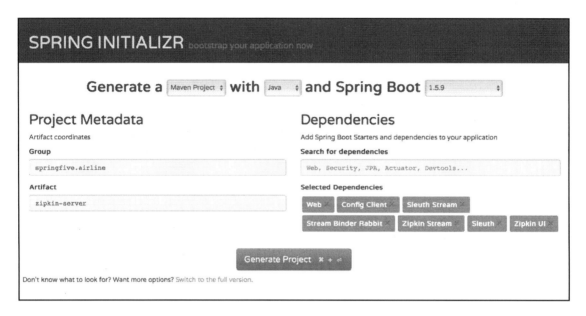

Awesome – take a look at the **Selected Dependencies** section, all of them are required. Pay
attention to the Spring Boot version. We choose 1.5.9, because there is no support for
Zipkin server in Spring Boot 2. It is not a problem because we do not need specific features
from Spring Boot 2.

Click on the **Generate Project** button and wait for the download to finish. Afterwards, open
the project in IDE.

In order to enable service discovery and store Spans on a database, we need to put the
following dependencies in our pom.xml:

```
<dependency>
 <groupId>org.springframework.cloud</groupId>
 <artifactId>spring-cloud-starter-netflix-eureka-
client</artifactId>
</dependency>

<dependency>
 <groupId>org.springframework.boot</groupId>
 <artifactId>spring-boot-starter-jdbc</artifactId>
```

```
</dependency>

<dependency>
 <groupId>mysql</groupId>
 <artifactId>mysql-connector-java</artifactId>
 <version>6.0.6</version>
</dependency>
```

The first dependency is for the service discovery client and the others are to JDBC connections to MySQL. It makes our project dependencies fully configured.

Let's create our `main` class to start our Zipkin server. The class is pretty standard but with some new annotations:

```
package springfive.airline;

import org.springframework.boot.SpringApplication;
import
org.springframework.boot.autoconfigure.SpringBootApplication;
import org.springframework.cloud.netflix.eureka.EnableEurekaClient;
import
org.springframework.cloud.sleuth.zipkin.stream.EnableZipkinStreamSe
rver;

@SpringBootApplication
@EnableZipkinStreamServer
@EnableEurekaClient
public class ZipkinServerApplication {

 public static void main(String[] args) {
  SpringApplication.run(ZipkinServerApplication.class, args);
 }

}
```

The `@EnableEurekaClient` annotation enables the application to connect to the Eureka server. The new annotation, `@EnableZipkinStreamServer`, instructs the framework to connect with the configured broker to receive the `Spans`. Remember, it can be done using the Spring Cloud Stream Binder.

Configuring boostrap.yaml and application.yaml

In the section, we created our `main` class. Before we run it, we should create our two configuration files. The `bootstrap.yaml` inside the `src/main/resources` directory and the `application.yaml` on our GitHub repository. They will be downloaded via Config Server and provided by the Zipkin server project.

Let's start with `bootstrap.yaml`:

```yaml
spring:
  application:
    name: zipkin
  cloud:
    config:
      uri: http://localhost:5000
      label: master
```

Nothing special, we have configured our Config Server address.

Let's jump to our `application.yaml`:

```yaml
server:
  port: 9999

spring:
  rabbitmq:
    port: 5672
    host: localhost
  datasource:
    schema: classpath:/mysql.sql
    url:
jdbc:mysql://${MYSQL_HOST:localhost}/zipkin?autoReconnect=true
    driver-class-name: com.mysql.cj.jdbc.Driver
    username: root
    password: root
    initialize: true
    continue-on-error: true
  sleuth:
    enabled: false

zipkin:
  storage:
    type: mysql

logging:
  level:
    ROOT: INFO
```

```
eureka:
  client:
    serviceUrl:
      defaultZone: http://localhost:8761/eureka/
```

There are some interesting things here. In the `spring.rabbitmq` node, we have configured our RabbitMQ broker connection. It will be used to receive `Spans`. In the `spring.datasource`, we have configured the MySQL connection. The Zipkin server will use it to store data. Also, we have configured how to execute the DDL script to create the `zipkin` database.

The `spring.sleuth` node was configured to not produce any `Span` because it is a server, not a client application, and we will not perform a trace on the Zipkin server.

The `zipkin` node had been used to configure the Zipkin server storage type, MySQL, in our case.

Let's run it!!!

Running the Zipkin server

We have configured the Zipkin server properly, so now we will be able to run it properly.

We can run the main class `ZipkinServerApplication`. We can use the IDE or Java command line, after running the following output:

```
2018-01-16 14:37:47.396  INFO [zipkin,,,] 3715 --- [main] o.s.i.endpoint.EventDrivenConsumer        : Adding {message-handler:inbound.sleuth.sleuth} as a subscriber to the 'bridge.sleuth
2018-01-16 14:37:47.396  INFO [zipkin,,,] 3715 --- [main] o.s.i.endpoint.EventDrivenConsumer        : started inbound.sleuth.sleuth
2018-01-16 14:37:47.397  INFO [zipkin,,,] 3715 --- [main] o.s.c.support.DefaultLifecycleProcessor   : Starting beans in phase 2147483647
2018-01-16 14:37:47.474  INFO [zipkin,,,] 3715 --- [main] s.b.c.e.t.TomcatEmbeddedServletContainer  : Tomcat started on port(s): 9999 (http)
2018-01-16 14:37:47.475  INFO [zipkin,,,] 3715 --- [main] .s.c.n.e.s.EurekaAutoServiceRegistration  : Updating port to 9999
2018-01-16 14:37:47.479  INFO [zipkin,,,] 3715 --- [main] s.airline.ZipkinServerApplication         : Started ZipkinServerApplication in 13.782 seconds (JVM running for 14.068)
```

Good job – the Zipkin server is running now. We can take a look at the index page to see what it looks like.

Go to Zipkin page; the page should look like the following screenshot:

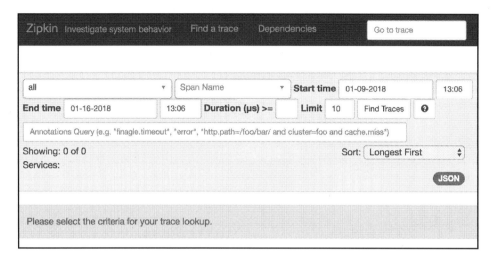

Also, we can check the RabbitMQ panel to find the queue created by the Zipkin server. Go to the RabbitMQ Queues (`http://localhost:15672/#/queues`) section, the page should look like this:

Looking at the queues, the project has created the `sleuth.sleuth` queue, well done.

The Zipkin server is ready. For now, we will not have any `Span`, because there is no application sending data to Zipkin. We will do that in the next chapter.

Spring Cloud Gateway

The API Gateway pattern helps us to expose our microservices through a single known entrypoint. Usually, it acts as an entrypoint to external access and redirects the call to internal microservices.

There are many benefits when we adopt the API Gateway in our application. The first one can be recognized easily, it makes the API consumption easy for the clients, which means the clients do not need to know the different microservices endpoints.

Other benefits are a consequence of the first one. When we have a unique entrypoint, we can address some cross-application concerns such as filtering, authentication, throttling, and rate limit, as well.

It is an essential part when we adopt the microservices architecture.

The Spring Cloud Gateway enables us to have these features in a Spring-managed bean, in a Spring way using Dependency Injection and other features provided by the Spring Framework.

The project was built on the Spring Framework 5, which uses the Project Reactor as a basis. There are some interesting features provided, such as Hystrix Circuit Breaker integration and with the Spring Cloud Discovery client, as well.

Look at the diagram to understand the benefits of the API Gateway:

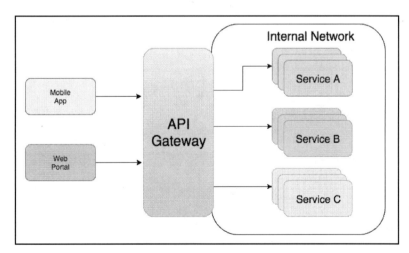

The full documentation of the API Gateway Pattern can be found at: http://microservices.io/patterns/apigateway.html.

Creating the Spring Cloud Gateway project

We will use the Spring Initializr to create our Spring Cloud Gateway project; we will need to add some dependencies manually. Let's go to the **Spring Initializr** page and create our project:

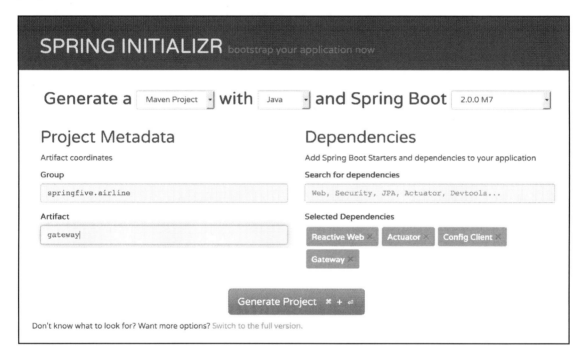

There is a brand new dependency Gateway, it enables us to work with Spring Cloud Gateway. Then click on **Generate Project** and wait for the download to complete.

After that, we need to add a missing dependency. The missing dependency is required by the Gateway to interact with the Eureka server; the name of the dependency is `spring-cloud-starter-netflix-eureka-client`. Then, let's add the dependency on our `pom.xml`, we will need to add the following snippet:

```
<dependency>
 <groupId>org.springframework.cloud</groupId>
 <artifactId>spring-cloud-starter-netflix-eureka-client</artifactId>
</dependency>
```

Excellent, our project is configured correctly to work with the Eureka server. In the following section, we will configure the project to work with the Config Server as well.

Creating the Spring Cloud Gateway main class

There is no secret to this part. The Spring Cloud Gateway works in the same way as the common Spring Boot applications. There is a `main` class which will start the embedded server and starts the whole application.

Our `main` class should look like this:

```
package springfive.airline.gateway;

import org.springframework.boot.SpringApplication;
import org.springframework.boot.autoconfigure.SpringBootApplication;
import org.springframework.cloud.netflix.eureka.EnableEurekaClient;

@EnableEurekaClient
@SpringBootApplication
public class GatewayApplication {

 public static void main(String[] args) {
  SpringApplication.run(GatewayApplication.class, args);
 }

}
```

As we can see, it is a pretty standard Spring Boot application, configured with `@EnableEurekaClient` to work with the Eureka server as a service discovery implementation.

Configuring the Spring Cloud Gateway project

The primary project structure is ready. We will create the project configurations in this section. To achieve this, we need to carry out the following steps:

- Add a `gateway.yaml` file to GitHub
- Create the `bootstrap.yaml` in the Gateway project

We are using the Spring Cloud Config Server, so it is necessary to create the new file in GitHub because the Config Server will try to find the file on the repository. In our case, we are using GitHub as a repository.

The second task is necessary because the `bootstrap.yaml` file is processed before the application is fully ready to run. Then, during this phase, the application needs to look up the configuration file and to achieve this, the application needs to know the `repository`, in our case, the Config Server. Remember the address of the Config Server always needs to be placed on the `bootstrap.yaml`.

Let's create our `gateway.yaml` file – the file should look like this:

```
server:
  port: 8888
eureka:
  client:
    serviceUrl:
      defaultZone: http://localhost:8761/eureka/
logging:
  level: debug
```

The `eureka.client` node in the YAML file is responsible for configuring the Eureka Client configurations. We need to configure our Eureka server address instance. It should be pointed to the correct address.

 There are more options for the Eureka Configuration Client properties. The full documentation can be found in `https://github.com/Netflix/eureka/wiki/Configuring-Eureka`; the Netflix team maintains Eureka.

Then, we need to create our `bootstrap.yaml` file on the Gateway project. This file will instruct the Spring Framework to look up the configuration file on the Config Server and then download the required file to finish the application bootstrap. Our file should look like this:

```
spring:
  application:
      name: gateway
  cloud:
    config:
      uri: http://localhost:5000
      label: master
```

Pretty simple. The `application.name` is required to instruct the framework to look up the correct file. Usually, there are many configuration files for different applications and environments as well.

On the `cloud.config` node, we need to put in the Spring Cloud Config Server address, which we configured in the previous sections.

The project final structure should look like this:

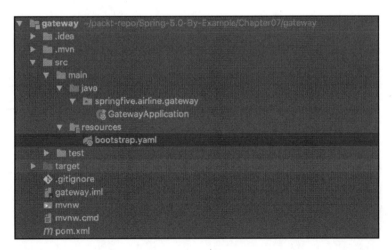

Look at the screenshot. There is no `application.yaml` in the classpath. This gives us several advantages; there is no configuration file in classpath projects, which helps us a great deal in managing the microservices configurations.

In the next section, we will run it and explain the whole application bootstrap process. Let's do it.

Running the Spring Cloud Gateway

The project is well-configured, so now it is time to run it. We can use the Java command line or IDE. There is no difference either way.

The Config Server and Eureka server need to stay up; it is mandatory that the Gateway project works correctly. Then, we can run the project.

Run the project and look at the logs. We can see some interesting stuff, such as the project connecting to the Config Server and download the configuration and after this, it connects to the Eureka server and self-registers. The following diagram explains the application bootstrap flow:

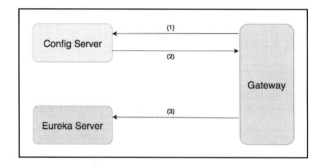

Let's look at what the different flows are and understand them:

1. The Gateway application requests the configuration file
2. The Config Server serves the config file
3. The Gateway application registers to the Eureka server

Awesome, our Gateway application is connected to our infrastructure services.

Checking the Eureka server

Our Gateway is running. Now, we can check the Eureka server page to confirm this information.

Go to `http://localhost:8761/`, and check the **Instances currently registered with Eureka** section. We should see the Gateway application, as shown in the following screenshot:

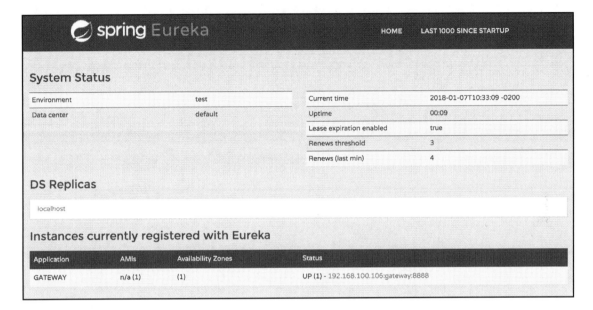

Excellent. It worked well. The Gateway application is successfully registered, and it can be looked up via the service discovery. Our Gateway will connect to the Eureka server to get the service available and distribute the requested calls to the correct services.

Well done. Now, we can create our routes in the Gateway. We will do this in the next chapter when we create our airline microservices.

Creating our first route with Spring Cloud Gateway

Our Gateway is running. Before we start the real routes for our Airline application, let's try to use some fake routes to test the Spring Cloud Gateway behaviors. We will use the `https://httpbin.org/` site, which helps us to test some routes.

Let's create a class with the `@Configuration` annotation to provide the routes for the Spring Container. Let's create a package called `springfive.airline.gateway.infra.route`, then create the following class:

```
package springfive.airline.gateway.infra.route;


import java.util.function.Function;
import org.springframework.cloud.gateway.route.RouteLocator;
import org.springframework.cloud.gateway.route.builder.PredicateSpec;
import org.springframework.cloud.gateway.route.builder.RouteLocatorBuilder;
import
org.springframework.cloud.gateway.route.builder.RouteLocatorBuilder.Builder
;
import org.springframework.context.annotation.Bean;
import org.springframework.context.annotation.Configuration;

@Configuration
public class SampleRoute {

  private Function<PredicateSpec, Builder> addCustomHeader = predicateSpec
-> predicateSpec
      .path("/headers")
      .addRequestHeader("Book", "Spring 5.0 By Example")
      .uri("http://httpbin.org:80");

  @Bean
  public RouteLocator sample(RouteLocatorBuilder builder) {
    return builder.routes()
        .route("custom-request-header", addCustomHeader)
        .route("add-query-param", r ->
r.path("/get").addRequestParameter("book", "spring5.0")
            .uri("http://httpbin.org:80"))
        .route("response-headers", (r) -> r.path("/response-headers")
            .addResponseHeader("book","spring5.0")
            .uri("http://httpbin.org:80"))
        .route("combine-and-change", (r) ->
r.path("/anything").and().header("access-key","AAA")
            .addResponseHeader("access-key","BBB")
            .uri("http://httpbin.org:80"))
        .build();
  }

}
```

There are some different types to configure routes; the first one we extracted is the function to a private attribute called `addCustomHeader`, which will be used in the `custom-request-header` route. We will use **curl** to test some routes created previously.

The first one we will test is the `custom-request-header`, the route was configured to route to: `http://httpbin.org:80` and the path will be `/headers`. This service will return the Request Headers sent to the server. Take a look at `addCustomHeader`, we have configured it to add a custom header to the Request. It will be **Book** as the key and **Spring 5.0 By Example,** as the value. Let's call the gateway URL, using curl:

```
curl http://localhost:8888/headers
```

The output should look like this:

```
{
  "headers": {
    "Accept": "*/*",
    "Book": "Spring 5.0 By Example",
    "Connection": "close",
    "Host": "httpbin.org",
    "User-Agent": "curl/7.54.0"
  }
}
```

Let's analyze the output. The first thing to look at is we have called the localhost address. The `Host` key in the Request shows `httpbin.org`, it means the Spring Cloud Gateway has changed the address. Awesome, but we expected it. The second one is where we have added the `Book` key, and bingo, there it is in the Request Headers. The Gateway worked as expected, and with a few lines of code, we did some interesting stuff.

Let's do one more test. We will test the `combine-and-change`, this route is configured to answer the `/anything` with the Request `Header access-key: AAA`, so the command line should be:

```
curl -v -H "access-key: AAA" http://localhost:8888/anything
```

As we can see, the -v argument makes the call in verbose mode, it is useful for debugging purposes and the -H indicates the Request Headers. Let's look at the output:

```
*   Trying ::1...
* TCP_NODELAY set
* Connected to localhost (::1) port 8888 (#0)
> GET /anything HTTP/1.1
> Host: localhost:8888
> User-Agent: curl/7.54.0
> Accept: */*
> access-key: AAA
>
< HTTP/1.1 200 OK
< access-key: BBB
< Connection: keep-alive
< Server: meinheld/0.6.1
< Date: Wed, 10 Jan 2018 00:49:29 GMT
< Content-Type: application/json
< Access-Control-Allow-Origin: *
< Access-Control-Allow-Credentials: true
< X-Powered-By: Flask
< X-Processed-Time: 0.00110197067261
< Content-Length: 329
< Via: 1.1 vegur
<
{
  "args": {},
  "data": "",
  "files": {},
  "form": {},
  "headers": {
    "Accept": "*/*",
    "Access-Key": "AAA",
    "Connection": "close",
    "Host": "httpbin.org",
    "User-Agent": "curl/7.54.0"
  },
```

Awesome. If you look at the access-key value, the Gateway changed to a requested value BBB. Good job guys. There are some endpoints to test, feel free to test as you want.

You can find the httpbin documentation at: https://httpbin.org/. There are some interesting other methods to test HTTP.

Putting the infrastructure on Docker

Our infrastructure is ready and it enables us to develop the application. We can create a Docker compose file to spin up the infrastructure services; during the development life cycle, components such as Eureka, Config Server, Trace Server, and API Gateway do not suffer changes because they interact as an infrastructure.

Then, it enables us to create component images and use them in the `docker-compose.yaml` file. Let's list our components:

- Config Server
- Eureka
- Zipkin
- RabbitMQ
- Redis

We know how to create Docker images using the Fabric8 Maven plugin, we have done this several times in the previous chapters – let's do it.

Let's configure one as an example, keep in mind we need do the same configuration for all projects, Eureka, Gateway, Config Server, and Gateway. The following snippet configures the `docker-maven-plugin` to generate a Docker image:

```
<plugin>
  <groupId>io.fabric8</groupId>
  <artifactId>docker-maven-plugin</artifactId>
  <version>0.21.0</version>
  <configuration>
    <images>
      <image>
        <name>springfivebyexample/${project.build.finalName}</name>
        <build>
          <from>openjdk:latest</from>
          <entryPoint>java -Dspring.profiles.active=docker -jar
/application/${project.build.finalName}.jar</entryPoint>
          <assembly>
            <basedir>/application</basedir>
            <descriptorRef>artifact</descriptorRef>
            <inline>
              <id>assembly</id>
              <files>
                <file>
                  <source>target/${project.build.finalName}.jar</source>
                </file>
```

```
        </files>
      </inline>
    </assembly>
    <tags>
      <tag>latest</tag>
    </tags>
    <ports>
      <port>8761</port>
    </ports>
  </build>
  <run>
    <namingStrategy>alias</namingStrategy>
  </run>
  <alias>${project.build.finalName}</alias>
      </image>
    </images>
  </configuration>
</plugin>
```

It is a pretty simple configuration. A simple Maven plugin with a couple of configurations. Then, after the plugin configuration, we are able to generate the Docker image. The command to generate Docker images is:

```
mvn clean install docker:build
```

It will generate a Docker image for us.

The projects configured can be found on GitHub; there are so many configurations to do as in the previous chapters. We need to configure the `docker-maven-plugin` and generate the Docker images.

 Fully configured projects can be found in the chapter seven folder. The GitHub repository is: `https://github.com/PacktPublishing/Spring-5.0-By-Example/tree/master/Chapter07`.

After the images have been created, we are able to create a Docker compose file defining the whole thing. The `docker-compose-infra-full.yaml` file should look like this:

```
version: '3'
services:

  config:
    hostname: config
    image: springfivebyexample/config
    ports:
```

```
        - "5000:5000"
      networks:
        - airline
  rabbitmq:
    hostname: rabbitmq
    image: rabbitmq:3.7.0-management-alpine
    ports:
      - "5672:5672"
      - "15672:15672"
    networks:
      - airline
  mysql:
    hostname: mysql
    image: mysql:5.7.21
    ports:
      - "3306:3306"
    environment:
      - MYSQL_ROOT_PASSWORD=root
      - MYSQL_DATABASE=zipkin
    networks:
      - airline
  redis:
    hostname: redis
    image: redis:3.2-alpine
    ports:
      - "6379:6379"
    networks:
      - airline

  zipkin:
    hostname: zipkin
    image: springfivebyexample/zipkin
    ports:
      - "9999:9999"
    networks:
      - airline
networks:
  airline:
    driver: bridge
```

There are some interesting things to pay attention to here. It is very important that all container instances are attached to the same Docker network called `airline`. Pay attention to the ports exposed by the containers, it is important to enable service discovery features in Docker.

Then, we can execute the instruction to spin up the whole infrastructure; it can be done using the following command:

```
docker-compose -f docker-compose-infra-full.yaml up -d
```

The following output should appear:

```
Creating network "docker_airline" with driver "bridge"
Creating docker_zipkin_1      ... done
Creating docker_rabbitmq_1    ... done
Creating docker_mysql_1       ... done
Creating docker_config_1      ... done
Creating docker_gateway_1     ... done
Creating docker_discovery_1 ... done
```

Also, we can execute the following instruction to check the container's execution:

```
docker-compose -f docker-compose-infra-full.yaml ps
```

It will list the running containers, as shown in the following screenshot:

```
       Name                Command            State                                  Ports
--------------------------------------------------------------------------------------------------------------------------------
docker_config_1      /bin/sh -c java -Dspring.p ...   Up      0.0.0.0:5000->5000/tcp
docker_discovery_1   /bin/sh -c java -Dspring.p ...   Up      0.0.0.0:8761->8761/tcp
docker_mysql_1       docker-entrypoint.sh mysqld      Up      0.0.0.0:3306->3306/tcp
docker_rabbitmq_1    docker-entrypoint.sh rabbi ...   Up      15671/tcp, 0.0.0.0:15672->15672/tcp, 25672/tcp, 4369/tcp, 5671/tcp, 0.0.0.0:5672->5672/tcp
docker_redis_1       docker-entrypoint.sh redis ...   Up      0.0.0.0:6379->6379/tcp
docker_zipkin_1      /bin/sh -c java -Dspring.p ...   Up      0.0.0.0:9999->9999/tcp
```

All applications are up and running. Well done.

To remove the containers, we can use:

```
docker-compose -f docker-compose-infra-full.yaml down
```

It will remove the containers from the stack.

Excellent job, our infrastructure is fully operational in Docker containers. It is a base for starting to create our microservices.

Summary

In this chapter, we have built the essential infrastructures services adopting the microservices architectural style.

We have learned how Spring Framework eliminates the infrastructure code from our microservices and enables us to create these services, using a couple of annotations.

We understand how it works under the hood; it is extremely important to debug and troubleshoot when the application gets some errors in the production stage.

Now, we are ready to create scalable, fault tolerant, and responsive systems. We have built the foundations of our system.

In the next chapter, we will start to build our Airline Ticket System, understand how to connect the new microservices with the whole infrastructure, and enable service discovery and other amazing features.

See you there.

8

Circuit Breakers and Security

In the previous chapter, we configured the microservices that will act in our infrastructure, and we created a Eureka server to work as a service discovery for our solution. Also, we have created a Config Server application that will serve as the configurations for our microservices.

In this chapter, we will create microservices to interact with our previous infrastructure. We will discover how to apply service discovery features for our business microservices and understand how the Circuit Breaker pattern can help us to bring resilience to our applications.

During the chapter, we will understand how the microservices can communicate with other services through the HTTP asynchronous call powered by the Spring WebFlux client.

By the end of this chapter, we will have learned how to:

- Connect microservices with service discovery
- Pull the configuration from the configuration server
- Understand how Hystrix brings resilience to microservices
- Show the Edge API strategy
- Present the Spring Boot Admin

Understanding the service discovery power

We will create our first microservice with business requirements. We will create a `planes` microservice, which will maintain data about company planes, such as characteristics, model, and some other attributes.

The `planes` microservice will be used to serve plane characteristics for our second microservice, the `flights` microservice. It needs to get some plane information to be able to create a flight, such as the number of seats.

The `planes` microservice is an excellent candidate to start with because there is no business-related dependency to be created.

Our `planes` microservice will be useful soon. Time to create it. Let's go.

Creating the planes microservice

As we have been doing in the previous chapters, we will use the Spring Initializr for that purpose. The following dependencies should be selected, as shown in the following screenshot:

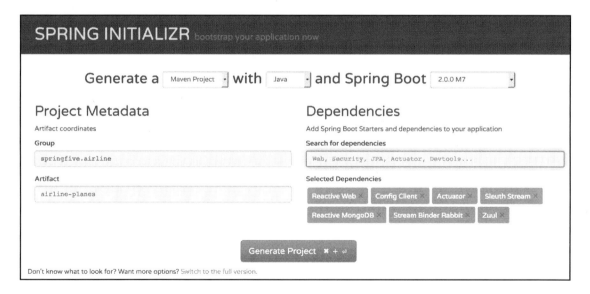

There are some necessary dependencies. The **Stream Binder Rabbit** and **Sleuth Stream** dependencies are necessary to enable us to the send data spans, and to enable application trace, across to the RabbitMQ message broker. We will use MongoDB to act as a database for this specific application, so we need **Reactive MongoDB** for that. **Config Client** is mandatory for all microservices present in the solution. We will not have any application configuration on the classpath. The **Actuator** provides production-ready metrics and information about the running application; it's an essential characteristic of the microservice's architectural style. Moreover, **Zuul** will be essential to enable us to connect the application with our Edge API. We will learn more about it during the course of the chapter.

We can now press the **Generate Project** button to download the project. Open the project on the IDE.

The `planes` microservice will be created using the Spring Boot 2 framework because we are interested in implementing the reactive foundation for our plane service.

Also, we need to include one more dependency, and it can be done using the following snippet on our `pom.xml`:

```
<dependency>
  <groupId>org.springframework.cloud</groupId>
  <artifactId>spring-cloud-starter-netflix-eureka-client</artifactId>
</dependency>
```

The `spring-cloud-starter-netflix-eureka-client` enables the service discovery, powered by the Eureka server in our application.

Coding the planes microservice

We will add some features on the application. For this specific application, we will create CRUD functionalities with Spring Reactive WebFlux.

The `Plane` class represents the plane model in our microservices and the class should be like this:

```
package springfive.airline.airlineplanes.domain;

import com.fasterxml.jackson.annotation.JsonInclude;
import com.fasterxml.jackson.annotation.JsonInclude.Include;
import java.util.Set;
import lombok.Builder;
import lombok.Data;
```

```
import lombok.NonNull;
import org.springframework.data.annotation.Id;
import org.springframework.data.mongodb.core.mapping.Document;
import springfive.airline.airlineplanes.resource.data.PlaneRequest;

@Data
@Document(collection = "planes")
@JsonInclude(Include.NON_NULL)
public class Plane {

  @Id
  String id;

  String owner;

  PlaneModel model;

  Set<Seat> seats;

  String notes;

  @Builder
  public static Plane newPlane(String owner,PlaneModel planeModel,Set<Seat>
seats,String notes){
    Plane plane = new Plane();
    plane.owner = owner;
    plane.model = planeModel;
    plane.seats = seats;
    plane.notes = notes;
    return plane;
  }

  public Plane fromPlaneRequest(@NonNull PlaneRequest planeRequest){
    this.owner = planeRequest.getOwner();
    this.model = planeRequest.getModel();
    this.seats = planeRequest.getSeats();
    this.notes = planeRequest.getNotes();
    return this;
  }

}
```

The interesting point is the @Document annotation. It enables us to configure the name of the MongoDB collection for our domain. The @Builder annotation creates an implementation of the Builder pattern using the annotated method.
The Project Lombok library provides this feature (https://projectlombok.org). Also, the project has some exciting features, such as @Data, which creates getters/setters, equals, and hashCode implementation automatically for the annotated class.

As we can see, there are some domain models in this class. These models do not need explanation here, and the full source code can be found in the GitHub project at https:// github.com/PacktPublishing/Spring-5.0-By-Example/tree/master/Chapter08/airline-planes.

The reactive repository

Our Plane class needs a repository to persist the data to a database. We will use a reactive repository for MongoDB provided by the Spring Reactive MongoDB implementation. We will use the ReactiveCrudRepository as it makes our repositories reactive. Our repository should be like this:

```
package springfive.airline.airlineplanes.repository;

import org.springframework.data.repository.reactive.ReactiveCrudRepository;
import springfive.airline.airlineplanes.domain.Plane;

public interface PlaneRepository extends
ReactiveCrudRepository<Plane,String>{
}
```

The implementation is the same as it was in the previous Spring Data versions, except for the new reactive interface. Now, we can create our service layer in the next section.

Creating the Plane service

Our PlaneService will be responsible for creating a kind of glue between the PlaneRepository and PlaneResource; the latter one we will create in the next section. The implementation should be like this:

```
package springfive.airline.airlineplanes.service;

import lombok.NonNull;
import org.springframework.stereotype.Service;
```

```
import reactor.core.publisher.Flux;
import reactor.core.publisher.Mono;
import springfive.airline.airlineplanes.domain.Plane;
import springfive.airline.airlineplanes.repository.PlaneRepository;
import springfive.airline.airlineplanes.resource.data.PlaneRequest;

@Service
public class PlaneService {

  private final PlaneRepository planeRepository;

  public PlaneService(PlaneRepository planeRepository) {
    this.planeRepository = planeRepository;
  }

  public Flux<Plane> planes(){
    return this.planeRepository.findAll();
  }

  public Mono<Plane> plane(@NonNull String id){
    return this.planeRepository.findById(id);
  }

  public Mono<Void> deletePlane(@NonNull Plane plane){
    return this.planeRepository.delete(plane);
  }

  public Mono<Plane> create(@NonNull PlaneRequest planeRequest){
    final Plane plane = Plane.builder().owner(planeRequest.getOwner())
        .planeModel(planeRequest.getModel()).seats(planeRequest.getSeats())
        .notes(planeRequest.getNotes()).build();
    return this.planeRepository.save(plane);
  }

  public Mono<Plane> update(@NonNull String id,@NonNull PlaneRequest
planeRequest){
    return this.planeRepository.findById(id)
        .flatMap(plane -> Mono.just(plane.fromPlaneRequest(planeRequest)))
        .flatMap(this.planeRepository::save);
  }

}
```

There is nothing special in this class, and the PlaneService will invoke the
PlaneRepository to persist the Plane in a database. As we can see, we have used
lambdas extensively. Java 8 is a requirement to run Spring Boot 2 applications.

Take a look at how the Builder pattern enables us to write clean code. It is much easier to read this code; we did it using the `chaining` method provided by Lombok.

The REST layer

We will use Spring WebFlux to expose our REST endpoints, and then we need to return `Mono` or `Flux` in our methods. The REST implementation should be like this:

```
package springfive.airline.airlineplanes.resource;

import java.net.URI;
import javax.validation.Valid;
import org.springframework.http.HttpStatus;
import org.springframework.http.ResponseEntity;
import org.springframework.web.bind.annotation.DeleteMapping;
import org.springframework.web.bind.annotation.GetMapping;
import org.springframework.web.bind.annotation.PathVariable;
import org.springframework.web.bind.annotation.PostMapping;
import org.springframework.web.bind.annotation.PutMapping;
import org.springframework.web.bind.annotation.RequestBody;
import org.springframework.web.bind.annotation.RequestMapping;
import org.springframework.web.bind.annotation.RestController;
import org.springframework.web.util.UriComponentsBuilder;
import reactor.core.publisher.Flux;
import reactor.core.publisher.Mono;
import springfive.airline.airlineplanes.domain.Plane;
import springfive.airline.airlineplanes.resource.data.PlaneRequest;
import springfive.airline.airlineplanes.service.PlaneService;

@RestController
@RequestMapping("/planes")
public class PlaneResource {

  private final PlaneService planeService;

  public PlaneResource(PlaneService planeService) {
    this.planeService = planeService;
  }

  @GetMapping
  public Flux<Plane> planes() {
    return this.planeService.planes();
  }

  @GetMapping("/{id}")
```

```
    public Mono<ResponseEntity<Plane>> plane(@PathVariable("id") String id) {
      return this.planeService.plane(id).map(ResponseEntity::ok)
        .defaultIfEmpty(ResponseEntity.notFound().build());
    }

    @PostMapping
    public Mono<ResponseEntity<Void>> newPlane(
        @Valid @RequestBody PlaneRequest planeRequest, UriComponentsBuilder
uriBuilder) {
      return this.planeService.create(planeRequest).map(data -> {
        URI location = uriBuilder.path("/planes/{id}")
          .buildAndExpand(data.getId())
          .toUri();
        return ResponseEntity.created(location).build();
      });
    }

    @DeleteMapping("/{id}")
    public Mono<ResponseEntity<Object>> deletePlane(@PathVariable("id")
String id) {
      return this.planeService.plane(id).flatMap(data ->
this.planeService.deletePlane(data)
        .then(Mono.just(ResponseEntity.noContent().build())))
        .defaultIfEmpty(new ResponseEntity<>(HttpStatus.NOT_FOUND));
    }

    @PutMapping("/{id}")
    public Mono<ResponseEntity<Object>> updatePlane(@PathVariable("id")
String id,@Valid @RequestBody PlaneRequest planeRequest) {
      return this.planeService.update(id,planeRequest)
        .then(Mono.just(ResponseEntity.ok().build()));
    }

}
```

Take a look at the `plane` method. When `planeService.plane(id)` returns the empty Mono, the REST endpoint will return `notFound` like this implementation: `ResponseEntity.notFound().build()`. It makes the code extremely easy to understand.

On the `newPlane` method, we will return the `location` HTTP header with the new entity ID recently created.

Running the plane microservice

Before we run the plane microservice, we will create the `plane` microservice's `main` class. It will be responsible for starting the application. To do that, we need to include a couple of Spring Annotations. The class implementation can be like this:

```
package springfive.airline.airlineplanes;

import org.springframework.boot.SpringApplication;
import org.springframework.boot.autoconfigure.SpringBootApplication;
import org.springframework.cloud.netflix.eureka.EnableEurekaClient;
import org.springframework.cloud.netflix.zuul.EnableZuulProxy;

@EnableZuulProxy
@EnableEurekaClient
@SpringBootApplication
public class AirlinePlanesApplication {

 public static void main(String[] args) {
  SpringApplication.run(AirlinePlanesApplication.class, args);
 }

}
```

The Spring Annotations will be connected with the Zuul proxy. Also, we need to connect the application with the Eureka server and configure the application automatically. These behaviors can be done using `@EnableZuulProxy`, `@EnableEurekaClient`, and `@SpringBootApplication`.

Now, we will create a `bootstrap.yaml` file to instruct the Spring Framework to search the configuration file on the Config Server, created in the previous chapter. The file should be like this:

```
spring:
  application:
    name: planes
  cloud:
    config:
      uri: http://localhost:5000
      label: master
```

We have configured the Config Server address; it was a piece of cake.

Now, we need to add the `application.yaml` file on the GitHub repository, because the Config Server will try to find the file in the repository.

The file can be found on GitHub at `https://github.com/PacktPublishing/Spring-5.0-By-Example/blob/master/config-files/flights.yaml`.

We can run the application on the IDE or via the command line; it is up to you. Check that the Config Server, Eureka, MongoDB, and RabbitMQ are up and running before trying to run it.

We can use the Docker compose file located on GitHub (`https://github.com/PacktPublishing/Spring-5.0-By-Example/blob/master/Chapter07/docker/docker-compose-infra-full.yaml`). It contains RabbitMQ, Config Server, Eureka, MongoDB, MySQL, Redis, and Zipkin containers ready to use. If you are using it, run it using the following command: `docker-compose -f docker-compose-infra-full.yaml up -d`.

Let's check the output. We can check it in different ways: on a console, and on the Eureka server. Let's do it.

Check the console. Let's try to find a line about `DiscoveryClient`. The `planes` microservice is trying to connect to the Eureka server:

```
INFO [planes,,,] 8938 --- [InfoReplicator-0] com.netflix.discovery.DiscoveryClient    : DiscoveryClient_PLANES/192.168.100.101:planes:50001: registering service...
INFO [planes,,,] 8938 ---              main] o.s.i.endpoint.EventDrivenConsumer       : Adding {logging-channel-adapter:_org.springframework.integration.errorLogger} as a subscriber to the 'errorChannel'
INFO [planes,,,] 8938 ---              main] o.s.i.channel.PublishSubscribeChannel    : Channel 'planes:50001.errorChannel' has 1 subscriber(s).
INFO [planes,,,] 8938 ---              main] o.s.i.endpoint.EventDrivenConsumer       : started _org.springframework.integration.errorLogger
INFO [planes,,,] 8938 ---              main] o.s.i.e.SourcePollingChannelAdapter      : started SleuthStreamSpanReporter.poll.inboundChannelAdapter
INFO [planes,,,] 8938 ---              main] o.s.c.support.DefaultLifecycleProcessor  : Starting beans in phase 2147482647
INFO [planes,,,] 8938 ---              main] o.s.c.support.DefaultLifecycleProcessor  : Starting beans in phase 2147483647
INFO [planes,,,] 8938 --- [InfoReplicator-0] com.netflix.discovery.DiscoveryClient    : DiscoveryClient_PLANES/192.168.100.101:planes:50001 - registration status: 204
INFO [planes,,,] 8938 ---              main] o.s.b.w.embedded.tomcat.TomcatWebServer  : Tomcat started on port(s): 50001 (http) with context path ''
INFO [planes,,,] 8938 ---              main] s.c.a.e.s.EurekaAutoServiceRegistration  : Updating port to 50001
INFO [planes,,,] 8938 ---              main] s.s.s.AirlinePlanesApplication           : Started AirlinePlanesApplication in 17.153 seconds (JVM running for 18.25)
INFO [planes,,,] 8938 --- [on(4)-127.0.0.1] org.mongodb.driver.connection            : Opened connection [connectionId{localValue:3, serverValue:26}] to localhost:27017
```

There is some important information on the log files here. The first line indicates which application is trying to register with the Eureka server. The next four lines are about Sleuth. The Sleuth framework is registering the RabbitMQ queues and channels.

We need to find the following line:

```
Started AirlinePlanesApplication in 17.153 seconds (JVM running for 18.25)
```

Also, we can check the Eureka server, and we can see the **PLANES** application there, like this:

Instances currently registered with Eureka			
Application	AMIs	Availability Zones	Status
PLANES	n/a (1)	(1)	UP (1) - 192.168.100.101:planes:50001

Awesome, our plane microservice is operational.

> We can try our microservices using Postman. This application enables us to call our APIs using the intuitive IDE to interact with our microservice. The application permits us to group some HTTP calls into collections. The planes collection can be found on GitHub at `https://github.com/PacktPublishing/Spring-5.0-By-Example/blob/master/postman/planes.postman_collection`.

We have finished our first microservices. In the next section, we will create our `flights` microservice, which will consume the plane's data.

Flights microservice

Our plane's microservices are up and running. It will be important for now because the flight's microservice needs to get the plane's data to create the flight's entities.

We will introduce the Netflix Ribbon, which will act as a client load balancer for our applications, and we will consume the service discovery to look up the service's address from the service registry.

Cloning the Flight microservice project

We did this task many times in the previous chapter. We can download the project source code on GitHub at `https://github.com/PacktPublishing/Spring-5.0-By-Example/tree/master/Chapter08/airline-flights`. In the next section, we will dive deep into Ribbon and how it can help us on distributed systems.

Netflix Ribbon

The Ribbon is an open source project created and maintained by the Netflix company. The project is licensed under Apache 2.0 and can be used for commercial purposes.

The Ribbon provides a client-side software load balancing algorithm for the **IPC (Inter-Process Communication)**. The project supports most popular protocols, such as TCP, UDP, and HTTP in an asynchronous manner.

There are more interesting features, such as service discovery integration, which enables integration in dynamic and elastic environments such as the cloud. For this purpose, we will look at our Eureka server. Both projects are maintained by the Netflix team. It fits well for our use case.

Another interesting feature is fault tolerance. The Ribbon client can find the live servers on the configured list and send the request. Also, the down servers will not receive any request.

The following diagram explains how the Ribbon works:

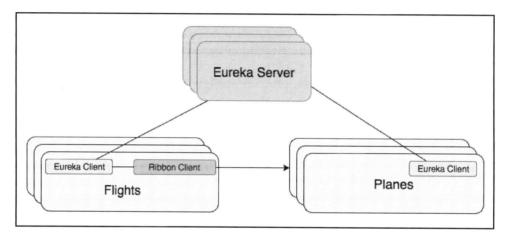

As we can see, the **Ribbon Client** can communicate with Eureka and then redirect the request for the desired microservice. In our case, the `flights` microservice will use the Ribbon client and get the service registry from Eureka and redirect the call to a live `planes` microservice instance. It sounds like an amazing solution.

Understanding the discovery client

Now, we will learn about service discovery and how it works in complex and dynamic environments. The basic idea of service discovery is to maintain the services repository and provide service addresses for the callers.

It requires some complex tasks to achieve this goal. There are two main behaviors to understand:

- The first one is the register. As we know, the service discovery needs to store the services information, such as the address and name, and then during the service bootstrap, it needs to send the information to the service registry.
- In the the second operation, the service discovery clients need to query the service registry, asking for the desired service name, for instance. Then the service registry will send the service information to the client.

Now we understand the basics, as illustrated in the following diagram:

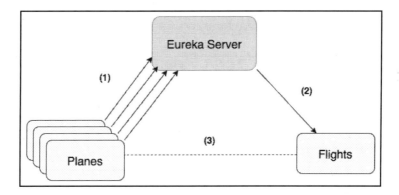

As you can see in the preceding diagram:

1. The first part is the service registration.
2. At the second stage, the service client will get the service address from the Eureka server.
3. Then the client can call based on the service information.

Let's do it in the code.

Service discovery and load balancing in practice

Now we will write some code to interact with our service discovery and load balance infrastructure. Now we know how it works, it will help us to understand the source code.

We will create a `DiscoveryService` class which will discover the addresses from a requested service name. The class code should be like this:

```
package springfive.airline.airlineflights.service;

import org.springframework.cloud.client.discovery.DiscoveryClient;
import org.springframework.cloud.client.loadbalancer.LoadBalancerClient;
import org.springframework.stereotype.Service;
import reactor.core.publisher.Flux;
import reactor.core.publisher.Mono;

@Service
public class DiscoveryService {

  private final LoadBalancerClient lbClient;

  private final DiscoveryClient dClient;

  public DiscoveryService(LoadBalancerClient lbClient, DiscoveryClient
dClient) {
    this.lbClient = lbClient;
    this.dClient = dClient;
  }

  public Flux<String> serviceAddressFor(String service) {
    return Flux.defer(() ->
Flux.just(this.dClient.getInstances(service)).flatMap(srv ->
      Mono.just(this.lbClient.choose(service))
    ).flatMap(serviceInstance ->
      Mono.just(serviceInstance.getUri().toString())
    ));
  }

}
```

As we can see, we inject two objects: the `LoadBalanceClient`, which acts as a client load balancer, that is, Netflix Ribbon; and the `DiscoveryClient`, which will find the instance from a requested service.

We use the lambda `Flux.defer()` to organize the flow, and then we will look up the service instances from Eureka server. We use `this.dClient.getInstances(service)` for that. It will return a list of service names after we look up the service URI from the load balancing. This will be done using `this.lbClient.choose(service)`. Then we will return the `Flux` of service instances addresses.

It is time to see how the client code can use the `DiscoveryService` object. The client code can be like this:

```
public Mono<Plane> plane(String id) {
  return
discoveryService.serviceAddressFor(this.planesService).next().flatMap(
      address -> this.webClient.mutate().baseUrl(address + "/" +
this.planesServiceApiPath + "/" + id).build().get().exchange()
      .flatMap(clientResponse -> clientResponse.bodyToMono(Plane.class)));
}
```

This code can be found in the `PlaneService` class on the project. Remember the `serviceAddressFor()` method returns a `Flux` of service addresses. We will get the first one, using the `next()` method. Then we are able to transform the service address to a valid address to reach the plane microservice.

Now, we will test the service connections. We need to do the following tasks:

1. Run the Config Server, Eureka, the `planes` microservice, and the `flights` microservice
2. Create a `plane` entity on the `planes` microservice
3. Create a `flight` entity on the `flights` microservice

Check whether all services listed previously are up and running. Then we will create a `plane` entity using the following JSON:

```
{
  "owner" : "Spring Framework Company",
  "model" : {
    "factory" : "Pivotal",
    "model" : "5.0",
    "name" : "Spring 5.0",
    "reference_name" : "S5.0"
  },
  "seats" : [
    {
      "identity" : "1A",
      "row" : "1",
      "right_side" : { "seat_identity" : "2A"},
      "category" : {
        "id" : "A",
        "name": "First Class"
      }
    },
    {
```

```
      "identity" : "2A",
      "row" : "1",
      "left_side" : { "seat_identity" : "1A"},
      "category" : {
        "id" : "A",
        "name": "First Class"
      }
    },
    {
      "identity" : "3A",
      "row" : "1",
      "left_side" :{ "seat_identity" : "2A"},
      "category" : {
        "id" : "A",
        "name": "First Class"
      }
    }
    ],
   "notes": "The best company airplane"
}
```

We need to call the `planes` microservice in `http://localhost:50001/planes` using the HTTP `POST` method. We can find the request to create planes in the `Planes Collection` on Postman. When we have called the create plane API, we will get a new plane ID. It can be found in the HTTP response headers, as shown in the following image, on Postman:

Postman is a tool that helps developers to test APIs. Postman provides a friendly **GUI (Graphic User Interface)** to make requests. Also, the tool supports environments and it can be helpful to test different environments, such as development, test, and production.

Take a look at the `location` HTTP response header. The HTTP status code is important as well. We will use the plane ID `5a6a6c636798a63817bed8b4`, created just now, to create a new flight.

We can find the list of HTTP status code at *W3 Org* (`https://www.w3.org/Protocols/rfc2616/rfc2616-sec10.html`). Keep this in mind, as it is very important to follow the correct status code. It is considered a best practice when we are creating REST APIs.

The Flight Collection can be found on GitHub at `https://github.com/PacktPublishing/Spring-5.0-By-Example/blob/master/postman/flights.postman_collection`. There is a **Create Flight** request we want to execute, but before that, we need to change our plane ID created previously. Take a look at the following screenshot:

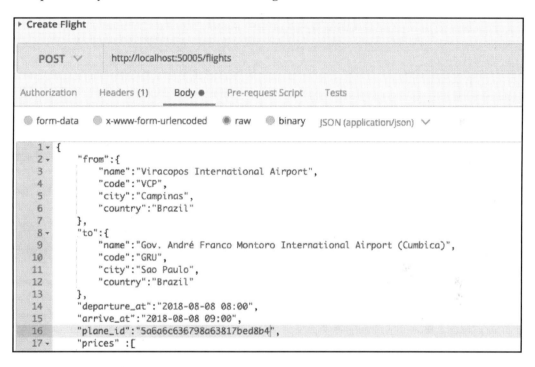

The plane ID has changed to that of our plane previously created. Now we can execute the request. The `flights` microservices has the same behavior as a `planes` microservice. It will return the location response with the new flight ID. In my case, the new ID generated is like the following image:

Now, we can find the flight by ID. The request can be found at Flight Collection; the name is Flight by Id. We can execute this request, and the result should be like this:

```json
{
    "id": "5a6a6f1e6798a6383a89fb09",
    "from": {
        "name": "Viracopos International Airport",
        "code": "VCP",
        "city": "Campinas",
        "country": "Brazil"
    },
    "to": {
        "name": "Gov. André Franco Montoro International Airport (Cumbica)",
        "code": "GRU",
        "city": "Sao Paulo",
        "country": "Brazil"
    },
    "departureAt": "2018-08-08T08:00:00",
    "arriveAt": "2018-08-08T09:00:00",
    "plane": {
        "id": "5a6a6c636798a63817bed8b4",
        "model": {
            "factory": "Pivotal",
            "model": "5.0",
            "name": "Spring 5.0"
        }
    },
```

Take a look at the `plane` JSON node. We don't have any data about a plane in the `flight` microservice. This information came in from the `planes` microservice. We have used service discovery and client load balancing. Well done!

Let's take a look at the debug provided by the IDE. We want to see the plane service address:

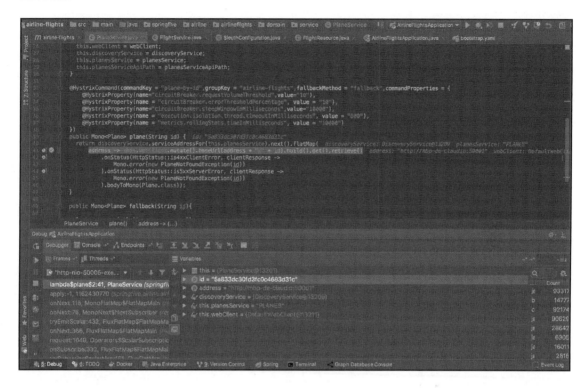

On the **Variables** panel, we can see the **address** variable. The value came in from service discovery and client load balancing. It is the **Service IP** or **Domain Name**. Now we are able to call the requested service transforming the URL.

Awesome, our infrastructure works very well, now we are able to find services using the infrastructure, but there is something important to pay attention to. We will discover it in the next section.

When the services fail, hello Hystrix

Sometimes the infrastructure can fail, especially the network. It can cause some problems in microservices architecture because in general there are many connections between services. It means at runtime that the microservices depend on other microservices. Normally these connections are done using the REST APIs through the HTTP protocol.

It can cause a behavior called **cascade failure**; that is, when one part of the microservices system fails, it can trigger the other microservices failure, because of the dependencies. Let's illustrate this:

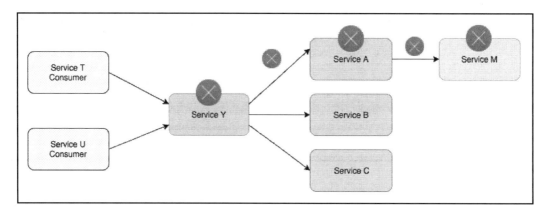

If **Service Y** fails, **Service A** and **Service M** potentially can fail as well.

We have a pattern to help us when this happens: the Circuit Breaker.

Hystrix in a nutshell

Hystrix is a library that helps developers to manage interactions between services. The project is open source, maintained by the community, and is under the Netflix GitHub.

The Circuit Breaker pattern is a pattern that helps to control the system integrations. The idea is quite simple: we will wrap the remote call in a function or object, and we will monitor these calls to keep track of the failures. If the calls reach the limit, the circuit will open. The behavior is like that of an electrical circuit breaker, and the idea is the same—protect something to avoid breaking the electrical system:

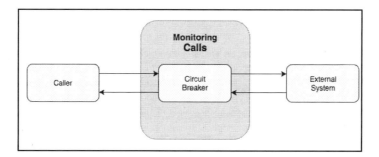

Hystrix implements the Circuit Breaker pattern and has some interesting behaviors, such as fallback options. Hystrix provides resilience for our applications. We are able to provide a fallback, stop cascading failures, and give the operational control.

The library provides high-level configurations and it can be configured through an annotation if we are using Spring Cloud Hystrix.

 The Circuit Breaker pattern was described by Martin Fowler. You can find more information about it on Martin Fowler's Page at https://martinfowler.com/bliki/CircuitBreaker.html

Spring Cloud Hystrix

As we expected, Spring Boot integrates with Netflix Hystrix. The integration can be done using a couple of annotations and by configuring the annotations with Hystrix properties. We will protect the planes microservice interactions we are coding in the flight service. We now have a method that tries to get the plane's data.

Let's take a look at that method:

```
@HystrixCommand(commandKey = "plane-by-id",groupKey = "airline-
flights",fallbackMethod = "fallback",commandProperties = {
@HystrixProperty(name="circuitBreaker.requestVolumeThreshold",value="10"),
      @HystrixProperty(name = "circuitBreaker.errorThresholdPercentage",
value = "10"),
@HystrixProperty(name="circuitBreaker.sleepWindowInMilliseconds",value="100
00"),
      @HystrixProperty(name =
"execution.isolation.thread.timeoutInMilliseconds", value = "800"),
      @HystrixProperty(name = "metrics.rollingStats.timeInMilliseconds",
value = "10000")
   })
public Mono<Plane> plane(String id) {
  return
discoveryService.serviceAddressFor(this.planesService).next().flatMap(
      address -> this.webClient.mutate().baseUrl(address + "/" +
this.planesServiceApiPath + "/" + id).build().get().exchange()
      .flatMap(clientResponse -> clientResponse.bodyToMono(Plane.class)));
}
```

There are some configurations for this command. The first configuration is `commandKey`. The basic idea here is to create a name for the command. It will be useful for panel control. The second one, `groupKey`, is the command used to group the commands. It also helps in grouping commands data together on dashboards. There is the concept of a rolling window. The idea is to group the request in a gap of time; it is used to enable metrics and statistics.

`circuitBreaker.requestVolumeThreshold` configures the number of requests in a rolling window that will trip at the circuit. For example, if we have a rolling window configured to be open for 10 seconds, if we have nine requests in a gap of 10 seconds, the circuit will not open because we have configured it to 10 in our command. Another configuration is `circuitBreaker.sleepWindowInMilliseconds`, where the basic idea is to give an amount of time, after tripping the circuit, to reject requests before trying again to allow attempts.

The last one is `execution.isolation.thread.timeoutInMilliseconds`. This property configures the timeout for the command. It means that if the time configured is reached, the circuit breaker system will perform a fallback logic and mark the command as a timeout.

 The `Hystrix` library is highly customizable, and there are a lot of properties to use. The full documentation can be found at `https://github.com/Netflix/Hystrix/wiki/configuration`. We can use these properties for different use cases.

Spring Boot Admin

The Spring Boot Admin project is a tool that helps developers in production environments. The tool shows Spring Boot application metrics in an organized dashboard, and it makes it extremely easy to see application metrics and much more information.

The tool uses the data from the Spring Boot Actuator as an information source. The project is open source and has a lot of contributors and is an active project in the community as well.

Running Spring Boot Admin

It is a piece of cake to set up the application. We will need a new Spring Boot application, and to connect this new application with our service discovery implementation. Let's do it right now.

We can find the code on GitHub at `https://github.com/PacktPublishing/Spring-5.0-By-Example/tree/master/Chapter08/admin`. If you want to create a new application, go ahead; the process is similar to what we did in the previous chapters.

The project is a Spring Boot regular application, with two new dependencies:

```
<dependency>
  <groupId>de.codecentric</groupId>
  <artifactId>spring-boot-admin-server</artifactId>
  <version>1.5.6</version>v
</dependency>

<dependency>
  <groupId>de.codecentric</groupId>
  <artifactId>spring-boot-admin-server-ui</artifactId>
  <version>1.5.6</version>
</dependency>
```

These dependencies are about `admin-server` and `admin-server-ui`. The project does not support Spring Boot 2 yet, but this is not a problem as we do not need reactive stuff for this; it is a monitoring tool.

We have configured our mandatory dependencies. We will need a service discovery because we have one in our infrastructure. We need it to provide the service discovery feature, and minimize the configurations for our Spring Boot Admin application. Let's add the Eureka client dependency:

```
<dependency>
  <groupId>org.springframework.cloud</groupId>
  <artifactId>spring-cloud-starter-netflix-eureka-client</artifactId>
</dependency>
```

Awesome, our dependencies are configured properly. Then we can create our main class. The main class should be like this:

```
package springfive.airline.admin;

import de.codecentric.boot.admin.config.EnableAdminServer;
import org.springframework.boot.SpringApplication;
import org.springframework.boot.autoconfigure.SpringBootApplication;
```

```
import org.springframework.cloud.netflix.eureka.EnableEurekaClient;

@EnableAdminServer
@EnableEurekaClient
@SpringBootApplication
public class AdminApplication {

  public static void main(String[] args) {
    SpringApplication.run(AdminApplication.class, args);
  }

}
```

The main difference here is that `@EnableAdminServer` will configure the Spring Boot Admin application and set up the server for us. As we expected, we will use the Config Server application to store our `application.yaml`. In order to achieve this, we need to create our `bootstrap.yaml`, which should be like this:

```
spring:
  application:
    name: admin
  cloud:
    config:
      uri: http://localhost:5000
      label: master
```

No difference at all, `bootstrap.yaml` is configured to look up the configuration file from the Config Server.

Time to create our `application.yaml` file, to which we need to add some configuration to set the new health check URL, since the actuator on Spring Boot 2 was moved, prefixed by *actuator*. Our new health check URL should be `/actuator/health`.

Our configuration file should be like this:

```
server:
  port: 50015

eureka:
  client:
    serviceUrl:
      defaultZone: http://localhost:8761/eureka/
spring:
  boot:
    admin:
      discovery:
```

```
converter:
    health-endpoint-path: /actuator/health
```

We have configured the Eureka server address and set the health check URL.

Now we can run our main class called `AdminApplication`. We can use the Java command line or IDE; there is no difference at all.

Run it!

We should see the following line at the log file:

Awesome, our application is ready to use. Now we can go to the main page. Go to `http://localhost:50015/#/` (main page), then we can see the following page:

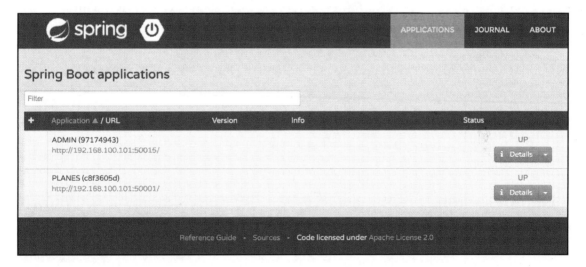

Look how it is easier to see any outage or strange behaviors in our microservices. Remember the key point in microservices architecture is monitoring. It is really necessary in order to have a good environment.

Spring Cloud Zuul

The Spring Cloud Gateway is the natural choice when we adopt the microservices architecture, but nowadays the Spring Cloud Gateway does not have support enabled for service discovery features, such as the Eureka server. It means we will have to configure it route by route. This does not sound good.

We have the Zuul proxy as a gateway for our microservices environment, but keep in mind the Spring Cloud Gateway is the best choice when the project has support for service discovery.

Let's create the Zuul proxy project.

Understanding the EDGE service project

The EDGE service is a service that provides dynamic routing, monitoring, resiliency, and security. The basic idea here is to create a reverse proxy for our microservices.

This service will act as a proxy for our microservices and will be exposed as a central access point. The Spring Cloud Zuul integrates with the Eureka server. It will increase our resiliency because we will use the service discovery feature provided by the Eureka server.

The following image demonstrates how we will use the **Edge Service** in our architecture:

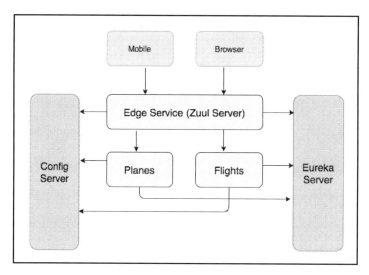

As we can see, the **Zuul Server** will connect to the service discovery server, to get the list of available services. After that the Zuul service will redirect to the requested service.

Look at the diagram. There is no interaction with the clients, that is, **Mobile** and **Browser**, and our microservices.

Spring Cloud Zuul also supports interesting features, such as:

- **pre**: This can be used to set some data in RequestContext; it is executed before the request is routed
- **route**: This handles the request routing
- **post**: This filters which one acts after the request is routed
- **error**: When some errors happen, we can use the error feature to handle the request

We will not use these features, but keep in mind that they can be very useful. Remember, our Zuul server is our gateway to the internet.

Creating the EDGE server

We will use the Zuul server to act as an API gateway for our applications. Now it's time to create our project. As there is no relevant difference involved in creating this project, we will take a look at specific Zuul parts.

The dependency required is:

```
<dependency>
    <groupId>org.springframework.cloud</groupId>
    <artifactId>spring-cloud-starter-netflix-zuul</artifactId>
</dependency>
```

It will configure for us the Zuul server dependencies.

Now we can add the project's main class. The class should be like this:

```
package springfive.airline.edge;

import org.springframework.boot.SpringApplication;
import org.springframework.boot.autoconfigure.SpringBootApplication;
import org.springframework.cloud.netflix.eureka.EnableEurekaClient;
import org.springframework.cloud.netflix.zuul.EnableZuulProxy;
import org.springframework.stereotype.Controller;
```

```
@Controller
@EnableZuulProxy
@EnableEurekaClient
@SpringBootApplication
public class EdgeServerApplication {

  public static void main(String[] args) {
    SpringApplication.run(EdgeServerApplication.class, args);
  }

}
```

The new thing here is `@EnableZuulProxy`. It will set up a Zuul server endpoint and configure reverse proxy filters. Then we will be able to forward a request to microservices applications. Zuul integrates with the Eureka server, so we do not need to configure it manually. The auto-configuration will find the services at the time of the discovery client implementation.

We can run the application via the command line or IDE, it is up to you.

Then we can see the routes configured. Go to `http://localhost:8888/routes` and we will able to see the routes:

We have some routes configured. We did this using the `application.yaml` file. The file should be like this:

```
zuul:
  routes:
    planes:
      path: /api/v1/planes/**
      serviceId: planes
    flights:
      path: /api/v1/flights/**
```

```
        serviceId: flights
    fares:
      path: /api/v1/fares/**
      serviceId: fares
    passengers:
      path: /api/v1/passengers/**
      serviceId: passengers
```

Let's understand this configuration. We have created a node called `planes`. This node configures a `path` (that is the URI) and configures the service name, by `serviceId`, registered in the Eureka server.

Let's do a simple test. We will:

- Configure the new URL path for the planes service
- Test the request using the Zuul server

Open the `PlaneResource` class located in the `planes` microservice project.

The `RequestMapping` is configured like this:

```
@RequestMapping("/planes")
```

Change it to something like this:

```
@RequestMapping("/")
```

Remember we can use the Zuul server as a router, so we do not need this information anymore. With the URI path on the source code, we are able to use the configuration file.

Run the `planes` microservice again. The following services need to be running:

- Config Server
- Eureka server
- Planes microservice
- API Edge

Then we can call the `planes` microservices using the Zuul proxy. Let's do it using cURL:

```
curl http://localhost:8888/api/v1/planes
```

Let's understand this a little bit. The port `8888` points to the **Zuul Server**, and we have configured it in `application.yaml`. When the path is `/api/v1/planes/**`, the **Zuul Server** will redirect to the `planes` microservices. The basic flow is:

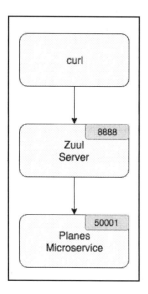

The request is coming to the **Zuul Server**, and then the **Zuul Server** will redirect it to the requested microservice. The result should be like this; in my case, I have some planes in the database:

[{"id":"5a633a596798a675a9e671a5","owner":"Spring Framework Company","model":{"factory":"Pivotal","model":"5.0","name":"Spring 5.0","reference_name":"55.0"},"seats":[{"identity":"1A","row":1,"category":{"id":"A","name":"First Class"},"right_side":{"seat_identity":"2A"}},{"identity":"2A","row":1,"category":{"id":"A","name":"First Class","left_side":{"seat_identity":"1A"}},{"identity":"3A","row":1,"category":{"id":"A","name":"First Class"},"left_side":{"seat_identity":"2A"}}],"notes":"The best company airplane"},{"id":"5a6a6c63d6798a65817bed8b4","owner":"Spring Framework Company","model":{"factory":"Pivotal","model":"5.0","name":"Spring 5.0","reference_name":"55.0"},"seats":[{"identity":"1A","row":1,"category":{"id":"A","name":"First Class"},"right_side":{"seat_identity":"2A"}},{"identity":"2A","row":1,"category":{"id":"A","name":"First ClassMacBook-Pro-de-Claudio:Library c

Awesome, our API Gateway is fully operational. We will use it for all services in the same port, and only the URI will be changed to point to the desired `serviceId`.

We can configure the port like in other Spring Boot applications. We chose the `8888` port in this case.

Summary

In this chapter, we have learned about some important microservice patterns and how they can help us to deliver a fault-tolerant, resilient, and error-prone application.

We have practiced how to use the service discovery feature provided by the Spring Framework and how it works at the application runtime, and we made some debug tasks to help us to understand how it works under the hood.

The Hystrix project, hosted by Netflix, can increase our application's resilience and fault tolerance. When working with remote calls, in this section, we made some Hystrix commands and understood how Hystrix is a useful implementation of the Circuit Breaker pattern.

At the end of the chapter, we are able to understand the microservices drawbacks and how to solve the common problems in a distributed environment.

Now we know how to solve the common problems of microservices architectural style using the Spring Framework.

In the next chapter, we will finish our *Airline Ticket System*, using the configured tools to monitoring the microservices' health and look at how it helps developers during the operation time when the microservices are running in the production stage.

See you there.

9
Putting It All Together

There are some challenges to face when we adopt the microservices architectural style. The first one handles operational complexity; services such as service discovery and load balancer help us to tackle these points. We solved these challenges in the previous chapters and got to know some important tools while doing so.

There are some other important key points to handle in microservices adoption. The effective way to monitor what happens in our microservices environments is to monitor how many times microservices consume other microservices resources, such as HTTP APIs, and how many times they fail. If we have near real-time statistics, it can save the developer days of troubleshooting and error investigations.

In this chapter, we will create some services which help us monitor the Hystrix commands and aggregate the command's statistics in a distributed environment.

Security is an important characteristic in microservices architecture, especially because of the distributed characteristic adopted by the microservices architecture. There are a lot of microservices in our architecture; we cannot share state between services, so the stateless security fits well for our environment.

The OAuth 2.0 protocol specification has this important characteristic: the stateless implementation. Spring Cloud Security provides support for OAuth 2.0.

Finally, we will Dockerize our microservices to use the images in Docker compose files.

In this chapter, we will learn about:

- Implementing the Turbine server to aggregate Hystrix streams
- Configuring the Hystrix Dashboard to use Turbine and input data

- Creating a mail service that will integrate an email API
- Understanding Spring Cloud Security
- Dockerizing our microservices

The airline Bookings microservice

The airline `Bookings` microservice is a standard Spring Boot Application. There are some interactions with other services, such as the `flights` microservice.

These interactions were created using Hystrix to bring some desired behaviors, such as fault-tolerance and resilience, to the airline `Bookings` microservice.

There are some business rules on this service, they are is not important to the learning context now, so we will skip the project creation and execution sections.

 The full source code can be found at GitHub (`https://github.com/PacktPublishing/Spring-5.0-By-Example/tree/master/Chapter09/airline-booking`); let's check it out and take a look at some code.

The airline Payments microservice

The Airline `Payments` is a microservice that gives payments confirmation for our Airline Ticket System. For learning purposes, we will jump this project because there are some business rules, nothing important in the Spring Framework context.

We can find the full source code on GitHub (`https://github.com/PacktPublishing/Spring-5.0-By-Example/tree/master/Chapter09/airline-payments`).

Learning about the Turbine server

There are some integrations in our microservices group; the `Bookings` microservice calls the `Fares` microservice and the `Passengers` microservice, these integrations are done using Hystrix to make it more resilient and fault tolerant.

However, in the microservices world, there are several instances of service. This will require us to aggregate the Hystrix command metrics by instance. Managing the instances panel by panel is not a good idea. The Turbine server helps developers in this context.

By default, Turbine pulls metrics from servers run by Hystrix, but it is not recommended for cloud environments because it can consume high values of network bandwidth and it will increase the traffic costs. We will use Spring Cloud Stream RabbitMQ to push metrics to Turbine via the **Advanced Message Queuing Protocol** (**AMQP**). Due to this, we will need to configure the RabbitMQ connections and put two more dependencies in our microservices, the dependencies are:

```
<dependency>
  <groupId>org.springframework.cloud</groupId>
  <artifactId>spring-cloud-netflix-hystrix-stream</artifactId>
</dependency>

<dependency>
  <groupId>org.springframework.cloud</groupId>
  <artifactId>spring-cloud-starter-stream-rabbit</artifactId>
</dependency>
```

These dependencies will enable the metrics to be sent to the Turbine server via the AMQP protocol.

The Turbine stream, by default, uses the port `8989`. We will configure it to run at `8010`, and we can use the `turbine.stream.port` property in the `application.yaml` to customize it.

The Turbine stream will be a Hystrix Dashboard data input to show the commands metrics.

> The full source code can be found on GitHub (`https://github.com/PacktPublishing/Spring-5.0-By-Example/tree/master/Chapter09/turbine`).

There are many configurations to customize the Turbine server. They make the server extremely adaptable for different use cases.

> We can find the Turbine documentation in the *Spring Cloud Turbine* section (`https://cloud.spring.io/spring-cloud-netflix/single/spring-cloud-netflix.html#_turbine`). There is a great deal of information, especially if you need to customize some configurations.

Creating the Turbine server microservice

Let's create our Turbine server. We will create a standard Spring Boot Application with a couple of annotations to enable Turbine stream and discovery client, as well.

The main class should be:

```
package springfive.airline.turbine;

import org.springframework.boot.SpringApplication;
import org.springframework.boot.autoconfigure.SpringBootApplication;
import org.springframework.cloud.netflix.eureka.EnableEurekaClient;
import
org.springframework.cloud.netflix.turbine.stream.EnableTurbineStream;

@EnableEurekaClient
@EnableTurbineStream
@SpringBootApplication
public class AirlineTurbineApplication {

 public static void main(String[] args) {
    SpringApplication.run(AirlineTurbineApplication.class, args);
 }

}
```

As we can see, `@EnableTurbineStream` will enable us to push Hystrix commands metrics via the RabbitMQ message broker, which is enough for us.

The Turbine server `application.yaml` file can be found on GitHub (`https://github.com/PacktPublishing/Spring-5.0-By-Example/blob/master/config-files/turbine.yaml`). There are a couple of configurations, such as discovery client and Turbine server configuration.

We can run the application, via the command line or IDE. Run it!

Make some calls to the `flights` microservice. The Create Flight API will call the `planes` microservice, which uses the Hystrix command, and will trigger some Hystrix command calls.

 We can use the Postman Collection located at GitHub (`https://github.com/PacktPublishing/Spring-5.0-By-Example/blob/master/postman/flights.postman_collection`). This collection has a Create Flight request, which will call the `planes` microservices to get plane details. It is enough to collect metrics.

Now, we can test whether our Turbine server is running correctly. Go to the Turbine stream endpoint and then the JSON data with metrics should be displayed like this:

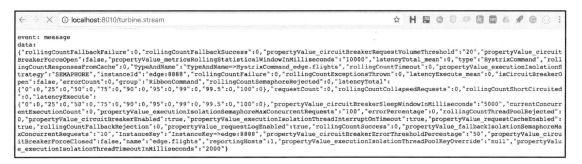

There are some Hystrix commands information, but as we can see, this information needs to be organized to make it useful for us. Turbine uses the **Server-Sent Events (SSE)** technology, which was introduced in `Chapter 6`, *Playing with Server-Sent Events*.

In the next section, we will introduce the Hystrix Dashboard. It will help us to organize and make this information useful for us.

Let's jump to the next section.

Hystrix Dashboard

The Hystrix Dashboard will help us to organize the Turbine stream information. As we saw in the previous section, the Turbine server sends information via SSE. It is done using JSON objects.

The Hystrix stream provides a dashboard for us. Let's create our Hystrix Dashboard microservice. The application is a standard Spring Boot Application annotated with `@EnableHystrixDashboard`. Let's add the dependency to enable it:

```
<dependency>
  <groupId>org.springframework.cloud</groupId>
  <artifactId>spring-cloud-starter-netflix-hystrix-
dashboard</artifactId>
</dependency>
```

Good, now we can create the main class for our application. The main class should look like this:

```
package springfive.airline.hystrix.ui;

import org.springframework.boot.SpringApplication;
import org.springframework.boot.autoconfigure.SpringBootApplication;
import org.springframework.cloud.netflix.eureka.EnableEurekaClient;
import
org.springframework.cloud.netflix.hystrix.dashboard.EnableHystrixDashbo
ard;

@EnableEurekaClient
@SpringBootApplication
@EnableHystrixDashboard
public class HystrixApplication {

  public static void main(String[] args) {
    SpringApplication.run(HystrixApplication.class, args);
  }

}
```

The full source code can be found at GitHub: `https://github.com/PacktPublishing/Spring-5.0-By-Example/tree/master/Chapter09/hystrix-ui`.

As we can see, this is a pretty standard Spring Boot Application annotated with `@EnableHystrixDashboard`. It will provide the Hystrix Dashboard for us.

Now, we can run the application via IDE or the Java command line. Run it!

The Hystrix Dashboard can be accessed using the following URL : `http://localhost:50010/hystrix`.

Then, go to the **Hystrix Dashboard** main page. The following page should be displayed:

Awesome – our **Hystrix Dashboard** is up and running. On this page, we can point to `hystrix.stream` or `turbine.stream` to consume and show the commands' metrics.

Keep this application running, we will use it later in this chapter.

Awesome job, guys, let's move to the next section.

Creating the Mail microservice

Now, we will create our `Mail` microservice. The name is self-explanatory, this component will be responsible for sending emails. We will not configure an **SMTP (Simple Mail Transfer Protocol)** server, we will use SendGrid.

SendGrid is an **SaaS (Software as a Service)** service for emails, we will use this service to send emails to our Airline Ticket System. There are some triggers to send email, for example, when the user creates a booking and when the payment is accepted.

Our `Mail` microservice will listen to a queue. Then the integration will be done using the message broker. We choose this strategy because we do not need the feature that enables us to answer synchronously. Another essential characteristic is the retry policy when the communication is broken. This behavior can be done easily using the message strategy.

We are using RabbitMQ as a message broker. For this project, we will use RabbitMQ Reactor, which is a reactive implementation of RabbitMQ Java client.

Creating the SendGrid account

Before we start to code, we need to create a SendGrid account. We will use the trial account which is enough for our tests. Go to the SendGrid portal (`https://sendgrid.com/`) and click on the **Try for Free** button.

Fill in the required information and click on the **Create Account** button.

In the main page, on the left side, click on **Settings**, then go to the **API Key** section, follow the image shown here:

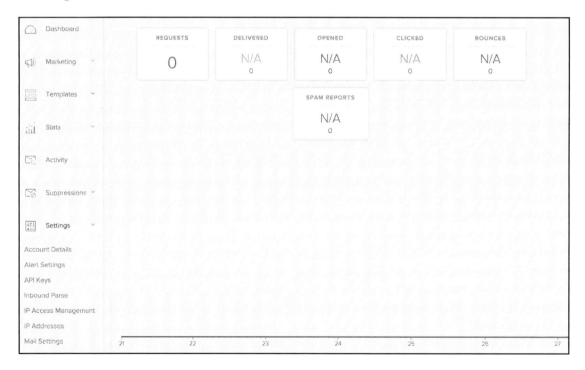

Then, we can click on the **Create API Key** button at the top-right corner. The page should look like this:

Fillin the **API Key** information and choose **Full Access**. After that the **API Key** will appear on your screen. Take a note of it in a safe place, as we will use it as an environment variable soon.

Goob job, our SendGrid account is ready to use, now we can code our `Mail` microservice.

Let's do it in the next section.

Creating the Mail microservice project

As we did in `Chapter 8`, *Circuit Breakers and Security,* we will take a look at essential project parts. We will be using Spring Initializr, as we have several times in the previous chapters.

The full source code can be found at GitHub (`https://github.com/ PacktPublishing/Spring-5.0-By-Example/tree/master/Chapter09/ mail-service`).

Adding RabbitMQ dependencies

Let's add the RabbitMQ required dependencies. The following dependencies should be added:

```
<dependency>
  <groupId>io.projectreactor.rabbitmq</groupId>
  <artifactId>reactor-rabbitmq</artifactId>
  <version>1.0.0.M1</version>
</dependency>

<dependency>
  <groupId>org.springframework.boot</groupId>
  <artifactId>spring-boot-starter-amqp</artifactId>
</dependency>
```

The first one is about the reactive implementation for RabbitMQ and the second one is the starter AMQP, which will set up some configurations automatically.

Configuring some RabbitMQ stuff

We want to configure some RabbitMQ exchanges, queues, and bindings. It can be done using the RabbitMQ client library. We will configure our required infrastructure for the `Mail` microservice.

Our configuration class should look like this:

```
package springfive.airline.mailservice.infra.rabbitmq;

// imports are omitted

@Configuration
public class RabbitMQConfiguration {

  private final String pass;

  private final String user;

  private final String host;

  private final Integer port;

  private final String mailQueue;

  public RabbitMQConfiguration(@Value("${spring.rabbitmq.password}") String
pass,
      @Value("${spring.rabbitmq.username}") String user,
      @Value("${spring.rabbitmq.host}") String host,
      @Value("${spring.rabbitmq.port}") Integer port,
      @Value("${mail.queue}") String mailQueue) {
    this.pass = pass;
    this.user = user;
    this.host = host;
    this.port = port;
    this.mailQueue = mailQueue;
  }

  @Bean("springConnectionFactory")
  public ConnectionFactory connectionFactory() {
    CachingConnectionFactory factory = new CachingConnectionFactory();
    factory.setUsername(this.user);
    factory.setPassword(this.pass);
    factory.setHost(this.host);
    factory.setPort(this.port);
    return factory;
  }
```

```
@Bean
public AmqpAdmin amqpAdmin(@Qualifier("springConnectionFactory")
ConnectionFactory connectionFactory) {
    return new RabbitAdmin(connectionFactory);
}

@Bean
public TopicExchange emailExchange() {
    return new TopicExchange("email", true, false);
}

@Bean
public Queue mailQueue() {
    return new Queue(this.mailQueue, true, false, false);
}

@Bean
public Binding mailExchangeBinding(Queue mailQueue) {
    return BindingBuilder.bind(mailQueue).to(emailExchange()).with("*");
}

@Bean
public Receiver receiver() {
    val options = new ReceiverOptions();
    com.rabbitmq.client.ConnectionFactory connectionFactory = new
com.rabbitmq.client.ConnectionFactory();
    connectionFactory.setUsername(this.user);
    connectionFactory.setPassword(this.pass);
    connectionFactory.setPort(this.port);
    connectionFactory.setHost(this.host);
    options.connectionFactory(connectionFactory);
    return ReactorRabbitMq.createReceiver(options);
}

}
```

There is interesting stuff here, but all of it is about infrastructure in RabbitMQ. It is important because when our application is in bootstrapping time, it means our application is preparing to run. This code will be executed and create the necessary queues, exchanges, and bindings. Some configurations are provided by the application.yaml file, look at the constructor.

Modeling a Mail message

Our `Mail` service is abstract and can be used for different purposes, so we will create a simple class to represent a mail message in our system. Our `Mail` class should look like this:

```
package springfive.airline.mailservice.domain;

import lombok.Data;

@Data
public class Mail {

    String from;

    String to;

    String subject;

    String message;

}
```

Easy, this class represents an abstract message on our system.

The MailSender class

As we can expect, we will integrate with the SendGrid services through the REST APIs. In our case, we will use the reactive `WebClient` provided by Spring WebFlux.

Now, we will use the SendGrid API Key created in the previous section. Our `MailSender` class should look like this:

```
package springfive.airline.mailservice.domain.service;

import org.springframework.beans.factory.annotation.Value;
import org.springframework.http.HttpStatus;
import org.springframework.http.ReactiveHttpOutputMessage;
import org.springframework.stereotype.Service;
import org.springframework.web.reactive.function.BodyInserter;
import org.springframework.web.reactive.function.BodyInserters;
import org.springframework.web.reactive.function.client.WebClient;
import reactor.core.publisher.Flux;
import reactor.core.publisher.Mono;
import springfive.airline.mailservice.domain.Mail;
import springfive.airline.mailservice.domain.service.data.SendgridMail;
```

```
@Service
public class MailSender {

  private final String apiKey;

  private final String url;

  private final WebClient webClient;

  public MailSender(@Value("${sendgrid.apikey}") String apiKey,
      @Value("${sendgrid.url}") String url,
      WebClient webClient) {
    this.apiKey = apiKey;
    this.webClient = webClient;
    this.url = url;
  }

  public Flux<Void> send(Mail mail){
    final BodyInserter<SendgridMail, ReactiveHttpOutputMessage> body =
BodyInserters
.fromObject(SendgridMail.builder().content(mail.getMessage()).from(mail.get
From()).to(mail.getTo()).subject(mail.getSubject()).build());
    return this.webClient.mutate().baseUrl(this.url).build().post()
        .uri("/v3/mail/send")
        .body(body)
        .header("Authorization","Bearer " + this.apiKey)
        .header("Content-Type","application/json")
        .retrieve()
        .onStatus(HttpStatus::is4xxClientError, clientResponse ->
            Mono.error(new RuntimeException("Error on send email"))
        ).bodyToFlux(Void.class);
  }

}
```

We received the configurations in the constructor, that is, the sendgrid.apikey and sendgrid.url. They will be configured soon. In the send() method, there are some interesting constructions. Look at BodyInserters.fromObject(): it allows us to send a JSON object in the HTTP body. In our case, we will create a SendGrid mail object.

In the onStatus() function, we can pass a predicate to handle the HTTP errors family. In our case, we are interested in the 4xx error family.

This class will process sending the mail messages, but it is necessary to listen to the RabbbitMQ queue, which we will do in the next section.

Creating the RabbitMQ queue listener

Let's create our `MailQueueConsumer` class, which will listen to the RabbitMQ queue. The class should look like this:

```
package springfive.airline.mailservice.domain.service;

import com.fasterxml.jackson.databind.ObjectMapper;
import java.io.IOException;
import javax.annotation.PostConstruct;
import lombok.extern.slf4j.Slf4j;
import lombok.val;
import org.springframework.beans.factory.annotation.Value;
import org.springframework.stereotype.Service;
import reactor.rabbitmq.Receiver;
import springfive.airline.mailservice.domain.Mail;

@Service
@Slf4j
public class MailQueueConsumer {

    private final MailSender mailSender;

    private final String mailQueue;

    private final Receiver receiver;

    private final ObjectMapper mapper;

    public MailQueueConsumer(MailSender mailSender, @Value("${mail.queue}")
String mailQueue,
        Receiver receiver, ObjectMapper mapper) {
      this.mailSender = mailSender;
      this.mailQueue = mailQueue;
      this.receiver = receiver;
      this.mapper = mapper;
    }

    @PostConstruct
    public void startConsume() {
      this.receiver.consumeAutoAck(this.mailQueue).subscribe(message -> {
        try {
          val mail = this.mapper.readValue(new String(message.getBody()),
Mail.class);
          this.mailSender.send(mail).subscribe(data ->{
            log.info("Mail sent successfully");
          });
```

```
      } catch (IOException e) {
        throw new RuntimeException("error on deserialize object");
      }
    });
  }

}
```

The method annotated with `@PostConstruct` will be invoked after `MailQueueConsumer` is ready, which will mean that the injections are processed. Then `Receiver` will start to process the messages.

Running the Mail microservice

Now, we will run our `Mail` microservice. Find the `MailServiceApplication` class, the main class of our project. The main class should look like this:

```
package springfive.airline.mailservice;

import org.springframework.boot.SpringApplication;
import org.springframework.boot.autoconfigure.SpringBootApplication;
import org.springframework.cloud.netflix.eureka.EnableEurekaClient;
import org.springframework.cloud.netflix.hystrix.EnableHystrix;
import org.springframework.cloud.netflix.zuul.EnableZuulProxy;

@EnableHystrix
@EnableZuulProxy
@EnableEurekaClient
@SpringBootApplication
public class MailServiceApplication {

  public static void main(String[] args) {
    SpringApplication.run(MailServiceApplication.class, args);
  }

}
```

It is a standard Spring Boot Application.

We can run the application in IDE or via the Java command line.

Run it!

We need to pass ${SENDGRID_APIKEY} and ${SENDGRID_URL} as environment variables. If you are running the application with the Java command line, the -D option allows us to pass environment variables. If you are using the IDE, you can configure in the **Run/Debug Configurations**.

Creating the Authentication microservice

We want to secure our microservices. Security is essential for microservices applications, especially because of the distributed characteristics.

On the microservices architectural style, usually, there is a service that will act as an authentication service. It means this service will authenticate the requests in our microservices group.

Spring Cloud Security provides a declarative model to help developers enable security on applications. There is support for commons patterns such as OAuth 2.0. Also, Spring Boot Security enables **Single Sign-On** (**SSO**).

Spring Boot Security also supports relay SSO tokens integrating with Zuul proxy. It means the tokens will be passed to downstream microservices.

For our architecture, we will use the OAuth 2.0 and JWT patterns, both integrate with Zuul proxy.

Before we do so, let's understand the main entities in OAuth 2.0 flow:

- **Protected resource**: This service will apply security rules; the microservices applications, in our case
- **OAuth authorization server**: The authentication server is a service between the application, which can be a frontend or a mobile, and a service that applications want to call
- **Application**: The application that will call the service, the client.
- **Resource Owner**: The user or machine that will authorize the client application to access their account

Let's draw the basic OAuth flow:

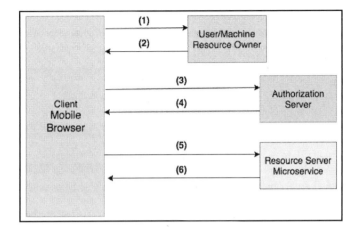

We can observe the following in this diagram:

1. The **Client** requests the authorization
2. The **Resource Owner** sends the authorization grant
3. The application client requests the access token from the **Authorization Server**
4. If the authorization grant is valid, the **Authorization Server** will provide the access token
5. The application calls the protected resource and sends the access token
6. If the **Resource Server** recognizes the token, the resource will serve for the application

These are the basics of the OAuth 2.0 authorization flow. We will implement this flow using Spring Cloud Security. Let's do it.

Creating the Auth microservice

As we have been doing in this chapter, we will take a look at the important parts. Let's start with our dependencies. We need to put in the following dependencies:

```
<dependency>
<groupId>org.springframework.cloud</groupId>
<artifactId>spring-cloud-starter-oauth2</artifactId>
</dependency>

<dependency>
```

```
      <groupId>org.springframework.security</groupId>
      <artifactId>spring-security-core</artifactId>
   </dependency>

   <dependency>
     <groupId>org.springframework.security</groupId>
     <artifactId>spring-security-config</artifactId>
   </dependency>
```

These dependencies will enable us to use the Spring Cloud Security features. Let's start to code our Authentication microservice.

Configuring the security

Let's start coding our `Auth` microservice. We will start with the authorization and authentication, as we want to protect all resources in our microservices, then we will configure `WebSecurityConfigureAdapter`. The class should look like this:

```
package springfive.airline.authservice.infra.security;

import org.springframework.beans.factory.annotation.Autowired;
import org.springframework.context.annotation.Configuration;
import
org.springframework.security.config.annotation.authentication.builders.Auth
enticationManagerBuilder;
import
org.springframework.security.config.annotation.method.configuration.EnableG
lobalMethodSecurity;
import
org.springframework.security.config.annotation.web.builders.HttpSecurity;
import
org.springframework.security.config.annotation.web.configuration.EnableWebS
ecurity;
import
org.springframework.security.config.annotation.web.configuration.WebSecurit
yConfigurerAdapter;
import org.springframework.security.crypto.password.PasswordEncoder;
import springfive.airline.authservice.service.CredentialsDetailsService;

@Configuration
@EnableWebSecurity
@EnableGlobalMethodSecurity(prePostEnabled = true)
public class SecurityConfig extends WebSecurityConfigurerAdapter {

  private final PasswordEncoder passwordEncoder;
```

```
    private final CredentialsDetailsService credentialUserDetails;

    public SecurityConfig(PasswordEncoder passwordEncoder,
        CredentialsDetailsService credentialUserDetails) {
      this.passwordEncoder = passwordEncoder;
      this.credentialUserDetails = credentialUserDetails;
    }

    @Override
    @Autowired
    protected void configure(AuthenticationManagerBuilder auth) throws
    Exception {
    auth.userDetailsService(this.credentialUserDetails).passwordEncoder(this.pa
    sswordEncoder);
    }

    @Override
    protected void configure(HttpSecurity http) throws Exception {
      http.csrf().disable()
          .authorizeRequests()
          .antMatchers("/login", "/**/register/**").permitAll()
          .anyRequest().authenticated()
          .and()
          .formLogin().permitAll();
    }

}
```

There is a lot of stuff here. Let's start with the @EnableWebSecurity, this annotation
enables Spring Security integrations with Spring MVC. @EnableGlobalMethodSecurity
provides AOP interceptors to enable methods security using the annotations. We can use
this feature by annotating the methods on a controller, for instance. The basic idea is to
wrap the methods call in AOP interceptors and apply security on the methods.

WebSecurityConfigurerAdapter enables us to configure the secure endpoints and some
stuff about how to authenticate users, which can be done using the
configure(AuthenticationManagerBuilder auth) method. We have configured our
CredentialsDetailsService and our PasswordEncoder to avoid plane password
between application layers. In this case, CredentialsDetailsService is the source of our
user's data.

In our method, configure(HttpSecurity http), we have configured some HTTP
security rules. As we can see, all users can access /login and /**/register/**. It's about
Sign In and *Sign Up* features. All other requests need to be authenticated by the
Authorization server.

The `CredentialsDetailsService` should look like this:

```
package springfive.airline.authservice.service;

import org.springframework.security.core.userdetails.UserDetailsService;
import
org.springframework.security.core.userdetails.UsernameNotFoundException;
import org.springframework.stereotype.Component;
import springfive.airline.authservice.domain.Credential;
import springfive.airline.authservice.domain.data.CredentialData;
import springfive.airline.authservice.repository.CredentialRepository;

@Component
public class CredentialsDetailsService implements UserDetailsService {

  private final CredentialRepository credentialRepository;

  public CredentialsDetailsService(CredentialRepository
credentialRepository) {
    this.credentialRepository = credentialRepository;
  }

  @Override
  public CredentialData loadUserByUsername(String email) throws
UsernameNotFoundException {
    final Credential credential =
this.credentialRepository.findByEmail(email);
    return
CredentialData.builder().email(credential.getEmail()).password(credential.g
etPassword()).scopes(credential.getScopes()).build();
  }

}
```

There is nothing special here. We need to override the `loadUserByUsername(String email)` method to provide the user data to Spring Security.

Let's configure our token signer and our token store. We will provide these beans using the `@Configuration` class, as we did in the previous chapters:

```
package springfive.airline.authservice.infra.oauth;

import org.springframework.beans.factory.annotation.Value;
import org.springframework.context.annotation.Bean;
import org.springframework.context.annotation.Configuration;
import org.springframework.security.crypto.bcrypt.BCryptPasswordEncoder;
import org.springframework.security.crypto.password.PasswordEncoder;
```

```
import
org.springframework.security.oauth2.provider.token.store.JwtAccessTokenConv
erter;
import
org.springframework.security.oauth2.provider.token.store.JwtTokenStore;

@Configuration
public class OAuthTokenProducer {

    @Value("${config.oauth2.privateKey}")
    private String privateKey;

    @Value("${config.oauth2.publicKey}")
    private String publicKey;

    @Bean
    public JwtTokenStore tokenStore(JwtAccessTokenConverter tokenEnhancer)
{
        return new JwtTokenStore(tokenEnhancer);
    }

    @Bean
    public PasswordEncoder passwordEncoder() {
        return new BCryptPasswordEncoder();
    }

    @Bean
    public JwtAccessTokenConverter tokenEnhancer() {
        JwtAccessTokenConverter converter = new JwtAccessTokenConverter();
        converter.setSigningKey(privateKey);
        converter.setVerifierKey(publicKey);
        return converter;
    }

}
```

We have configured our private and public keys in the application.yaml file. Optionally, we can read the jks files from the classpath as well. Then, we provided our token signer or token enhancer using the JwtAccessTokenConverter class, where we have used the private and public key.

In our token store, Spring Security Framework will use this object to read data from tokens, then set up the JwtAccessTokenConverter on the JwtTokenStore instance.

Finally, we have provided the password encoder class using the BCryptPasswordEncoder class.

Our last class is the Authorization server configuration. The configuration can be done using the following class:

Look at the `OAuth2AuthServer` class located on GitHub (`https://github.com/PacktPublishing/Spring-5.0-By-Example/blob/master/Chapter09/auth-service/src/main/java/springfive/airline/authservice/infra/oauth/OAuth2AuthServer.java`).

We have used `@EnableAuthorizationServer` to configure the Authorization server mechanism in our `Auth` microservice. This class works together with `AuthorizationServerConfigurerAdapter` to provide some customizations.

On `configure(AuthorizationServerSecurityConfigurer oauthServer)`, we have configured the security for token endpoints.

At `configure(AuthorizationServerEndpointsConfigurer endpoints)`, we have configured the endpoints of the token service such as, `/oauth/token` and `/oauth/authorize`.

Finally, on `configure(ClientDetailsServiceConfigurer clients)`, we have configured the client's ID and secrets. We used in-memory data, but we can use JDBC implementations as well.

The `Auth` microservice main class should be:

```
package springfive.airline.authservice;

import org.springframework.boot.SpringApplication;
import org.springframework.boot.autoconfigure.SpringBootApplication;
import org.springframework.cloud.netflix.eureka.EnableEurekaClient;
import org.springframework.cloud.netflix.zuul.EnableZuulProxy;

@EnableZuulProxy
@EnableEurekaClient
@SpringBootApplication
public class AuthServiceApplication {

  public static void main(String[] args) {
    SpringApplication.run(AuthServiceApplication.class, args);
  }

}
```

Here, we have created a standard Spring Boot Application with service discovery and Zuul proxy enabled.

Testing the Auth microservice

As we can see, the `Auth` microservice is ready for testing. Our microservice is listening to port `7777`, which we configured using the `application.yaml` file on GitHub.

Client credentials flow

Let's start with the client credentials flow.

Our application needs to be up on port `7777`, then we can use the following command line to get the token:

```
curl -s
442cf4015509eda9c03e5ca3aceef752:4f7ec648a48b9d3fa239b497f7b6b4d8019697bd@l
ocalhost:7777/oauth/token   -d grant_type=client_credentials  -d
scope=trust | jq .
```

As we can see, this *client ID* and *client secret* are from the `planes` microservice. We did this configuration at the `OAuth2AuthServer` class. Let's remember the exact point:

```
....
@Override
public void configure(ClientDetailsServiceConfigurer clients)throws
Exception {
  clients
      .inMemory()
      .withClient("ecommerce") // ecommerce microservice
      .secret("9ecc8459ea5f39f9da55cb4d71a70b5d1e0f0b80")
      .authorizedGrantTypes("authorization_code", "refresh_token",
"implicit",
          "client_credentials")
      .authorities("maintainer", "owner", "user")
      .scopes("read", "write")
      .accessTokenValiditySeconds(THREE_HOURS)
      .and()
      .withClient("442cf4015509eda9c03e5ca3aceef752") // planes
microservice
      .secret("4f7ec648a48b9d3fa239b497f7b6b4d8019697bd")
      .authorizedGrantTypes("authorization_code", "refresh_token",
"implicit",
          "client_credentials")
      .authorities("operator")
      .scopes("trust")
      .accessTokenValiditySeconds(ONE_DAY)
  ....
```

After you call the preceding command, the result should be:

```
{
  "access_token": "eyJhbGciOiJSUzI1NiIsInR5cCI6IkpXVCJ9.eyJzY29wZSI6WyJ0cnVzdCJdLCJleHAiOjE1MTczNTk4MjIsImFidGhvcml0aWVzIjpbIm9wZXJhdG9yIi, IsImpdaSI6IjM0N2YwYTg5LTgyODNtNDc3ZC05YmYyLT
ZmMTNiYThhYWQzYyIsImNsaWVudF9pZCI6IjQ0MnNmNDAxNTUwOBVkYTTjMDNiNWNhM2FjZWVmNzUyIn0.UsMLHIEIS3Urx_IMoif7foLqUK5X14htzAusdii9D2GsVnxUnZTYlfnwT734IQG50rHQeSGGZA8cQSNoyITYvoYSytBqSifiDsHJ
OgLwiN8DQF_I_eSbipStogy7T_tP-SkoyG4TnkUqAz13n1TmqN1Je-Mb3Iy8-P1AIsn9x5E",
  "token_type": "bearer",
  "expires_in": 86399,
  "scope": "trust",
  "jti": "347f0a89-8283-477d-9bf2-6a13ba8aad6c"
}
```

As we can see, the token was obtained with success. Well done, our client credentials flow was configured successfully. Let's move to the implicit flow, which will be covered in the next section.

Implicit grant flow

In this section, we will take a look at how to authenticate in our `Auth` microservice using the implicit flow.

Before we test our flow, let's create a user to enable authentication in the `Auth` microservice. The following command will create a user in the `Auth` service:

```
curl -H "Content-Type: application/json" -X POST -d '{"name":"John
Doe","email":"john@doe.com", "password" : "john"}'
http://localhost:7777/register
```

As we can see, the email is `john@doe.com` and the password is `john`.

We will use the browser to do this task. Let's go to the following URL:

```
http://localhost:7777/oauth/authorize?client_id=ecommerce&response_type
=token&scope=write&state=8777&redirect_uri=https://httpbin.org/anything
```

Let's understand the parameters:

The first part is the service address. To use the implicit grant flow, we need the path `/oauth/authorize`. Also we will use `ecommerce` as a client ID because we have configured it previously. `response_type=token` informs the implicit flow, `scope` is the scope as what we want in our case is write, `state` is a random variable, and `redirect_uri` is the URI to go after the `oauth` login process.

Put the URL in a web browser, and the following page should be displayed:

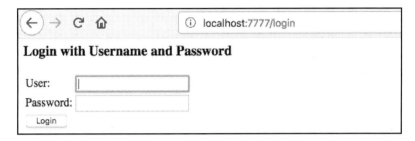

After typing the **User** and **Password**, the following page will be displayed to authorize our protected resources:

Click on the **Authorize** button. Then we will see the token in the browser URL like this:

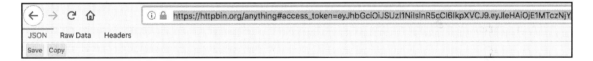

The full token can be viewed if we copy the browser URL.

Awesome job, guys, our Auth microservice is fully operational.

In the next sections, we will configure the Auth microservice to protect Zuul proxy downstream microservices, such as the planes microservices. Let's jump to the next section.

Protecting the microservices with OAuth 2.0

Now we will configure OAuth 2.0 to protect our microservices; in our case, our microservices are the resource servers. Let's start with the `planes` microservices. We will add the new dependency and configure the private and public keys. Also, we will configure our `JwtTokenStore`.

Let's do it.

Adding the security dependency

To add the newly required dependency, we will change the `pom.xml` of the `planes` microservice. We will add the following dependency:

```xml
<dependency>
  <groupId>org.springframework.cloud</groupId>
  <artifactId>spring-cloud-starter-oauth2</artifactId>
</dependency>
```

A piece of cake – our required dependency is configured properly.

In the next section, we will configure the `application.yaml` file.

Configuring the application.yaml file

To configure our private and public keys, we will use the `application.yaml` file. We did this configuration in the `Auth` microservice. The configuration is pretty easy. We need to add the following snippet:

```yaml
config:
  oauth2:
    privateKey: |
      -----BEGIN RSA PRIVATE KEY-----
      MIICXQIBAAKBgQDNQZKqTlO/+2b4ZdhqGJzGBDltb5PZmBz1ALN2YLvt341pH6i5
      mO1V9cX5Ty1LM70fKfnIoYUP4KCE33dPnC7LkUwE/myh1zM6m8cbL5cYFPyP099t
      hbVxzJkjHWqywvQih/qOOjliomKbM9pxG8Z1dB26hL9dSAZuA8xExjlPmQIDAQAB
      AoGAImnYGU3ApPOVtBf/TOqLfne+2SZX96eVU06myDY3zA4rO3DfbR7CzCLE6qPn
      yDAIiW0UQBs0oBDdWOnOqz5YaePZu/yrLyj6KM6Q2e9ywRDtDh3ywrSfGpjdSvvo
      aeL1WesBWsgWv1vFKKvES7ILFLUxKwyCRC2Lgh7aI9GGZfECQQD84m98Yrehhin3
      fZuRaBNIu348Ci7ZFZmrvyxAIxrV4jBjpACW0RM2BvF5oYM2gOJqIfBOVjmPwUro
      bYEFcHRvAkEAz8jsfmxsZVwh3Y/Y47BzhKIC5FLaads541jNjVWfrPirljyCy1n4
      sg3WQH2IEyap3WTP84+csCtsfNfyK7fQdwJBAJNRyobY74cupJYkW5OK4OkXKQQL
      Hp2iosJV/Y5jpQeC3JO/gARcSmfIBbbI66q9zKjtmpPYUXI4tc3PtUEY8QsCQQCc
```

```
        xySyC0sKe6bNzyC+Q8AVvkxiTKWiI5idEr8duhJd589H72Zc2wkMB+a2CEGo+Y5H
        jy5cvuph/pG/7Qw7sljnAkAy/feClt1mUEiAcWrHRwcQ71AoA0+21yC9VkqPNrn3
        w7OEg8gBqPjRlXBNb00QieNeGGSkXOoU6gFschR22Dzy
        -----END RSA PRIVATE KEY-----
    publicKey: |
        -----BEGIN PUBLIC KEY-----
        MIGfMA0GCSqGSIb3DQEBAQUAA4GNADCBiQKBgQDNQZKqTlO/+2b4ZdhqGJzGBDlt
        b5PZmBz1ALN2YLvt341pH6i5mO1V9cX5Ty1LM70fKfnIoYUP4KCE33dPnC7LkUwE
        /myh1zM6m8cbL5cYFPyP099thbVxzJkjHWqywvQih/qOOjliomKbM9pxG8Z1dB26
        hL9dSAZuA8xExjlPmQIDAQAB
        -----END PUBLIC KEY-----
```

Moreover, the user info URI will be done using the following configuration in YAML:

```
oauth2:
  resource:
    userInfoUri: http://localhost:7777/credential
```

Awesome – our application is fully configured. Now, we will do the last part: configuring to get the information token.

Let's do that.

Creating the JwtTokenStore Bean

We will create the `JwtTokenStore`, which will be used to get token information. The class should look like this:

```
package springfive.airline.airlineplanes.infra.oauth;

import org.springframework.beans.factory.annotation.Value;
import org.springframework.context.annotation.Bean;
import org.springframework.context.annotation.Configuration;
import org.springframework.security.oauth2.provider.token.store.JwtAccessTokenConverter;
import org.springframework.security.oauth2.provider.token.store.JwtTokenStore;

@Configuration
public class OAuthTokenConfiguration {

  @Value("${config.oauth2.privateKey}")
  private String privateKey;

  @Value("${config.oauth2.publicKey}")
```

```
    private String publicKey;

    @Bean
    public JwtTokenStore tokenStore() throws Exception {
      JwtAccessTokenConverter enhancer = new JwtAccessTokenConverter();
      enhancer.setSigningKey(privateKey);
      enhancer.setVerifierKey(publicKey);
      enhancer.afterPropertiesSet();
      return new JwtTokenStore(enhancer);
    }

}
```

Awesome – our token signer is configured.

Finally, we will add the following annotation to the main class, which should look like this:

```
package springfive.airline.airlineplanes;

import org.springframework.boot.SpringApplication;
import org.springframework.boot.autoconfigure.SpringBootApplication;
import org.springframework.cloud.netflix.eureka.EnableEurekaClient;
import org.springframework.cloud.netflix.zuul.EnableZuulProxy;
import
org.springframework.security.oauth2.config.annotation.web.configuration.Ena
bleResourceServer;

@EnableZuulProxy
@EnableEurekaClient
@EnableResourceServer
@SpringBootApplication
public class AirlinePlanesApplication {

 public static void main(String[] args) {
   SpringApplication.run(AirlinePlanesApplication.class, args);
 }

}
```

It will protect our application, and it will require the access token to access the application endpoints.

Remember, we need to do the same task for all microservices that we want to protect.

Monitoring the microservices

In the microservice architectural style, monitoring is a crucial part. There are a lot of benefits when we adopt this architecture, such as time to market, source maintenance, and an increase of business performance. This is because we can divide the business goals for different teams, and each team will be responsible for some microservices. Another important characteristic is optimization of computational resources, such as cloud computing costs.

As we know, there is no such thing as a free lunch, and this style brings some drawbacks, such as operational complexity. There are a lot of *small services* to monitor. There are potentially hundreds of different service instances.

We have implemented some of these services in our infrastructure but until now, we did not have the data to analyze our system health. In this section, we will explore our configured services.

Let's analyze right now!

Collecting metrics with Zipkin

We have configured our Zipkin server in the previous chapter. Now we will use this server to analyze our microservices data. Let's do it.

Make some calls to create a flight. The Create Flight API will call the **Auth Service** and the **Flight Service**. Look at the following diagram:

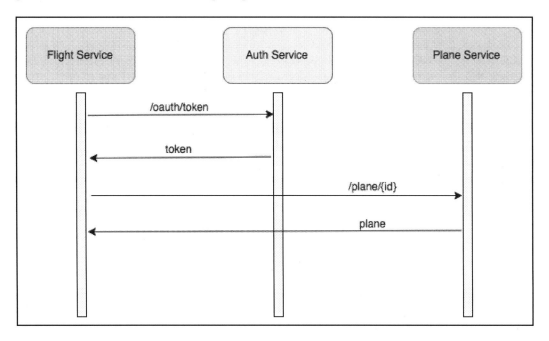

We will take a look at the `flights` microservice and the `planes` microservice communications. Let's analyze it:

Go to the Zipkin main page, `http://localhost:9999/`, select **flights**, and then click on **Find a trace**. The page should look like this:

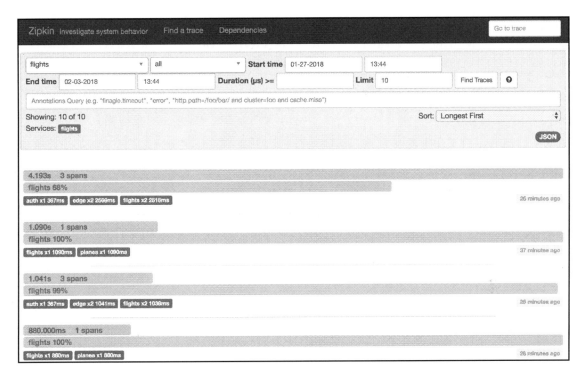

As we can see, there is some data on our Zipkin server. Click on **Span**, which has the
`flights` and `planes` tags, then we will take a look at this specific trace, and we will be
redirected to another page with specific span data, like this:

On this page, we can see important information, such as the total request time. Then click on the **planes** row, where we will be able to see detailed information, as in the following image:

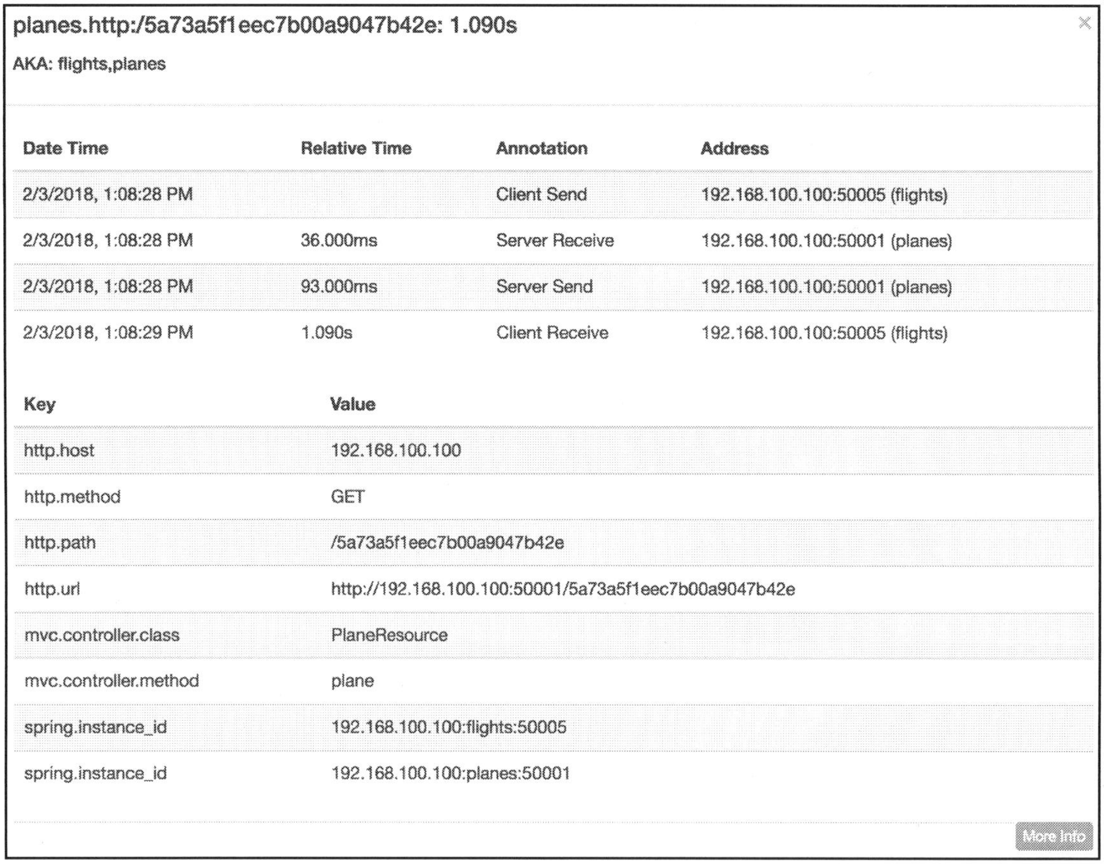

Look at the request information. There are some interesting things, such as `mvc.controller.class` and `mvc.controller.method`. These help developers to troubleshoot errors. Also in the first panel, we have the times of the service's interactions. It is very helpful to find microservices network latencies; for example, it makes environment management easier because we have visual tools to understand data better.

Also, the Zipkin server provides others interesting features to find microservices statistics, such as finding requests that have delayed for more than a specific time. It is very helpful for the operations guys.

We can find more information about Spring Cloud Sleuth on the documentation page (`http://cloud.spring.io/spring-cloud-static/spring-cloud-sleuth/2.0.0.M5/single/spring-cloud-sleuth.html`) or in the GitHub (`https://github.com/spring-cloud/spring-cloud-sleuth`) project page.

Collection commands statistics with Hystrix

Now, we want to monitor our Hystrix commands. There are several commands in our microservices and probably the most used will be the OAuth token requester, because we always need to have a token to call any microservice in our system. Our Turbine server and Hystrix UI were configured at the beginning of this chapter and we will use these services right now.

Remember, we are using `spring-cloud-netflix-hystrix-stream` as an implementation to send Hystrix data to the Turbine server, as it performs better than HTTP and also brings some asynchronous characteristics.

 Asynchronous calls can make the microservice more resilient. In this case, we will not use HTTP calls (synchronous calls) to register Hystrix Commands statistics. We will use the RabbitMQ queue to register it. In this case, we will put the message in the queue. Also, asynchronous calls make our application more optimized to use computational resources.

Run the Turbine server application and Hystrix UI application. Turbine will aggregate the metrics from the servers. Optionally, you can run several instances of the same service, such as `flights`. Turbine will aggregate the statistics properly.

Let's call the Create Flights API; we can use the Postman to do that.

Then we can see the real-time commands statistics. Before that, we will configure `turbine.stream` in our Hystrix Dashboard.

Go to the Hystrix Dashboard page: `http://localhost:50010/hystrix/`. The following page will be displayed:

Then we have some work to do. Let's configure our Turbine server stream. Our Turbine stream is running at `http://localhost:8010/turbine.stream`. Put this information below the **Hystrix Dashboard** information, and then we can click on the **Monitor Stream** button.

We will redirect to the Hystrix Commands Dashboard; we called the Create Flights API a few times ago. The commands metrics will be displayed, like the following image:

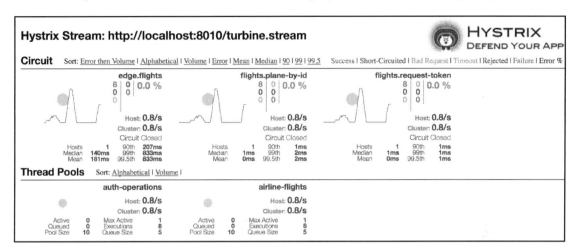

As we can see, we called the Create Flights API eight times. This API uses some commands, such as `flights.plane-by-id`, it calls the planes microservice, and the `flights.request-token` calls the `Auth` service.

Look how easy it is to monitor the commands. Operation guys like the Zipkin server can use this page.

Awesome job, guys, our services integrations are adequately monitored, which makes our microservices adoption more comfortable because we have useful applications to monitor our services instances.

Dockerizing the microservices

In the previous chapters, we have used the Fabric8 Maven Docker plugin to enable us to create Docker images, using the Maven goals.

Now, we need to configure our microservices to use this plugin to easily create images for us. It can be helpful to integrate with some Continuous Integration and Delivery tools, such as Jenkins, because we can call the `docker: build` goal easily.

Each project has the custom configurations, such as port and image name. We can find the configuration at the GitHub repository. Remember, the configuration is done using the pom.xml.

The following list has the GitHub repository addresses for all projects; the pom.xml has the Maven Docker plugin configuration:

- **Flights**: https://github.com/PacktPublishing/Spring-5.0-By-Example/blob/master/Chapter09/airline-flights/pom.xml
- **Planes**: https://github.com/PacktPublishing/Spring-5.0-By-Example/blob/master/Chapter09/airline-planes/pom.xml
- **Fares**: https://github.com/PacktPublishing/Spring-5.0-By-Example/blob/master/Chapter09/airline-fare/pom.xml
- **Bookings**: https://github.com/PacktPublishing/Spring-5.0-By-Example/blob/master/Chapter09/airline-booking/pom.xml
- **Admin**: https://github.com/PacktPublishing/Spring-5.0-By-Example/blob/master/Chapter09/admin/pom.xml
- **EDGE**: https://github.com/PacktPublishing/Spring-5.0-By-Example/blob/master/Chapter09/api-edge/pom.xml
- **Passengers**: https://github.com/PacktPublishing/Spring-5.0-By-Example/blob/master/Chapter09/airline-passengers/pom.xml
- **Auth**: https://github.com/PacktPublishing/Spring-5.0-By-Example/blob/master/Chapter09/auth-service/pom.xml
- **Mail**: https://github.com/PacktPublishing/Spring-5.0-By-Example/blob/master/Chapter09/mail-service/pom.xml
- **Turbine**: https://github.com/PacktPublishing/Spring-5.0-By-Example/blob/master/Chapter09/turbine/pom.xml
- **Zipkin**: https://github.com/PacktPublishing/Spring-5.0-By-Example/blob/master/Chapter09/zipkin-server/pom.xml
- **Payments**: https://github.com/PacktPublishing/Spring-5.0-By-Example/blob/master/Chapter09/airline-payments/pom.xml
- **Hystrix-dashboard**: https://github.com/PacktPublishing/Spring-5.0-By-Example/blob/master/Chapter09/hystrix-ui/pom.xml
- **Discovery**: https://github.com/PacktPublishing/Spring-5.0-By-Example/blob/master/Chapter09/eureka/pom.xml
- **Config Server**: https://github.com/PacktPublishing/Spring-5.0-By-Example/blob/master/Chapter09/config-server/pom.xml

Running the system

Now we can run our Docker containers using our images, which were created in the previous section.

We will split the services into two Docker compose files. The first one is about infrastructure services. The second one is about our microservices.

The stacks must be run on the same Docker network, because the service should be connected by the container hostname.

The Docker compose file for infrastructure can be found at GitHub: `https://github.com/PacktPublishing/Spring-5.0-By-Example/blob/master/stacks/docker-compose-infra.yaml`.

The Docker compose file for microservices can be found at GitHub: `https://github.com/PacktPublishing/Spring-5.0-By-Example/blob/master/stacks/docker-compose-micro.yaml`.

Now, we can run these files using the `docker-compose` commands. Type the following commands:

```
docker-compose -f docker-compose-infra.yaml up -d
docker-compose -f docker-compose-micro.yaml up -d
```

Then the full application will be up and running.

Well done, guys.

Summary

In this chapter, we have learned some important points on microservices architecture.

We were introduced to some important tools for monitoring the microservices environment. We have learned how the Turbine server can help us to monitor our Hystrix commands in distributed environments.

We were also introduced to the Hystrix Dashboard feature, which helps the developers and operations guys provide a rich dashboard with the commands statistics in near real time.

We learned how Spring Cloud Security enables security features for our microservices, and we implemented the OAuth 2 server, using JWT to enable resilience for our security layer.

Other Books You May Enjoy

If you enjoyed this book, you may be interested in these other books by Packt:

Mastering Spring 5.0
Ranga Rao Karanam

ISBN: 978-1-78712-317-5

- Explore the new features in Spring Framework 5.0
- Build microservices with Spring Boot
- Get to know the advanced features of Spring Boot in order to effectively develop and monitor applications
- Use Spring Cloud to deploy and manage applications on the Cloud
- Understand Spring Data and Spring Cloud Data Flow
- Understand the basics of reactive programming
- Get to know the best practices when developing applications with the Spring Framework
- Create a new project using Kotlin and implement a couple of basic services with unit and integration testing

Spring 5.0 Microservices - Second Edition
Rajesh R V

ISBN: 978-1-78712-768-5

- Familiarize yourself with the microservices architecture and its benefits
- Find out how to avoid common challenges and pitfalls while developing microservices
- Use Spring Boot and Spring Cloud to develop microservices
- Handle logging and monitoring microservices
- Leverage Reactive Programming in Spring 5.0 to build modern cloud native applications
- Manage internet-scale microservices using Docker, Mesos, and Marathon
- Gain insights into the latest inclusion of Reactive Streams in Spring and make applications more resilient and scalable

Leave a review - let other readers know what you think

Please share your thoughts on this book with others by leaving a review on the site that you bought it from. If you purchased the book from Amazon, please leave us an honest review on this book's Amazon page. This is vital so that other potential readers can see and use your unbiased opinion to make purchasing decisions, we can understand what our customers think about our products, and our authors can see your feedback on the title that they have worked with Packt to create. It will only take a few minutes of your time, but is valuable to other potential customers, our authors, and Packt. Thank you!

Index

integrations, testing 180
  monitoring 317
modules, Spring 8
MongoDB
  preparing 78, 79, 80

N

named client 18
Netflix Ribbon 267, 268
Netty
  about 13
  reference 13
null safety, Kotlin
  Elvis operator 131
  safe calls 131

O

OAuth 2.0 flow
  entities 304
OAuth 2.0, for protecting microservices
  about 314
  application.yaml file, configuring 314
  JwtTokenStore Bean, creating 315
  security dependency, adding 314
OpenJDK
  installing 26
OSI model
  reference 194

P

pagination 95
pgAdmin3
  about 88
  configuring 89
  installing 89
plane microservice
  running 265, 266
Plane service
  creating 261
planes microservice
  coding 259, 261
  creating 258, 259
  reactive repository 261
POJO (Plain Old Java Object) pattern 91

pom.xml
  configuring, for Spring Data JPA 82
PostgreSQL database
  preparing 80
Project Lombok library
  reference 261
Project Reactor
  about 105
  components 106
project
  creating, with Spring Initializr 133
projects, Spring Cloud
  Spring Cloud Bus 21
  Spring Cloud Config 19
  Spring Cloud Consul 20
  Spring Cloud Netflix 17
  Spring Cloud Security 21
  Spring Cloud Stream 22
publishers 106

Q

queues
  configuring, on Spring AMQP 162
  declaring, in yaml 162

R

RabbitMQ image
  pulling, from Docker Hub 158
RabbitMQ queues
  consuming, reactively 199, 200
RabbitMQ Reactor beans
  configuring 198
RabbitMQ server
  starting 158, 159
  starting, with Docker 158
RabbitMQ
  bindings 162
  exchanges 161
  queues 162
  Spring Application, integrating with 160
  Spring beans, declaring for 163
range expressions, Kotlin
  downTo case 130
  simple case 129

86371891R00199

Made in the USA
Middletown, DE
29 August 2018